THE DISABLED HIKER'S GUIDE TO NORTHERN CALIFORNIA

View of Enderts Beach

THE DISABLED HIKER'S GUIDE TO NORTHERN CALIFORNIA

OUTDOOR ADVENTURES ACCESSIBLE BY
CAR, WHEELCHAIR, AND ON FOOT

Syren Nagakyrie

FALCONGUIDES

ESSEX, CONNECTICUT

For Dad
Always California dreamin'

FALCONGUIDES®

An imprint of Globe Pequot, the trade division of
The Rowman & Littlefield Publishing Group, Inc.
4501 Forbes Blvd., Ste. 200
Lanham, MD 20706
www.rowman.com

Falcon and FalconGuides are registered trademarks and Make Adventure Your Story is a trademark of The Rowman & Littlefield Publishing Group, Inc.

Distributed by NATIONAL BOOK NETWORK

Copyright © 2024 Syren Nagakyrie

Photos by Syren Nagakyrie unless noted otherwise.

Maps by The Rowman & Littlefield Publishing Group, Inc.

British Library Cataloguing in Publication Information available

Library of Congress Cataloging-in-Publication Data

Names: Nagakyrie, Syren, author.
Title: The disabled hiker's guide to Northern California : outdoor adventures accessible by car, wheelchair, and on foot / Syren Nagakyrie.
Description: Essex, Connecticut : FalconGuides, [2024] | "Photos by Syren Nagakyrie unless noted otherwise. Maps by The Rowman & Littlefield Publishing Group, Inc."—Copyright page. | Includes bibliographical references. | Summary: "Covers the northern region of California from approximately Santa Cruz/Monterey to the Oregon state line. Includes drive-up adventures, wheelchair-accessible trails, and foot trails suitable for disabled hikers"— Provided by publisher.
Identifiers: LCCN 2024000638 (print) | LCCN 2024000639 (ebook) | ISBN 9781493073436 (paperback : acid-free paper) | ISBN 9781493073443 (epub)
Subjects: LCSH: Hiking for people with disabilities—California, Northern—Guidebooks. | Day hiking for people with disabilities—California, Northern—Guidebooks. | California, Northern—Description and travel. | California, Northern—Guidebooks. | BISAC: SPORTS & RECREATION / Hiking | TRAVEL / United States / West / Pacific (AK, CA, HI, OR, WA)
Classification: LCC GV199.56 N325 2024 (print) | LCC GV199.56 (ebook) | DDC 796.087—dc23/eng/20240212
LC record available at https://lccn.loc.gov/2024000638
LC ebook record available at https://lccn.loc.gov/2024000639

∞™ The paper used in this publication meets the minimum requirements of American National Standard for Information Sciences—Permanence of Paper for Printed Library Materials, ANSI/NISO Z39.48-1992.

CONTENTS

THE HIKES

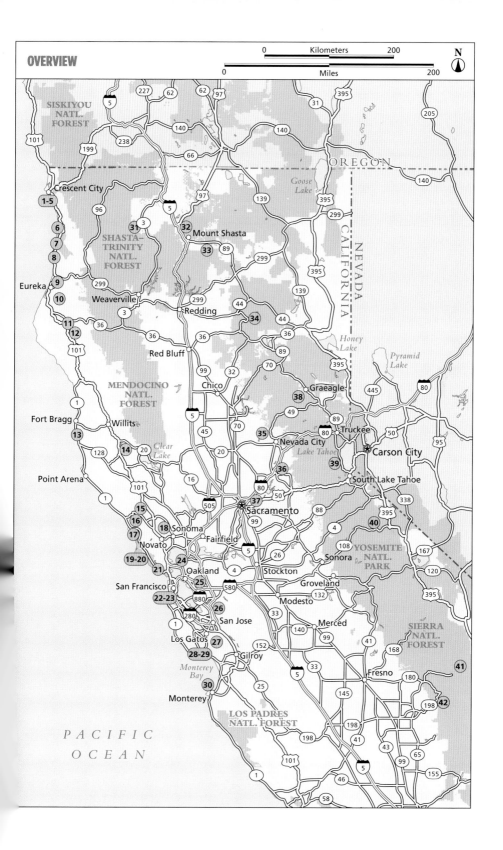

0   Kilometers   200

0   Miles   200

N

SISKIYOU
NATL.
FOREST

OREGON

CALIFORNIA

NEVADA

Crescent City

1-5

Mount Shasta

SHASTA-
TRINITY
NATL.
FOREST

Eureka

Weaverville

Redding

Goose
Lake

Honey
Lake

Pyramid
Lake

Red Bluff

MENDOCINO
NATL.
FOREST

Chico

Graeagle

Fort Bragg

Willits

Clear
Lake

Truckee

Nevada City

Lake Tahoe

Carson City

Point Arena

South Lake Tahoe

Sonoma

Sacramento

Novato

Fairfield

San Francisco

Oakland

Stockton

Groveland

YOSEMITE
NATL.
PARK

Sonora

Modesto

San Jose

Los Gatos

Gilroy

Merced

Monterey
Bay

SIERRA
NATL.
FOREST

Monterey

Fresno

LOS PADRES
NATL. FOREST

PACIFIC

OCEAN

ACKNOWLEDGMENTS

Thank you to the Disabled Hikers community—this book exists because of and for you. I also have immense appreciation for our partners who have committed to creating a more accessible outdoors, which includes organizations, parks, and many individuals who work in the field of outdoor recreation. Special thanks to the California State Parks Foundation for their support of this work.

Thank you to my friends, patrons, and backers for your support and encouragement. I thought writing a second book would be much easier than the first one, and you kept encouraging me when it proved just as challenging. Thanks to my first readers and field testers for your feedback, and the team at FalconGuides for all of your work in bringing this book to print. And, of course, thank you to my family for believing in me. Even though my father isn't here to see this book, I know he was proud of the work I am doing.

MEET YOUR GUIDE

Syren Nagakyrie is the founder of Disabled Hikers, a Disabled-led organization building community, access, and justice in the outdoors. Syren has multiple disabilities and chronic illnesses and is neurodivergent. They have loved the outdoors since childhood, but a lack of information and awareness made access very difficult. They have hiked and loved places across the country: the tropical lands of Florida, the Southern Appalachian and Blue Ridge Mountains, the Great Basin, and more. Inspired by the beauty and diversity of the Pacific Northwest, Syren founded Disabled Hikers and began writing trail guides in 2018.

Syren created a unique trail rating system called the Spoon Rating. They also lead group hikes and other events in the Pacific Northwest and beyond. Syren is a highly respected voice for disability justice, access, and belonging and regularly consults with parks, organizations, and other entities.

They believe that guidebook authors have a responsibility to give context on their ability, because ability influences the way we share information. Syren is primarily ambulatory with the use of a mobility aid, including a wheelchair periodically. They are generally able to hear, speak, and see clearly but can struggle with sensory processing and directions. A typical hike for Syren ranges from 1 to 3 miles, though they can do 4 to 6 miles followed by severe fatigue.

The information provided in this book is written as objectively as possible, and the author has tried to consider all types of disabilities and access needs. Given the incredible diversity and range of access needs within the disability community, the author recognizes that this information may be inadequate for some people.

You may contact the author through DisabledHikers.com.

BEFORE YOU HEAD OUT

This guide is designed to provide you with as much information as you may need to decide whether to attempt a trail. If you are someone who needs all of the information, read the entire chapter. If you just want a quick summary, then the opening overview, stats, and spoon rating should provide all you need. Below is an explanation of each section, what they mean, and how they were measured.

WHY GO?

This section provides a general description of the trail and highlights some of what you may experience. It also makes note of general trail design aspects to be aware of, such as traveling along a rocky cliff or making a water crossing.

THE RUNDOWN
Spoon Rating

The spoon rating is a system to identify how much effort a trail might take. The rating system is based in an understanding of Spoon Theory (a metaphor for the energy rationing that many disabled and chronically ill people have to do) by Christine Miserandino. It offers a representation of how accessible a hike is and how much effort it may take with consideration for how replenishing the experience may be.

Any one factor within a rating can shift without changing the overall rating. For example, a 5-mile-long trail with gentle elevation changes may be rated at 3 spoons, while a 3-mile-long trail with rocky terrain and steep grades may be rated at 5 spoons. Elevation gain, grade, trail surface, obstacles, and location (how difficult it is to reach the trail) have been generally weighed most heavily. Grades have been measured for trail lengths of 5 feet or more. In the rating system, a short grade is typically under 10 feet and a prolonged grade is over 30 feet.

Wheelchair accessibility has been determined based upon established accessibility guidelines, including the Architectural Barriers Act, Americans with Disabilities Act, and US Forest Service guidelines, as well as my personal experience. However, since the effort that wheelchair-accessible trails require can vary, and accessibility is influenced by the type of equipment used and the user's experience, it has been included as a factor in the rating system. Trails that meet all guidelines and would be accessible to most wheelchair users are listed in the Trail Finder as **ADA accessible** (a somewhat inaccurate term used for simplicity). For all other trails, **wheelchair accessible** means it is accessible to most wheelchair users with caution or assistance. **Wheelchair hikeable** means it may be accessible to experienced outdoor wheelchair users with adaptive equipment. However, I do not recommend making a determination about the accessibility of a trail based on this categorization alone. Please refer to the entire hike description before setting out on a wheelchair-friendly trail.

Since each person's ability and energy level is different and can change from day to day, I cannot tell you how difficult a trail might be for you—only you can decide that. While I have attempted to be as objective as possible, all rating systems have inherent subjectivity and what I consider a 1-spoon hike may still be different from what you consider a 1-spoon hike. The spoon rating, in combination with the thorough information provided in the guide, is meant to help you decide whether to attempt a trail, but it is not definitive. You may find trails that meet your particular needs in different ratings.

THE SPOON RATING SYSTEM

1 Spoon = 0–2 miles, level and even with grades under 8%, paved, very easy to navigate, probably wheelchair accessible

2 Spoons = 1–3 miles, short grades up to 12%, firm but unpaved surface with no obstacles, access takes a little planning, probably wheelchair hikeable

3 Spoons = 2–4 miles, generally gentle elevation changes with short grades up to 20%, firm surface with minimal obstacles, possibly wheelchair hikeable

4 Spoons = 3–5 miles, prolonged grades of 10–15%, elevation changes over 500 feet or longer than 0.5 mile, soft surface with obstacles, requires advance planning or basic trail map reading

5 Spoons = 5+ miles, prolonged grades of 15–20%, elevation changes of 1,000 feet or longer than 1 mile, trail has many obstacles, requires extensive planning or navigation

Type

This gives the layout of the trail. There are generally three types in this book: out-and-back, loop, and lollipop loop.

An **out-and-back trail** starts and ends at the same point and returns on the same route you went out on; you hike the same route in both directions. Read the hike description with this in mind—it means that all inclines will be declines on the way back and you'll have to cross difficult sections twice, for example.

A **loop** trail starts and ends at the same point, but returns on a different route. It can use multiple trails to form a loop, but in this guide loops are typically single trails that roughly circle a particular feature, such as a lake. The description follows the entire loop and will give you the direction of travel. Some loops may be easier for you to travel in the opposite direction given; a note has been made if this seems likely.

A **lollipop loop** is a variation of a loop trail. It combines an out-and-back section with a loop. You start and end at the same point but will travel out on one trail, then connect with the loop trail. You finish the loop at the same point where you began, and then return on the same trail you came in on.

Driving routes and overlooks are listed as a **scenic drive** or **scenic viewpoint**, respectively. These locations provide an immersive experience in nature without the need for a hike and are generally ADA accessible.

Distance

The distance is given for the entire length of the trail. For a loop, it represents the length of the entire hike, start to finish. For an out-and-back, it represents the total hike from the start to the recommended turnaround point and back. Many trails in this book continue beyond the recommended turnaround point, so you may see different mileages given in different sources.

Distance has been recorded using a GPS trail application, and compared with topographic maps, official trail listings, and other resources when available. However, recordings can be impacted by a number of factors, and sources may disagree on the mileage. In these circumstances, I have used the mileage from my recordings but may have made minor adjustments to ensure that landmarks and directions are accurate.

Elevation and Elevation Gain

The numbers given here represent the starting elevation above sea level, and the total elevation gained on the hike. If you have breathing difficulties, or you are used to only being near sea level, you may feel more shortness of breath at elevations above 3,000 feet due to slightly lower air pressure. Consult your doctor if you have concerns about being at higher elevations. With a few exceptions, most of the trails in this book are below 3,000 feet.

Many of the trails in this guide take rolling grades (going slightly up and then down), and elevation gain seldom occurs at a steady rate. Elevation profiles are provided to give you a visual representation of the length and grade of elevation changes. You can view these as a graph, with points representing elevation points on the trail. However, they shouldn't be viewed as an exact replica of the steepness of the trail. For example, a 10% grade will look steeper on a shorter trail than on a longer one.

Elevation has been recorded using a GPS trail application, and compared with trail listings, topographic maps, and other measurements when available.

Max Grade

The grade represents the steepness of a trail. Expressed as a percentage, it represents the amount of elevation gained over a length of trail, or rise over run. For example, a typical wheelchair ramp is between 2% and 5% grade, with a maximum 8.33% grade; a 15% grade is almost twice as steep as the steepest wheelchair ramp.

The max grade listed is the steepest section of the trail that is longer than 5 feet. The length of a grade greatly affects the amount of effort it takes; for example, a 5% grade for 100 feet may feel more difficult than a 15% grade for 20 feet. However, even a short, steep grade may make a trail inaccessible. Only you can decide how steep of a trail is appropriate for you, and it may take some trial and error to figure it out.

Grades were measured using a handheld clinometer and compared with GPS recordings and topographic maps. In some cases I have averaged several measurements along a section of trail, or made a best estimate based upon measurements and personal experience.

Max Cross Slope

The cross slope is the steepness of a trail on the horizontal axis; i.e., the grade of the surface from the inside to the outside of a section of trail. A steep cross slope requires more effort to hike, and may be difficult if you have problems with balance or sensory motor control, or a difference in length of limbs. A cross slope steeper than 2% is considered not wheelchair accessible, though some wheelchair users may be able to navigate a 5% cross slope, depending on the terrain and your equipment.

Typical Width

This is the width of the trail for the greatest distance. A trail that is narrower than 2 feet will allow people to travel single file, and passing will be difficult. A trail must be a minimum of 3 feet to be wheelchair accessible. A trail 4 feet or wider will be the most comfortable for passing or traveling as a group on foot.

Typical Surface

This is the material of the trail that you will be traveling on for the greatest distance. It may be paved, compact gravel, or natural. Natural surface means it has been unimproved other than creating the trail. The surface will be a combination of dirt and other natural elements depending on the terrain, and will likely have roots, rocks, and wet or muddy sections.

Trail Users

Who will you share the trail with? I have tried to stick to hiker-only trails as much as possible, but there are several mixed-use trails in the book. This can include trail runners, mountain bikers, or horseback riders. These other users may be traveling much faster than you, so you should always be alert. On mixed-use trails, bikers yield to hikers, hikers and bikers yield to horseback riders, and everyone yields to wheelchair users. However, this etiquette is not always followed, and you may need to yield the trail regardless of other users. You can also alert other trail users if it is difficult for you to yield, and ask them to let you pass.

A note on wheelchairs and other power-driven mobility devices (OPDMD) on trails: Generally speaking, any device that is designed for use by someone with a mobility disability and is also suitable for indoor use is allowed on public trails, unless the land manager has conducted a formal assessment to prove that such devices pose a safety risk. This includes devices such as track chairs and other motorized wheelchairs. In some instances, OPDMD such as golf carts and Segways, and self-powered devices such as handcycle bikes, may be allowed. More information about these rules is in the resources section. If you have questions about OPDMD use, contact the land manager using the provided contact information.

Season/Schedule

This lists the time of year that the area is open. However, some trails may be too difficult or dangerous during certain seasons, so the best season to visit is provided. For areas with designated opening and closing hours, that schedule is provided. Schedules and seasons can change depending on the weather and other factors, so always confirm before heading out.

Water Availability

Water availability describes any reliable source of water, including water fountains and surface water. Surface water (i.e., from creeks, rivers, or lakes) should always be filtered with a water filtration device designed specifically for outdoor use. Water sources can vary greatly, and often dry up in the summer, so confirm with the land manager if you intend to rely on surface water for your hike. Details about the water source are provided in the description.

Sun Exposure
This lists the amount of sun exposure or shade on the majority of the trail. **Full sun** means there is little to no shade, **partial shade** means either the entire trail is partially shaded or there are sections of the trail that are shaded, and **full shade** means that the majority of the trail is shaded by trees.

Amenities
This lists comfort stations that are available at the trailhead or along the trail, such as tables, benches, water fountains, and toilets. ADA accessible features will also be listed.

Pet-Friendly
This describes whether pets are allowed on the trail, and under which conditions (leashed or unleashed but under control at all times). I've also mentioned whether it is recommended to bring a pet—some trails technically allow them but aren't suitable for a variety of reasons.

Service dogs are allowed on all trails and recreation sites, inside buildings, and anywhere else their handler goes, even if pets are not allowed. Service dogs are trained to perform one or more specific task related to a person's disability, and their access is protected by the ADA. Emotional support animals and therapy animals do not qualify as service animals.

Cell Phone Reception
This is provided so that you know whether or not you'll be "off grid." It is up to you whether you go outdoors to escape technology or need to stay connected for safety, comfort, or potential emergencies. Cell reception can vary depending on network and weather conditions, and even when it is available it can be spotty. You should always tell someone where you are going and have a plan in case of emergencies. You may want to consider a personal locator beacon or other GPS device.

Special Notes
These are any special points to be aware of, particularly around terrain or sensory considerations. For example, there may be a note about the number of stairs or a source of loud, unexpected noise.

Nearest Town
The nearest town or city where you will have access to basic services such as gas, restrooms, and food is provided. Medical services may not be available in small towns, and the hours of other services may be limited.

Land Manager
The land manager is the entity that is primarily responsible for the trail or recreation site. It is typically a national forest, national park, or state, regional, or local park. Contact information is provided so that you can inquire about current conditions, closures, fee requirements, etc. Most land managers also have a website with pertinent information.

Pass/Entry Fee

Passes or day-use fees are required at most national parks, developed national forest recreation sites, and California state parks and state-managed developed recreation sites. However, there are plenty of exceptions to this rule, so the type of pass or entry fee is listed for each hike. Unless otherwise noted, display the pass in your vehicle. Some locations require you to carry a separate self-registration permit with you—this information is included in the pass/entry fee section and the hike description.

In general, two passes cover the vast majority of the hikes in this book: the America the Beautiful Interagency Pass and a California State Parks annual pass. If you have a permanent disability, you can receive a free lifetime America the Beautiful pass, called the Access Pass, which grants entry to all national parks, national monuments, and national forests and offers a discount on camping and some other fees. More information is provided in the resources section.

There are several variations of the California State Parks annual pass. The Golden Poppy Pass covers the locations in this book. As of 2023, the annual cost is $125. People with a permanent disability can apply for a lifetime disabled discount pass that grants 50% off vehicle day-use and camping fees. Honorably discharged veterans can qualify for a lifetime pass that grants free entrance and camping in state parks. If you receive SSI or CalWORKs or meet other income limitations, you can qualify for a free Golden Bear Pass. Free passes are also available to fourth-grade students and from public libraries, pending ongoing state funding. More information about state park passes can be found in the resources section.

Many land managers in the region are moving towards implementing day-use permitting and reservations at popular sites. None of those current sites are included in this book because it creates another barrier to access, but always verify pass requirements—the fines can be hefty.

Land Acknowledgment

Recognizing the Indigenous peoples of a place and their connection and stewardship with the land is an important practice. The land acknowledgment names the tribe(s) whose traditional lands include the place where the hike is located. Native place names and other points of cultural significance are included when appropriate. This information has been provided or verified by the tribe whenever possible. If information is not publicly available, the land acknowledgment has been left out. More information about the Indigenous peoples of the region is included in the opening sections. I have made my best effort to ensure the accuracy of this information, but summarizing 10,000 years of Indigenous history and 500 years of settlement and colonization is a difficult task for a hiking guide. Please use this as a starting point for your own research.

FINDING THE TRAILHEAD

Detailed directions to the trailhead or for the scenic drive are provided from an easily located starting point, typically the nearest town. I've also provided a description of the roadway—whether it is a highway, two-lane paved road, or single-lane dirt road—and any things to be aware of such as potholes or hidden curves. All of the trailheads in this book can be reached by a standard passenger car (I got to all of them in a Prius); however, some may require careful driving on unimproved dirt roads. In wet or snowy weather, these roads may be impassable without a four-wheel-drive and/or high-clearance vehicle. Many roads through popular recreation areas are closed in winter or during the spring melt or periods of heavy rain. You can verify road closures and other conditions on https://quickmap.dot.ca.gov.

The directions are as detailed and accurate as possible so that you can follow them using your car's odometer. However, odometer readings can vary among vehicles, so important landmarks and junctions are provided when available. Most of these trailheads can be easily located on smartphone map services, but they can be unreliable in remote areas and depend on good cell reception. You may be able to download the map area to your phone from the map service.

I've also included information on the parking area, including surface and the number of parking spots, especially accessible parking. I have attempted to differentiate between accessible parking that meets ADA guidelines (noted as ADA parking spots) and accessible parking that may be usable but does not meet guidelines (noted as designated accessible parking spots). Small parking areas at popular sites can fill quickly on weekends, though accessible parking is usually available if provided.

Public transit options are provided when available. With a little planning, many trailheads are accessible without a vehicle, and efforts are being made to enhance public transit services to trailheads.

The start section includes a short summary of the starting location for the hike.

THE HIKE

Every trail description is a step-by-step or roll-by-roll guide. Broken down to as little as every one-tenth mile, it should provide a tour of the entire trail from start to finish. Read it ahead of time to decide whether to attempt the trail, then bring it with you so you know what to expect up ahead. The descriptions focus less on providing information about the flora and fauna of a place—there are many guides already available that provide that information—but I have included unique and remarkable things to be attentive to, and some information about the ecosystem and other relevant natural features.

Many of the trails offer options that may be more or less accessible; for example, by changing the length, taking a side trip, or traveling in a different direction. Some trails may have a wheelchair-accessible portion. This information has been included in each description, and the trail will be listed in the Trail Finder under each applicable spoon rating.

Detailed information is also provided for every scenic drive and viewpoint, with turn-by-turn directions, optional side trips, and information about accessibility. Because the guidelines for wheelchair-accessible trails are so specific, those descriptions provide a little less detail but still cover directions, what you'll experience, and anything to be aware of.

MAPS

Maps illustrating the specific route are included for each hike, and they are as accurate as possible. I have tried to avoid the need for purchasing multiple maps, so the trails in this book are all generally well marked and easy to follow, and detailed map reading or navigation should not be required.

Your smartphone should be an adequate GPS device for the trails in this book. Always download a map to use offline—never rely on having cell reception.

Additional maps and brochures are typically available for free from the respective land managers. Check at national park and state park entrance stations and national forest visitor centers. Tourism visitor centers also usually stock maps for nearby recreation areas.

ELEVATION PROFILES

Elevation profiles are provided to give you a visual representation of the length and grade of elevation changes. You can view these as a graph, with points representing elevation points on the trail. However, they shouldn't be viewed as an exact replica of the steepness of the trail. For example, a 10% grade will look steeper on a shorter trail than a longer one.

MORE TERMS TO KNOW

I try to avoid jargon as much as possible, but there may be terminology in the guide that you are unfamiliar with. Here are a few more terms to know:

¾ **log bench:** A rustic bench made out of a log laid on the side with a ¼ section cut out and ¾ remaining to create a seat and backrest. They are usually rough and uneven.

Access aisles: The striped sections next to accessible parking spots and (occasionally) on accessible routes of travel that provide space for wheelchair ramps and mobility aids. These areas should never be blocked.

Armored crossing: A section of trail with large, closely placed rocks in the surface. The rocks are generally flat and smooth, but there may be some gaps or unevenness that make it difficult for someone using a wheelchair to cross.

Crowned: The trail is slightly higher in the center than on the edges. This creates a slight cross slope along the edges of the trail.

Fork: The trail you are traveling on splits into two or more directions. One or more directions may become a different trail.

Intersection: The trail you are traveling on crosses a different trail.

Rolling grade / rolls: The trail inclines and declines gently across a short distance, usually with a level area after every incline and decline.

Tactile elements: Three-dimensional or raised elements on a sign or map that provide information through the sense of touch.

MAP LEGEND

Municipal

≡⑤≡ Interstate Highway

≡⟨101⟩≡ US Highway

≡⟨128⟩≡ State Road

═══ Local Road

═ ═ ═ ═ Unpaved Road

·· — ·· State Border

Trails

— — — — — Featured Trail

— — — — Trail

━━━ Paved Trail

Water Features

Body of Water

Marsh

Beach

River/Creek

≋ Waterfall

Land Management

National Park/Recreation Area

Park/Preserve

Symbols

🪑 Bench

≍ Bridge

■ Building/Point of Interest

▲ Campground

🗼 Lighthouse

🅿 Parking

≍ Pass

▲ Peak

🏕 Picnic Area

🚻 Restrooms

🔭 Scenic View/Overlook

||||| Stairs/Boardwalk

🗼 Tower

○ Town

① Trailhead

❓ Visitor/Information Center

🚰 Water

♿ Wheelchair Accessible

INTRODUCTION

Northern California is a remarkable and diverse region of foggy coastlines, snowcapped mountains, and arid landscapes. It contains some of the world's mightiest trees and mountains and some of the most unique landscapes in the country. The Klamath Mountains in the northwest link California and Oregon and contain many unique species of plants found nowhere else in the world. The most southern portion of the Cascade Range dips into Northern California and includes the iconic volcano, Mount Shasta. Volcanic activity formed the geography of many areas in the state, but most especially in the Modoc Plateau. The Coastal Ranges run almost the length of Northern California and boundary some of the most highly populated parts of the state. The Central Valley, also called the Grand Valley, is one of the most defining characteristics of the state as a massive and fertile valley between the Coastal Ranges and Sierra Nevada. The Sierra Nevada rises like a spine along the eastern edge of the state, holding an equally defining identity for California.

With so many diverse landscapes and ecosystems in Northern California, it is no surprise the state is so popular. Over 15 million people currently call this region home. According to a report from the Outdoor Foundation, over half of the population participates in outdoor recreation, which is a $54.7 billion economy.

Of course, this popularity has had an impact, and outdoor recreation has been experiencing a boom in the past several years. While land managers and outdoor enthusiasts scramble to figure out how to adapt to increased use, many communities get left behind, including Disabled communities. Improving access to outdoor recreation is often viewed as a way to (a) make the experience less authentic for outdoor enthusiasts, and (b) make it too easy for people to enjoy the outdoors, thus bringing in more people.

But Disabled people deserve access to these places, and improving accessibility benefits everyone. That includes access to information. While this book is written specifically for people who are disabled, chronically ill, neurodivergent, or otherwise face access barriers to the outdoors, my hope is that non-disabled people will also recognize the importance of detailed, objective trail information. We all need information to decide whether or not to attempt a trail, and it should be easily available.

Climate change is continuing to have an impact on outdoor recreation. This book was written during some of the most challenging seasons in recent history—an ongoing pandemic; record-breaking snowstorms and flooding, which left many areas with severe damage; and large-scale wildfires. As climate change continues to impact the land upon which we recreate, many people who typically do not have to think about access are faced with unclear information and questions about whether or not they will be able to access their favorite places. As more of these changes take place, the experience of non-disabled hikers is going to more closely resemble that of disabled hikers. It is the perfect time to think more about accessibility in the outdoors, and who better to learn about access than from Disabled people?

I've always loved nature, but it took a long time for me to feel comfortable doing outdoor recreation. A lack of information that met my needs, limited understanding and acceptance of disability in the outdoors, and not seeing any other Disabled people represented in the community all contributed to feeling excluded from outdoor recreation. It just didn't feel like something that was meant for me. But nature has always offered a sense of belonging even when I felt excluded otherwise. That is why I started Disabled Hikers, a Disabled-led nonprofit organization to build more disability community and justice and challenge the dominant narrative of who is valid in the outdoors.

This book is designed to remove one of the barriers to experiencing the outdoors for people with disabilities: a lack of information written by Disabled people for Disabled people. I have attempted to include factors that are left out of other guides. Wheelchair accessibility has been expanded to include trails that meet standard accessibility guidelines and trails that may be hikeable for experienced hikers who use wheelchairs or have all-terrain equipment. Not all wheelchairs, or wheelchair users, are the same! Information on foot hiking trails has also been expanded to include the broad variety of people who are ambulatory and may or may not use mobility aids. Information for people with sensory disabilities is also included, along with considerations for people who are neurodivergent. I've also included scenic drives and viewpoints for people who want or need to experience the outdoors from their vehicles. That is a valid and sometimes necessary way to get outdoors—especially on the days when you don't have the spoons for a hike! Public transit options are provided for those who can't or don't want to drive. The overarching intent of this guide is to provide you with information so you can make your own decision about what you want to attempt.

The conditions under which this guide was written definitely impacted the places included in the book. There are areas that I could not include and popular sites that were inaccessible during this writing. Hopefully, future editions can include some of these locations. However, every location in this guide was selected for a reason—its beauty, opportunity to experience something unique, historical and cultural significance, or accessibility—and they each offer a significant "reward" to be worth the effort. I've tried to select a variety of hikes in every area to meet the needs of the most people. Unfortunately, as you may already know, there is a significant lack of trails that are suitable for disabled hikers in most areas. All of the hikes may not be accessible to you, but my hope is that something in this guide will offer you a new and meaningful experience.

With a little preparation, hiking opportunities abound year-round in Northern California, given the variety of elevations and ecosystems. Summer is typically dry and warm, and wildfire season is becoming longer with more campfire bans, so you will need to plan ahead if you're camping. The mountains burst into color with summer wildflowers, and the coast is usually cool and foggy. Winter can be wet and cold along the coast, and you will need to prepare for standing water and slippery conditions. But low-elevation hikes that are too hot in the summer become a wonderful destination in winter.

The shoulder seasons of spring and fall are really some of the best hiking in the area. Spring is typically muddy, but the creeks and waterfalls are usually at maximum flow, offering a glimpse of the astounding power of water in California. Fall usually brings the first rain showers in months, putting an end to wildfire season, and the forest suddenly seems to come alive in a final burst of green before putting on an encore of fall colors.

I hope this guide helps you to get out there and enjoy this beautiful area. You belong outdoors.

TRAIL FINDER

SCENIC DRIVES AND VIEWPOINTS
1. Crescent Beach
3. Howland Hill Scenic Drive
8. Moonstone Beach
13. Point Cabrillo Light Station
16. Sonoma County Scenic Drive
17. Doran Regional Park
20. Point Reyes National Seashore Beaches
27. Mount Umunhum Summit Overlook
33. McCloud River Falls
34. Lassen Volcanic National Park Scenic Drive
40. Sonora Pass Scenic Drive

ADA ACCESSIBLE
1. Crescent Beach
18. Valley of the Moon Trail
20. Point Reyes National Seashore Beaches
24. Point Pinole Regional Shoreline
27. Mount Umunhum Summit Overlook
33. McCloud River Falls
34. Lassen Volcanic National Park Scenic Drive
37. American River Parkway
40. Sonora Pass Scenic Drive

1 SPOON
1. Crescent Beach
6. Redwood Access and Revelation Trail Loop
8. Moonstone Beach
17. Doran Regional Park
18. Valley of the Moon Trail
20. Point Reyes National Seashore Beaches
21. Verna Dunshee Trail
22. Fort Funston
30. Asilomar Dunes Boardwalk
32. Sisson Meadow
37. American River Parkway

38. Frazier Falls
41. General Grant Tree Trail
42. Big Trees Trail

2 SPOONS
4. Stout Memorial Grove
5. Simpson-Reed / Peterson Memorial Trail
9. Arcata Marsh
11. Drury-Chaney Trail
12. Founders Grove
15. Riverfront Regional Park Lake Trail
20. Point Reyes National Seashore Beaches
23. Mori Point
26. Stream Trail
29. Old Cove Landing Trail
33. McCloud River Falls
36. Quarry Trail

3 SPOONS
2. Coastal Trail: Enderts Beach
7. Sue-meg State Park Loop
19. Bear Valley Trail
24. Point Pinole Regional Shoreline
31. Taylor Lake
33. McCloud River Falls
35. Buttermilk Bend Trail
39. Meeks Creek Meadow

4 SPOONS
10. Elk River Trail
13. Point Cabrillo Light Station
14. Shakota Trail
20. Point Reyes National Seashore Beaches
25. Nimitz Way

5 SPOONS
28. Henry Cowell Highlights Loop
33. McCloud River Falls

TRAIL NAME	TYPE	SPOON RATING	ADA ACCESSIBLE	WHEELCHAIR ACCESSIBLE	WHEELCHAIR HIKEABLE	RESTING AREAS	TACTILE FEATURES	AUDIO FEATURES	DIRECTIONAL SIGNAGE	PUBLIC TRANSIT
1. Crescent Beach	Viewpoint	1	X			X				
2. Coastal Trail: Enderts Beach	Out-and-back	3			X				X	
3. Howland Hill Scenic Drive	Scenic drive									
4. Stout Memorial Grove	Lollipop loop	2			X	X			X	
5. Simpson-Reed / Peterson Memorial Trail	Lollipop loop	2			X	X			X	
6. Redwood Access and Revelation Trail Loop	Lollipop loop	1		X		X	X		X	X
7. Sue-meg State Park Loop	Lollipop loop or out-and-back	3		X	X	X			X	X
8. Moonstone Beach	Scenic viewpoint	1								
9. Arcata Marsh	Loop	2		X		X			X	X
10. Elk River Trail	Out-and-back	4			X	X				X
11. Drury-Chaney Trail	Lollipop loop	2				X			X	
12. Founders Grove	Loop or out-and-back	2		X		X			X	X
13. Point Cabrillo Light Station	Loop, scenic viewpoint	4		X		X				X
14. Shakota Trail	Out-and-back	4								
15. Riverfront Regional Park Lake Trail	Out and back, loop	2			X	X				

TRAIL NAME	TYPE	SPOON RATING	ADA ACCESSIBLE	WHEELCHAIR ACCESSIBLE	WHEELCHAIR HIKEABLE	RESTING AREAS	TACTILE FEATURES	AUDIO FEATURES	DIRECTIONAL SIGNAGE	PUBLIC TRANSIT
16. Sonoma County Scenic Drive	Scenic drive			X		X				
17. Doran Regional Park	Lollipop loop, scenic viewpoint	1		X		X				
18. Valley of the Moon Trail	Out-and-back	1	X	X		X				
19. Bear Valley Trail	Out-and-back	3			X					
20. Point Reyes National Seashore Beaches	Scenic viewpoint, out-and-back	1, 2, 4	X		X	X				
21. Verna Dunshee Trail	Loop	1		X	X	X	X			
22. Fort Funston	Out-and-back	1		X		X	X		X	X
23. Mori Point	Out-and-back	2		X	X	X			X	X
24. Point Pinole Regional Shoreline	Loop	3	X	X	X	X				X
25. Nimitz Way	Out-and-back	4			X					
26. Stream Trail	Out-and-back	2	X	X		X				
27. Mount Umunhum Summit Overlook	Scenic viewpoint	1				X		X		
28. Henry Cowell Highlights Loop	Lollipop loop	5							X	
29. Old Cove Landing Trail	Loop	2			X	X				

TRAIL NAME	TYPE	SPOON RATING	ADA ACCESSIBLE	WHEELCHAIR ACCESSIBLE	WHEELCHAIR HIKEABLE	RESTING AREAS	TACTILE FEATURES	AUDIO FEATURES	DIRECTIONAL SIGNAGE	PUBLIC TRANSIT
30. Asilomar Dunes Boardwalk	Loop	1		X		X		X	X	X
31. Taylor Lake	Out-and-back	3								
32. Sisson Meadow	Out-and-back	1		X		X				
33. McCloud River Falls	Out-and-back, scenic viewpoint	2, 3, 5	X	X		X				
34. Lassen Volcanic National Park Scenic Drive	Scenic drive		X					X		
35. Buttermilk Bend Trail	Out-and-back	3		X	X	X				
36. Quarry Trail	Out-and-back	2				X				
37. American River Parkway	Out-and-back	1	X	X		X				X
38. Frazier Falls	Out-and-back	1		X		X			X	
39. Meeks Creek Meadow	Out-and-back	3			X					
40. Sonora Pass Scenic Drive	Scenic drive		X	X		X				
41. General Grant Tree Trail	Loop	1		X		X	X		X	
42. Big Trees Trail	Lollipop loop	1		X		X			X	

Top: View of the Sierras from Sonora Pass
Bottom: Douglas Flats picnic area

NORTH COAST

In the context of this guide, the North Coast includes the coastal area from the California state line south to Mendocino, and the Northern Coast Ranges south to Ukiah Valley. It is one of my favorite regions in Northern California. The Northern Coast Ranges run from the coast of Del Norte County to the north San Francisco Bay area, including the Mayacamas and Sonoma Mountains and the Marin Hills, but for geographic purposes I have grouped Sonoma- and Marin-area hikes with the Bay Area.

The North Coast is perhaps most renowned as redwood country. It is home to the only remaining old-growth coast redwood forests in the world, which once covered over 2 million acres from present-day Big Sur to southern Oregon but have been lost to logging and development. The 5% of old-growth forest that remains exists in a narrow 450-mile strip along the Northern California coast. While 75% of the ancient old growth is protected in state and national parks and preserves, the majority of coast redwood forests remain unprotected and subjected to continued logging and ecological devastation. Efforts to protect and revitalize the forest are ongoing, led by Indigenous people of the North Coast and collaborative projects like Redwoods Rising.

Historically, the focus on redwood conservation has been rooted in white supremacist ideals within the context of ongoing colonialization of the land. Two of the founders of the Save the Redwoods League, Madison Grant and Henry Fairfield Osborn, were well-known eugenicists who touted racist and anti-Semitic views. In this case, the remarkableness of redwoods was a stand-in for biological superiority, and these early founders equated preserving redwoods with preserving white supremacy (www.parks.ca .gov/?page_id=30473). Many of the early conservationists shared similar views. These roots have contributed to the ongoing exclusion of Black, Indigenous, and other people of color, Disabled people, and other marginalized communities from participating in outdoor recreation and conservation. California parks and conservation organizations have been reckoning with this history, as everyone who benefits from it must.

Long before the conservationist movement (or the need for one), Native people were (and continue to be) active stewards of the land. The rich and diverse lands of the North Coast are the traditional homelands of at least a dozen tribes, including the Tolowa Dee-ni', Yurok, Karuk, Wiyot, and Pomo, among others.

Taa-laa-waa-dvn (Tolowa Aboriginal Territory) encompasses the area of Daa-ghestlh-ts'a' (Wilson Creek) to the south, Ts'aa-xwii-chit (Sixes River) to the north, east to Taa-xuu-me' (Applegate watershed) in the Coast Range, and west to the Pacific Ocean horizon. Dan'-taa-dvn (Del Norte County) sits at the center of this territory, which was split by the enforced border of the California-Oregon state line (www.tolowa-nsn .gov/35/About-Us). The Tolowa Dee-ni' Nation have repurchased Xaa-wan'-k'wvt Village, a major center of life and culture in the estuary of the Smith River.

Yurok homelands extend from the mouth of the Klamath River to Slate Creek and along the Pacific Ocean from Damnation Creek to Little River (www.yuroktribe.org/our-history). I highly recommend stopping by the visitor center at Chah-pekw O' Ket'-toh (Stone Lagoon), formerly known as the Stone Lagoon Visitor Center, located along US 101 between Orick and Sue-meg State Park. Chah-pekw O'Ket'-toh is one of more than seventy village locations within Yurok Ancestral Territory. The Yurok Tribe co-manages the visitor center; it is the first visitor center to be jointly managed by a Tribal government and California State Parks. The visitor center contains numerous inter-pretive signs and exhibits on Ner'-er-ner' (Coastal Yurok) culture, including basketry, a media room built in replica of a traditional Yurok home, and information about the plants and animals of the area. The Yurok Tribe offers many authentic guiding services for visitors.

Wiyot traditional territory includes the Little River south to Bear River Ridge, and east to Berry Summit and Chalk Mountain (www.wiyot.us/148/Cultural). Many village sites and shell middens surround Wigi (Humboldt Bay), and the Tribe is actively work-ing to preserve and restore Wiyot land through projects such as the Dishgamu Humboldt Community Land Trust.

Pomo territory is vast, encompassing the coastline from the Eel River to the Russian River and inland to Clear Lake. The Ukiah Valley is the heart of Pomo territory; *yō'kaia* is the Pomo term from which the town of Ukiah takes its name—it means "deep valley" and references the Pomo people who lived in the southern portion of the valley (*We Are the Land: A History of Native California*, by Damon B. Atkins and William J. Bauer Jr.). Pomo people lived in several distinct groups, each with unique dialects of the Pomo lan-guage. There are twelve Pomo rancherias around the Ukiah Valley, though several were terminated during the era of the Federal Termination Act. Pomo Land Back is actively working to protect Jackson Demonstration State Forest in Pomo homelands.

1 CRESCENT BEACH

WHY GO?

Crescent Beach is a wide, 3-mile-long stretch of sandy beach that is perfect for picnicking, strolling, or riding with a suitable wheelchair. This day-use area provides an opportunity to enjoy a picnic right on the beach. There is easy access to the ocean, and beach wheelchairs are available to borrow.

THE RUNDOWN

Spoon rating: 1 spoon, ADA accessible
Type: Scenic viewpoint
Distance: Negligible
Elevation: 5 feet
Elevation gain: None
Max grade: 2%
Max cross slope: None
Typical width: 4 feet
Typical surface: Concrete
Season/schedule: Open year-round. Best spring through fall, but summer can be foggy.
Water availability: None
Sun exposure: Full sun
Amenities: Accessible picnic tables and vault toilets, grill, fire rings, trash cans

Pet-friendly: Yes, on leash
Cell phone reception: Yes
Special notes: Collecting driftwood is prohibited. People frequently allow their dogs off leash on the beach, so be careful if you have a service dog.
Nearest town: Crescent City
Land manager: Redwood National and State Parks, Redwood National Park, (707) 464-6101
Pass/entry fee: None
Land acknowledgment: A Tolowa Dee-ni' village once existed at a nearby creek, now known as Nickel Creek. Tolowa people continue to gather here for fishing and collecting of shellfish and other cultural traditions.

FINDING THE TRAILHEAD

Getting there: From Crescent City, head south on US 101 to Enderts Beach Road. Turn right, then continue 0.7 mile and turn right at the sign for Crescent Beach. **GPS:** 41.43382, -124.09070

Parking: Large paved parking lot with 1 van-accessible parking spot directly in front of the accessible path; you could parallel park along the edge of the parking area for additional accessible parking. Plenty of space for large vehicles and RVs.

Start: The accessible path to the picnic area begins to the left of the accessible parking spot.

THE HIKE

A sidewalk-style path with edge guards leads to two picnic areas. Both areas have accessible picnic tables, but it may be tight to navigate if you use a large wheelchair. The picnic area on the right is less than 20 feet from the parking lot. It is further back from the beach and has a somewhat obstructed view, but it is less likely for sand to be on the pad surrounding the table. It does not have a grill. The second picnic area is about 30 feet straight ahead. It overlooks the beach, but the path may be sandy due to wind and people tracking sand onto it. A grill stands approximately 4 feet high just off the pad. An interpretive sign provides information about the Tolowa and their traditions.

Fire rings on the beach close to the parking area

The path to picnic tables on the beach

The picnic table nearest to the beach

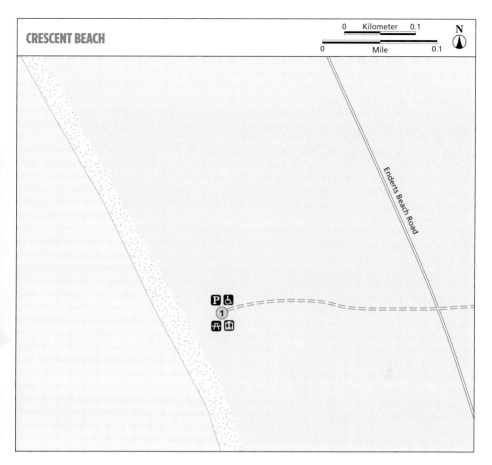

There are several fire rings and additional picnic tables on the firm, grassy area between the parking lot and the beach. Access to the beach is pretty level, but there may be driftwood to navigate in the winter. Beach wheelchairs—the kind with balloon wheels that have to be pushed by someone else—are available to borrow from a locked storage container on-site. To reserve one, call the park at the number above or visit the Crescent City Park Information Center at 1111 Second Street. A valid form of ID is required.

Once you are finished here, I recommend continuing down Enderts Beach Road to the Crescent Beach Overlook. There is a small parking area just before the end of the road. A short, paved path leads to a deck with incredible views of the ocean, the harbor, and the rocky coastline. It's a great place to enjoy sunset.

2 COASTAL TRAIL: ENDERTS BEACH

WHY GO?

This hike offers a little bit of everything that makes coastal trails so special: lush coastal forest, incredible views, a creek canyon, and an opportunity for tide pooling. This section is less technical than other portions of the Coastal Trail, but it loses 180 feet of elevation over 0.5 mile, making it a bit of a climb on the way back. Access to the beach requires navigating boulders. Plan to arrive at low tide if you want to visit the beach; a negative tide is the best time to check out the tide pools.

THE RUNDOWN

Spoon rating: 3 spoons, partially wheelchair hikeable. The first 0.2 mile is relatively flat, followed by a prolonged average 7% grade. Exposed cliffs and eroded areas may be a hazard.
Type: Out-and-back
Distance: 1.4 miles
Elevation: 207 feet
Elevation gain: 200 feet
Max grade: 18%
Max cross slope: 5%
Typical width: 3 feet
Typical surface: Compacted gravel
Trail users: Hikers, bikers
Season/schedule: Open year-round. Best spring through fall, but summer can be foggy.

Water availability: None
Sun exposure: Mostly shaded on the trail, no shade at the beach
Amenities: Accessible vault toilet, trash cans
Pet-friendly: No
Cell phone reception: None
Nearest town: Crescent City
Land manager: Redwood National and State Parks, Redwood National Park, (707) 464-6101
Pass/entry fee: None
Land acknowledgment: A Tolowa Dee-ni' village existed at Nickel Creek. This area continues to be a part of Tolowa people's cultural traditions.

FINDING THE TRAILHEAD

Getting there: From Crescent City, head south on US 101 to Enderts Beach Road. Turn right, then continue 2.3 miles to the end of the road. **GPS:** 41.705706, -124.142813
Parking: Paved parking lot at the end of the road and 1 van-accessible spot at the trailhead. There is a 1.5-inch lip from the concrete to the gravel trail surface.
Start: The trailhead is just behind the wooden barrier at a trailhead board.

THE HIKE

The trail follows an old roadbed—this used to be Redwood Highway and was the main route of travel along the coast, though it was likely a trail used by Indigenous people long before that. It starts with large, rough gravel on a 10% decline for 10 feet, then levels out and continues on a 4- to 6-foot-wide trail surfaced with loosely compacted small gravel. You are traveling along the cliff through a forest of Sitka spruce and red alder, with views

of the ocean below you. There is a 2% incline with a 5% cross slope towards the inside of the trail for about 20 feet. At 0.1 mile you leave the forest, and it opens up along the cliff with views of sea stacks and the coastline. The surface becomes a compacted mix of small and large gravel.

At 0.2 mile the trail curves slightly left, and you come to a couple sections of old landslides. There were two concrete barriers on the edge of the trail when I visited; the trail may be closed if the landslides continue. The trail is level and 4 feet wide at the first old landslide, but there is a sharp drop-off on the cliff edge and the gravel is loose, so be cautious. The second section was pretty uneven with some rocks on the surface, but it may be graded by the time this book is published.

At 0.3 mile the trail begins descending. Take a 5–8% decline with a slightly eroded 8% cross slope to the inside of the trail for about 30 feet. It then generally levels out again and reenters the forest. A print interpretive sign on the left provides information about the resilience of coastal forests. Continue hiking on the firmly packed gravel trail; it is slightly uneven and rolling. You'll pass some large trees with branches that are bent due to the windy, salty conditions of the coast. At 0.4 mile the trail takes a long 2–5% decline and narrows to 3 feet, continuing a little uneven with occasional exposed rocks rising up to 2 inches. Ferns, berries, chickweed, and mint line the trail in the summer, giving it a lush green feeling.

At 0.5 mile the trail forks at a sign. The Coastal Trail continues straight ahead—it is steep and difficult, so I don't recommend it. The Creekside Trail goes left—this is a narrow, pretty footpath that continues 0.2 mile along Nickel Creek. It's a nice optional detour. Go right to continue to Enderts Beach. The trail follows the creek canyon, continuing 3 feet wide on a generally 8% decline for about 0.1 mile. At 0.6 mile it levels out for a couple hundred feet, but there are lots of rolls and bumps in the trail and some

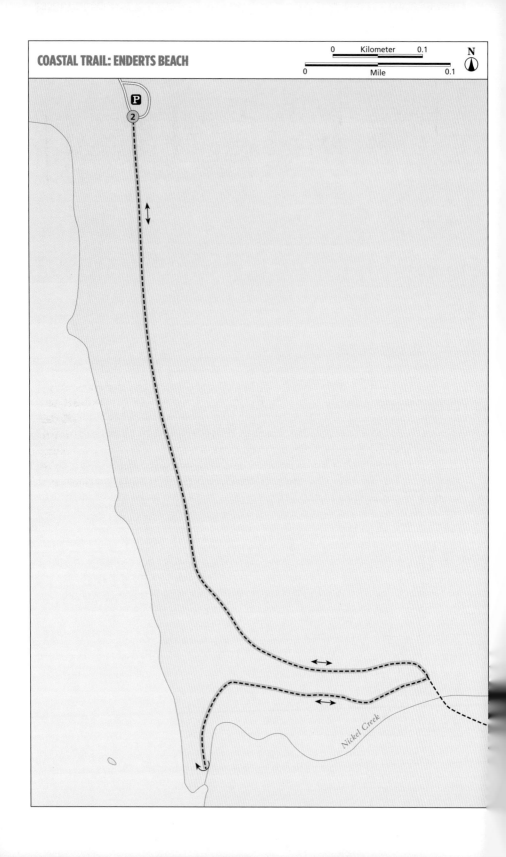

Nickel Creek

The wide gravel section of trail approaching an old landslide

potentially muddy areas. The trail then inclines at 5% for 100 feet or so, as you travel through a tunnel of low-growing spruce, then levels out as you continue through a shrubby area with blackberry vines and pass an interpretive sign about tide pools and the animals you may find there.

At 0.7 mile you reach the coastline and the trail curves sharply left. This is the steepest section of the trail. Take a 10–12% decline for about 100 feet as you approach the beach, increasing to 18% for about 50 feet. The trail ends on a rocky cliff that juts over the beach. Nickel Creek flows out to sea on your left. The views from here are worth the trip, and there are plenty of places to sit on the rocks, but to reach the beach you have to climb down the rocks to your right—it can be slippery, so be careful. I recommend using hiking poles to help with balance climbing down. There is a cool natural rock arch on the beach and lots of tide pools at low tide. When you're ready for the return climb, head back the way that you came.

MILES AND DIRECTIONS

0.0 Start at the trailhead at the end of Enderts Beach Road.

0.5 Go right at the fork.

0.7 Reach the coastline. Climb down the rocks to get to the beach.

1.4 Arrive back at the trailhead.

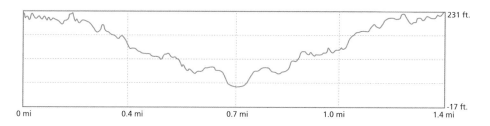

3 HOWLAND HILL SCENIC DRIVE

WHY GO?
This scenic driving route in Jedediah Smith Redwoods State Park brings you up close to giant old-growth redwoods without having to leave your car. The 10-mile-long road follows the Mill Creek canyon and offers a backcountry experience. There are many trailheads along the way, including Stout Grove (hike 4), and access to the Smith River at the end. This is my favorite drive in redwood country.

THE RUNDOWN

Type: Scenic drive
Distance: 18 miles round-trip. Allow at least an hour to complete the drive.
Elevation: 175 feet
Typical width and surface: Single-lane or narrow two-lane dirt road with few pullouts. Drivable in a standard vehicle. Recreational vehicles, vehicles pulling trailers, and oversize vehicles are prohibited.
Season/schedule: Open year-round with occasional closures in winter and spring. Best fall through spring before the road gets dusty in the summer.
Water availability: None
Sun exposure: Shaded

Amenities: Vault toilets at trailheads
Pet-friendly: Yes, allowed on leash on the road and in vehicles
Cell phone reception: Very spotty
Nearest town: Services available in Crescent City and Hiouchi
Land manager: Redwood National and State Parks, (707) 464-6101
Pass/entry fee: None
Land acknowledgment: This route travels through Tolowa Dee-ni' territory. Hiouchi, the name of the small town and visitor center in Jedediah Smith State Park, is an anglicized version of the Tolowa word Xaa-yuu-chit, which means "high-status stream/river."

FINDING THE TRAILHEAD

Getting there: From Crescent City, head 1 mile south on US 101 to Elk Valley Road and turn left. Continue for 1 mile to Howland Hill Road and turn right.
GPS: 41.758315, -124.167470
Start: Set your odometer on Howland Hill Road at Elk Valley Road.

THE DRIVE
Howland Hill Road begins as a two-lane paved residential street. You will pass the Sovereign Nation of Elk Valley Rancheria Tribal headquarters, which houses a museum. At 1.0 mile you enter Jedediah Smith Redwoods State Park and Howland Hill turns into a narrow two-lane paved road. The speed limit is 15 mph, but I recommend taking your time on this drive. The road is curvy as it climbs uphill, traveling through large Douglas firs and small redwoods. There is a drop-off on the left, which may be disconcerting to some travelers.

At 1.7 miles you reach what appears to be an intersection. There is a small parking area on the left, a gated road on the right, and another gate in front of you—continue straight on Howland Hill Road, watching out for a small bump as you pass through the open gate. The road transitions to dirt and you immediately come to a grove of very

Howland Hill Road curving between old-growth redwoods

large old-growth redwoods. You pass in between these giant trees on a wide single lane with pullouts on either side. Mill Creek is below you on the right, and redwoods and sword ferns cover the hillsides.

At 2.0 miles you drive underneath a large tree that is partially leaning over the road. You will lose cell service around this point. Continue along the beautiful fern-filled canyon, surrounded by giant old growth. At approximately 2.3 miles there is a slight curve with poor visibility, followed by a hairpin curve at 2.5 miles.

At 3.2 miles you drive between an old fallen tree that has been cut out and is rotted out through the middle—it is pretty neat to look into the interior of a tree from your car. At 3.5 miles, at a curve in the road, you pass another old blowdown with a huge root ball. There are several pullouts and some social trails that go off into the woods. Just beyond this is another giant redwood at a pullout. This tree has a partial goosepen—a hole in the base of the tree—that is at least 5 feet high. It is a popular picture spot, but always respect the trees by not climbing on them.

At 3.6 miles you pass through another gate and come to the trailhead for the Boy Scout Tree. The full trail is difficult, but the first 0.25 mile or so is level enough to stretch your legs, and there are old-growth redwoods at the trailhead. Two accessible vault toilets and one van-accessible parking spot are located here.

At 4.0 miles there are several places where the road narrows to one lane for about a car length as it passes between trees, with pullouts on both sides. At 4.3 miles you reach the Grove of the Titans trailhead, with another vault toilet and one van-accessible parking spot. Boardwalks were recently installed on this trail, which leads to some of the biggest trees in the park. However, there are a lot of steps and about 150 feet of elevation gain in 0.7 mile.

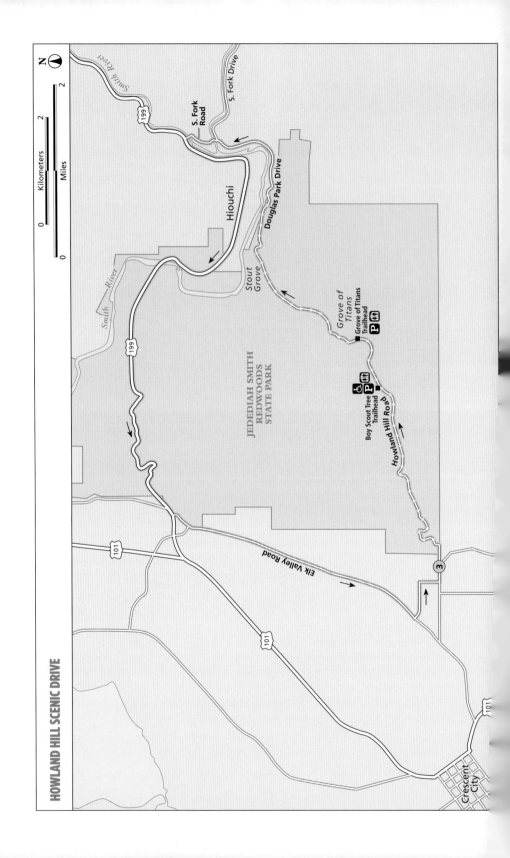

HOWLAND HILL SCENIC DRIVE

Howland Hill Road

After the trailhead there is one sharp curve and then the road narrows to one lane and crosses a single-lane bridge over the creek, with good visibility as you approach the bridge. The road widens again, with a few more sections of single lane passing between trees. At about 5.0 miles the canopy starts opening up and there are fewer large old growth trees.

At 5.4 miles the road narrows to one lane with a drop-off on the left to the creek canyon below you, but there are pullouts. The road may be a little more rutted and potholed here. You then enter another grove of redwoods, and at 5.8 miles reach the turnoff for Stout Memorial Grove (hike 4). A small sign points to the left for the grove.

Continuing past Stout Grove, the road widens back out and there are several pullouts. At 6.5 miles you cross Cedar Creek on a wide bridge, followed by a few sharp curves. Enter another grove of larger redwoods, then at 6.8 miles you pass a trailhead for the River Trail—from this trailhead, the River Trail heads north and west along the Smith River to Stout Grove. You'll start to notice houses across the river. There is another steep drop-off on the left and the road narrows to one lane with pullouts as you start heading downhill.

At 7.1 miles you pass through a gate. Continue straight past another pullout parking area with a gated road. Howland Hill Road becomes Douglas Park Drive and transitions to a paved one lane. Douglas Park Drive continues to be curvy as you enter a residential area. At 7.5 miles the road becomes paved two lanes along the Smith River. You will drive through a wooden covered bridge over Sheep Pen Creek.

At 8.4 miles you reach a T-intersection—go left on S. Fork Road towards US 199, crossing a bridge over the Smith River. There are very pretty river canyon views here. Cross another bridge over the Middle Fork Smith River, then reach a stop sign at a T-intersection. Go left on US 199 to return to Crescent City.

4 STOUT MEMORIAL GROVE

WHY GO?
Stout Memorial Grove is one of the most majestic old-growth red-wood forests in Jedediah Smith Redwoods State Park. Located on the banks of the Smith River, the grove experiences periodic flood-ing, which limits the growth of understory plants. The redwoods tower 300 feet above a forest floor carpeted in giant sword ferns and low-growing sorrel, creating an awe-inspiring experience. This trail is popular for good reason. I recommend a visit during the shoul-der season when the crowds are diminished and the forest is misty, though it is also stunning on a sunny day.

THE RUNDOWN

Spoon rating: 2 spoons, possibly wheelchair hikeable. After a brief, steep decline the trail is wide and flat with benches along the way.
Type: Lollipop loop
Distance: 0.7 mile
Elevation: 128 feet
Elevation gain: 33 feet gain, 26 feet loss
Max grade: 12%
Max cross slope: 2%
Typical width: 4 feet, minimum 38 inches
Typical surface: Firm soil and compacted gravel covered in tree needles
Trail users: Hikers
Season/schedule: Open year-round. Best in spring and fall.

Water availability: None—access to the Smith River is difficult.
Sun exposure: Shaded
Amenities: Accessible vault toilets, benches
Pet-friendly: No
Cell phone reception: Yes
Nearest town: Hiouchi
Land manager: Redwood National and State Parks, Jedediah Smith Redwoods State Park, (707) 464-6101
Pass/entry fee: None
Land acknowledgment: Tolowa Dee-ni' ancestral territory. The Smith River is known as Nii~-li~ in the Tolowa language.

FINDING THE TRAILHEAD
Getting there: From the Hiouchi Visitor Center, turn left on US 199. Continue 2 miles to S. Fork Road and turn right, cross the river twice, then turn right on Douglas Park Road. In 1.3 miles, continue straight onto Howland Hill Road. The turnoff for Stout Grove will be on the right in 1 mile. Continue 0.1 mile on a paved one-lane road to the parking area. **GPS:** 41.789652, -124.084808

Parking: Circular paved parking lot with 15 parking spots and 1 van-accessible spot near the restrooms.

Start: The exit of the parking loop, next to a large trailhead sign in the north corner.

THE HIKE
The trail begins at the end of the parking loop, to the right of a large trailhead sign with a photo and description of the forest. The pavement at the trailhead is very cracked and broken, with a couple holes and lips up to 2 inches. It may be difficult to navigate using

The Stout Grove trail through old-growth redwoods

The trail passing between blowdowns

The Stout Tree

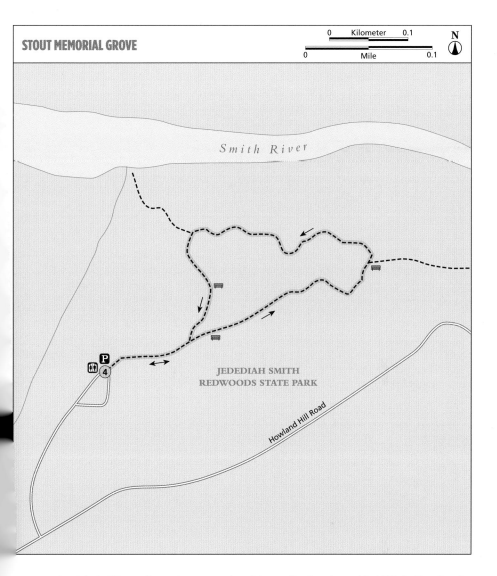

a wheelchair. The trail continues paved and immediately takes a 10–12% decline for the first hundred feet, then decreases to 5–8% for another couple hundred feet.

At 0.1 mile you reach the Stout Grove Loop. You can go either direction, but this description goes right at the loop. The trail is generally flat and compacted gravel along the entire loop, with a few slight dips and rolls. You are surrounded by towering old-growth redwoods, including standing snags and blowdowns—these are important features of a healthy old-growth forest.

At 0.2 mile there is a slight rise and roll on the trail for a couple feet and then it continues generally level, passing between large old-growth trees. You'll pass a couple snags that are almost completely eroded out and marked by evidence of past fires.

There is a bench at 0.3 mile, and then the trail forks. Go left to continue on the Stout Grove Loop. The River Trail is on the right—it leads about 0.5 mile along the Smith

River before connecting with Howland Hill Road and is an optional detour if you want to extend your hike. Continuing on the Stout Grove Loop, there may be some light noise from the highway in the distance, but you can mostly only hear the river.

At 0.4 mile you pass between several large snags and tumbles of old fallen trees, which makes for a very visually interesting experience. There are lots of interesting things to touch as well, including new redwood growth, roots of fallen trees, and tall sword ferns as the trail passes closely next to a blowdown on the right. The trail takes an 8% decline for a few feet with some exposed roots—there is about 3 feet of clearance around the roots—and then inclines again slightly. The trail continues a little more uneven with some slight rolls and cross slopes—evidence of impacts from fallen trees. You will pass between two old blowdown trees with exposed root bases on either side of the trail; another tree trunk lies vertically between them. The trail is about 38 inches wide here.

At 0.5 mile you reach another fork in the trail. Go left to continue on the loop. The Hiouchi Trail to the Jedediah Smith Campground goes to the right. At 0.6 mile you come to the Stout Tree, the largest tree in the grove. A gravel ramp leads up to a wooden platform, allowing an up-close experience of the tree. It is a popular photo spot. The loop ends just beyond the Stout Tree—go right to return to the parking lot.

MILES AND DIRECTIONS

0.0 Start at the trailhead at the end of the parking lot.

0.1 Reach the beginning of the loop. Go right.

0.3 Go left at the fork to stay on the loop.

0.5 Go left at the fork to stay on the loop.

0.6 Reach the end of the loop. Go right.

0.7 Arrive back at the parking lot.

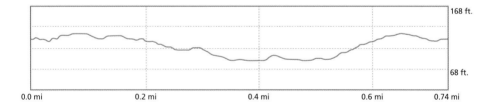

168 ft.

68 ft.

0.0 mi   0.2 mi   0.4 mi   0.6 mi   0.74 mi

5 SIMPSON-REED / PETERSON MEMORIAL TRAIL

WHY GO?

This is one of the more unique trails in Jedediah Smith Redwoods State Park. The forest is a distinctive mix of old-growth redwoods, hemlock trees, and vine maples, with tall sword ferns and redwood sorrel carpeting the ground. The grove is between two streams on the bank of the Smith River, creating a lush and damp environment that is perfect for a variety of wildlife, including rough-skinned newts and red-legged frogs. It is especially lovely in autumn, when the vine maples and other understory plants change color. This trail is designated as an ADA accessible trail by the park, but there are some trouble areas.

THE RUNDOWN

Spoon rating: 2 spoons, wheelchair hikeable with caution. The trail is generally firm and level, with some narrow spots and exposed roots. Not recommended for standard wheelchairs.
Type: Bisected lollipop loop
Distance: 0.93 mile
Elevation: 160 feet
Elevation gain: 49 feet gain, 56 feet loss
Max grade: 3%
Max cross slope: 8%
Typical width: 5 feet, minimum 18 inches
Typical surface: Firm soil and compacted gravel covered with redwood needles

Trail users: Hikers
Season/schedule: Open year-round
Water availability: None
Sun exposure: Shaded
Amenities: Accessible vault toilet, bench, trash cans
Pet-friendly: No
Cell phone reception: None
Nearest town: Hiouchi
Land manager: Redwood National and State Parks, Jedediah Smith Redwoods State Park, (707) 464-6101
Pass/entry fee: None
Land acknowledgment: Tolowa Dee-ni' ancestral territory

FINDING THE TRAILHEAD

Getting there: From the Hiouchi Visitor Center, turn right (west) on US 199. Continue 2.2 miles to Walker Road and turn right. It is easy to miss the turn-off—there is a pullout with parallel parking on US 199 just before you reach Walker Road (you can park here if there is no parking on Walker Road). The trailhead is about 200 feet down Walker Road. **GPS:** 41.81197, -124.10865

Parking: Two designated accessible spots at the trailhead—neither are painted with an access aisle, but there is usable space in between. About a dozen parking spots are scattered at pullouts along the road.

Start: The trailhead is behind the accessible parking area to the left of the vault toilet.

The trail passing between two large redwoods

THE HIKE

The trail begins generally 4 feet wide on a slightly uneven and rolling compacted gravel surface. It is generally firm, but there are some places with loose gravel. There is a steep cross slope at a natural drainage point near the beginning of the trail. The most level section is about 3 feet wide, so you may need to take care as you cross it.

In less than 0.1 mile, you pass several large blowdowns and then reach the trail fork at the beginning of the loop. I went right on the loop for this guide, but if you are hiking with a wheelchair or walker, I recommend going left to avoid a narrow section of trail. Just ignore the sign pointing behind you that reads Exit. Going right, the trail curves around an old fallen tree and passes closely between two young redwoods with about 3 feet of clearance. There is another section of narrow trail between two blowdowns—it may be pinched to 26 inches wide by plants growing along the edge and some exposed roots up to 2 inches high. The trail widens out again to 4 to 5 feet. You are surrounded by lots of large old-growth redwoods and waist-high sword ferns, but there may be some noise from the highway. You may also notice some very tall redwoods with candelabra crowns—this can happen when a redwood loses its top from breakage or cutting, and the crown regrows from many different sprouts along the wound.

At 0.1 mile there's a 5% cross slope towards the right for about 4 feet at a natural drainage. You then pass a small sign for the Simpson-Reed Trail—continue straight ahead, being mindful of some exposed roots in the center of the trail. You are traveling just below some of the large trees with candelabra crowns. The trail curves right around an old-growth redwood with exposed roots on the right side of the trail. Pass another blowdown on the left with piles of broken wood on the right; the trail then curves right and left over a few slightly uneven, rolling sections.

At 0.2 mile the trail splits around a few trees. The original trail route goes to the left, but there was a 6-inch-high, 6-inch-wide log across the trail at my visit. The more obvious

The trail passing narrowly around trees

route passes narrowly between two redwoods—new growth at the base of one of the trees pinches the trail to about 18 inches wide. This is supposed to be corrected, but you may want to confirm with the park. Beyond this pinch point, the trail widens out to 5 feet.

At 0.3 mile you have a nice view of the creek to the right. The trail curves to the right, passing between old growth, then you reach a fork in the trail at 0.4 mile. Go right on the Peterson Memorial Trail. (The Simpson-Reed Trail continues to the left, bisecting the loop—you can go that way if you would like to shorten the hike by 0.25 mile.) Cross a sturdy, level wooden bridge with handrails. Take a slight rise, then the trail curves left and crosses a footbridge with edge barriers. The trail continues on a compact gravel surface, passing through old-growth redwoods, maples, and hemlocks. One of the maples has grown over the trail and taken root on either side, creating a cool arch across the trail with over 6 feet of clearance underneath. The trail surface gets a little uneven and rolling with a slight cross slope, but it is generally pretty flat. You are continuing deeper into the old-growth forest, and any highway noise you heard at the beginning of the trail should fade.

There is a root across the trail at 0.5 mile, but it can be navigated with 3 feet of clearance on the right. The trail curves right around an old rotted-out tree, then you enter another grove of old growth. At 0.6 mile the trail curves sharply left along the creek. There is one unprotected drop-off with a 5–8% cross slope.

Cross another bridge over the creek at 0.7 mile—it is level, with smooth boards and handrails, but may be slippery so be careful. This is a nice spot to take in the experience for a moment; the creek is lush with plants, and you are surrounded by large redwoods. You then reach the intersection with the other side of the Simpson-Reed Trail loop—go right. You then come to a memorial grove along the creek. There is a bench with an armrest and space to pull over beside it. A wooden fence protects the drop-off. This is the only bench on the trail and a nice place to take a break. Continuing past the bench, there are some really nice old-growth trees, including several big fallen trees that are

The bench overlooking the creek

A large burled redwood

growing into nurse logs with new trees sprouting from their trunks, another sign of healthy old-growth forest.

At 0.8 mile there is an interpretive sign about fire in the redwoods and some huge old-growth trees with massive burls at the base towering hundreds of feet above you. Some roots across the trail rise up to 3 inches above the surface, so navigate with care around the trees. The trail continues 5 feet wide on firm compacted gravel. At 0.9 mile it curves right and left and then splits around a large fallen tree—go right to see the exposed roots, but the trail continues to the left of the blowdown and narrows to 4 feet wide. You may start to notice road noise again. You then reach the end of the loop—go right to return to the trailhead.

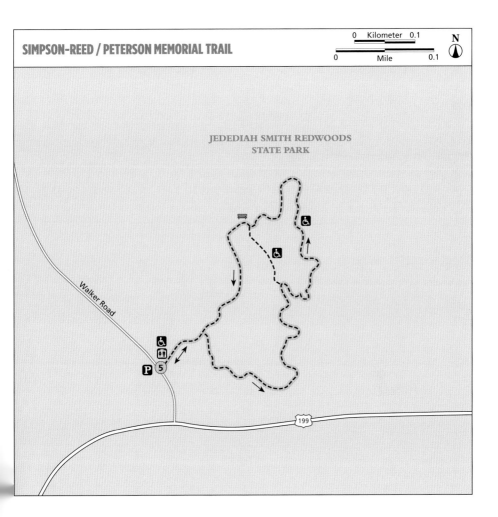

JEDEDIAH SMITH REDWOODS
STATE PARK

Walker Road

199

MILES AND DIRECTIONS

0.0 Begin at the trailhead sign to the left of the toilet.

0.03 Go right at the fork for the loop trail.

0.4 Go right to continue on the Peterson Memorial Trail.

0.7 Go right at the fork to continue on the loop.

0.9 Reach the end of the loop. Go right.

0.93 Arrive back at the trailhead.

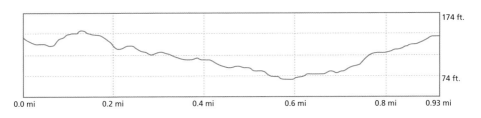

6 REDWOOD ACCESS AND REVELATION TRAIL LOOP

WHY GO?

This route combines the Redwood Access Trail and the Revelation Trail to create a half-mile ADA accessible loop through lush redwood forest. The Revelation Trail was designed to be accessible for visitors who are blind or low vision; it has guide ropes along the length of the trail and around features such as uprooted trees so that visitors can engage multiple senses. A platform encircles a large redwood tree for an up-close experience.

THE RUNDOWN

Spoon rating: 1 spoon, wheelchair accessible with two 5–8% inclines for a few feet
Type: Lollipop loop
Distance: 0.55 mile
Elevation: 150 feet
Elevation gain: 20 feet gain, 23 feet loss
Max grade: 8%
Max cross slope: 2%
Typical width: 5 feet, minimum 3 feet
Typical surface: Compact gravel
Trail users: Hikers
Season/schedule: Open year-round
Water availability: Water fountains
Sun exposure: Shaded

Amenities: Flush restrooms, trash cans, benches, picnic tables, visitor center
Pet-friendly: No
Cell phone reception: None
Special notes: Overhead and protruding objects on the Revelation Trail. Some areas of guide rope may be missing.
Nearest town: Orick
Land manager: Redwood National and State Parks, Prairie Creek Redwoods State Park, (707) 464-6101
Pass/entry fee: None
Land acknowledgment: Yurok ancestral territory

FINDING THE TRAILHEAD

Getting there: From Orick, head north on US 101 for 5 miles. Take exit 753 for Newton B Drury Scenic Parkway. Turn left and continue 1.1 miles to Prairie Creek Road. Turn left and the visitor center is on the right. **GPS:** 41.363760, -124.022936. **Note:** The parkway is closed on the first Saturday of the month from October to May for Hike and Bike Day.

Parking: There is 1 accessible parking spot directly in front of the visitor center, and 2 spots just past the visitor center on Prairie Creek Road. A parking lot across the road from the visitor center has about 20 spots but they are time limited. Additional parking is on Prairie Creek Road.

Public transit: From the market in Orick, take Redwood Coast Transit route 20 towards Crescent City. The first stop is on the parkway at the Prairie Creek Visitor Center—go left on Prairie Creek Road to reach the visitor center.

Start: The trailhead at the right rear corner of the visitor center.

The trail with a guide rope through the forest

THE HIKE

This trail has multiple access points. I recommend starting at the trailhead on the right side of the visitor center—this will avoid a section that is at a steep cross slope. There is a new trail access information sign here for the Redwood Access Trail. The trail starts 3 feet wide as it travels to the right of the visitor center, then you come to a wooden trail sign that marks the dedication of this trail in 1981 for International Year of the Disabled. Go to the right at the sign. The trail widens to 5 feet, and you immediately enter a grove of large redwoods. Continue on the level, firm trail through redwoods, sword ferns, and other understory plants. At 0.1 mile there is an old, very low log bench on the right.

At 0.2 mile you reach a signed trail intersection. Go right to continue on the Access Trail to the Revelation Trail. Wooden poles with guide ropes line the right side of the trail, guiding visitors along a wonderful sensory-scape of sword ferns and mossy trees. You soon reach a large tree that has fallen along the side of the trail. It is over 5 feet high and covered in moss, ferns, and other plants. A moss-covered maple also grows low and protrudes over the trail here; the lowest branch is over 6 feet high, but the trunk of the tree is a couple feet into the trail corridor, so be cautious if you are following the guide rope.

Shortly after, some guide rope may be missing as the trail leads to a viewing area of the creek on the right. There is a sturdy bench with an armrest and a small sign that provides information on the salmon that spawn in the creek. Unfortunately, none of the many signs on the trail are in Braille, but visitors can download an audio brochure from the park website. Immediately past the viewing area you reach another trail intersection—go left to stay on the Revelation Trail. The guide rope is on the left on this section of the loop. There is one short 8% incline, then the trail curves slightly left and continues generally 5 feet wide, though ferns may narrow it to 4 feet.

The trail with a guide rope traveling next to the large fallen tree

The platform surrounding the large redwood

REDWOOD ACCESS AND REVELATION TRAIL LOOP

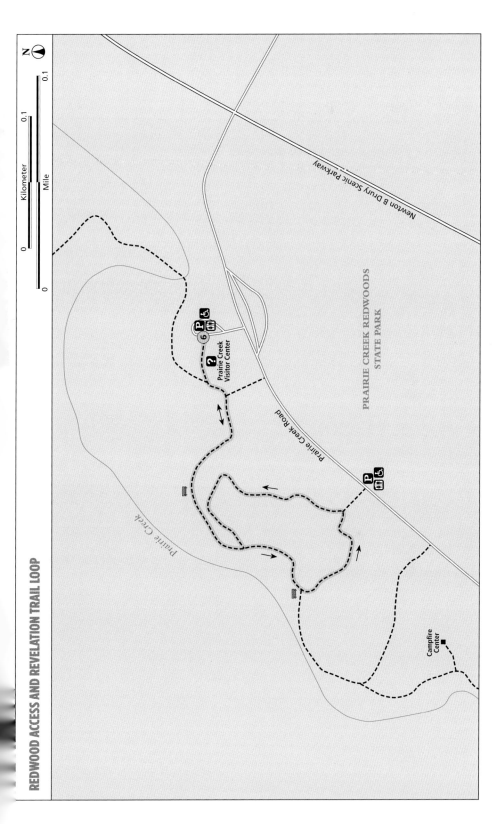

At 0.3 mile you arrive at a wood board ramp to a platform encircling a large redwood. Handrails line the ramp and platform. There is one partially collapsed board at the transition between the trail and the ramp, but still about 3 feet of level clearance. The ramp turns right, then left, and then closely circles the tree—you are close enough to easily touch the bark and follow the tree around the platform.

In front of the platform, a short gravel path leads to another parking lot with two accessible parking spots (one is van accessible), accessible gendered restrooms, a water fountain, and trash cans. There are no guide ropes from the parking area to the boardwalk, but otherwise it also makes a good place to begin the hike.

Go left from the platform. There are guide ropes on both sides of the trail for a short distance, then only on the right side. You will pass a fallen tree with exposed roots close enough to the trail to touch. There is a short 5% incline as the trail curves right, and a few slightly uneven spots with medium-size gravel that may make the surface a little unsteady. Large redwoods and lush forest surround you, and you pass close enough to several trees to touch them.

At 0.4 mile you reach the end of the Revelation Trail loop. Go right on the Access Trail to return to the trailhead.

MILES AND DIRECTIONS

0.0   Begin at the trailhead on the north side of the visitor center. Go right at the wooden sign for the Access Trail.

0.2   Reach an intersection with the Revelation Trail. Go right.

0.25 Reach another intersection with the Revelation Trail. Go left.

0.3   Reach a platform around a large redwood tree.

0.4   Reach the end of the Revelation Trail. Go right on the Access Trail.

0.55 Arrive back at the trailhead.

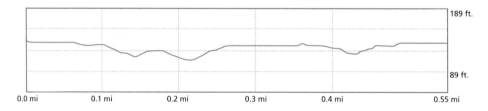

189 ft.

89 ft.

0.0 mi   0.1 mi   0.2 mi   0.3 mi   0.4 mi   0.55 mi

7 SUE-MEG STATE PARK LOOP

WHY GO?

Sue-meg (pronounced "sue-may") State Park was once known as Patrick's Point State Park. The name was officially changed in 2021 to Sue-meg, which has been the name used by Yurok people for this place since time immemorial. It is an incredibly special place of lush forest, coastal cliffs, and tall rocks protruding from the landscape. It is also an opportunity to learn more about Yurok culture at Suemêg Village, a re-created village used by Yurok people, and at numerous signs and exhibits. This route takes you to a few of the most popular and accessible locations in the park.

THE RUNDOWN

Spoon rating: 3 spoons. The most wheelchair-accessible portion of the loop is Suemêg Village to Ceremonial Rock, and the overlook at Patrick's Point.
Type: Lollipop loop or out-and-back
Distance: 2.1 miles (lollipop loop)
Elevation: 223 feet
Elevation gain: 151 feet gain, 148 feet loss
Max grade: 9%
Max cross slope: 5%
Typical width: 5 feet
Typical surface: Aggregate (combination of small and large gravel and soil)
Trail users: Hikers

Season/schedule: Open year-round, dawn to dusk
Water availability: Fountains at visitor center
Sun exposure: Mostly shaded
Amenities: Restrooms, benches, picnic tables
Pet-friendly: No
Cell phone reception: None
Nearest town: Trinidad
Land manager: California State Parks, Sue-meg State Park, (707) 677-3570
Pass/entry fee: Day-use fee. California State Parks annual passes are accepted.
Land acknowledgment: Ner'-er-nerh / Coastal Yurok

FINDING THE TRAILHEAD

Getting there: From Trinidad, head north on US 101 for 5 miles. Take exit 734 for Patrick's Point Drive. Turn left, and then right onto the Park Entrance Road. Go through the entrance booth and turn right to the visitor center. **GPS:** 41.134831, -124.155389

Parking: Large paved parking lot at the visitor center with 3 designated accessible spots. However, the only spot with a wide-enough access aisle is in the corner of the parking lot. The only curb cut is in front of the visitor center—it is steep but usable.

Public transit: From the Trinidad Park and Ride, take Redwood Coast Transit route 20 towards Crescent City. The eighth stop is at the park entrance station; walk across the street to reach the visitor center.

Start: The Suemêg Village trailhead to the right of the visitor center at the far end of the parking lot.

Suemêg Village

THE HIKE

This loop takes in several of the most popular sites in Sue-meg State Park. For ease of reading, I've divided the hike description by site with options to visit each individually. Of course, you can complete the entire hike by following the description from start to finish. There are a lot of interconnecting trails in the park, but they are generally well-signed. Be sure to pick up a map from the entrance kiosk or visitor center, or download the route if you are using a trail app, as cell service is spotty at best.

SUEMÊG VILLAGE

The Suemêg Village trail begins to the right of the visitor center at the far end of the parking area. It starts paved on an 8% incline for a few feet as you approach a Yurok Tribe canoe, with an interpretive sign about bringing the Ohl'Wo'Yoch (canoe) to life. The trail continues 5 feet wide on packed gravel with a 5% incline for about 30 feet. You then come to a T-intersection with a sign pointing left to Ceremonial Rock and right to Suemêg Village. Go right for the accessible route. Continue through a forest of Sitka spruce with ferns, salal, and other understory plants surrounding you. Take a 2% incline, then continue straight past a fork on the right for the Native Plant Garden. The trail curves to the left and briefly transitions to natural surface, then returns to compacted large gravel.

At 0.2 mile you reach the village. Continue straight ahead at the fork to a paved path that leads to an interpretive sign about the village and then to accessible gendered restrooms, trash cans, and a few picnic tables beneath an overhang. Additional picnic tables are located throughout the grounds. You have to travel over rolling, uneven, grassy terrain

Typical trail through the forest

to visit the buildings in the village. It's approximately 0.3 mile to circle the village. Please be respectful if you do visit the buildings—the village is actively used by Yurok people as a space for ceremony, education, and other cultural practices.

CEREMONIAL ROCK

To continue to Ceremonial Rock, make a right back onto the trail when you leave the village. You almost immediately reach a T-intersection with a sign for Ceremonial Rock. Go left. The trail continues 5 feet wide on level and compacted gravel. There may be lots of mushrooms to identify (but never pick!) in the fall, and also some large Sitka spruce and Douglas fir to enjoy.

At 0.3 mile you reach another T-intersection—go right to Ceremonial Rock (left takes you back to the visitor center but it is not accessible). The trail is slightly crowned here. You immediately reach another fork—continue slightly left to stay on the main trail. Curve right around a large Sitka spruce, then go left at the next T-intersection (Red Alder Campground is just off to the right—this is where you'll come in if you park near the campground). You then pass the turnoff for Agate Beach on the right; continue straight, following signs for Ceremonial Rock. The trail continues 5 feet wide on compacted medium-size gravel. Curve slightly left next to a large Sitka spruce and take a 5% incline for a few feet.

At 0.4 mile you pass a huge boulder on the left and the trail takes a couple slight inclines and declines. You'll start to notice the rock rising above the forest on the right. The trail curves slightly left, and then you arrive at the fork for Ceremonial Rock at 0.5

View of Wedding Rock from the overlook

mile. There is a good bench at the trail intersection and a rather rustic one to the right on the loop trail. The loop trail around the rock is narrow and rocky with a few stone steps. Getting to the top of the rock requires climbing dozens of very steep, slippery stone steps. I hiked it and regretted the decision immediately, especially on the way back down. So, I recommend hanging out at one of the benches or checking out the trail around the base of the rock as much as you are comfortable.

For a shorter route, you can park near the Red Alder Campground or in one of the parking areas along the northern portion of Park Entrance Road and take the Ceremonial Rock Trail (described below).

RIM TRAIL AND PATRICK'S POINT

Continue past Ceremonial Rock on the Ceremonial Rock Trail (or return to the trail and go right if you explored around the rock). Take an 8% decline for about 30 feet and curve slightly right. The trail continues 5 feet wide on compacted large gravel with some loose pieces on the surface. It rises and falls on 5% grades for a few feet, then you pass another large boulder on the left.

At 0.6 mile you take a 5% incline for about 5 feet, passing between two large trees, and then have to cross Park Entrance Road. There are textured plates on both sides of the road to indicate the crossing but no crosswalk, so proceed with caution. Continue straight ahead to the Rim Trail. The trail is slightly uneven and curves slightly right, then you cross an armored crossing. The trail surface is firm and even, but there is an unprotected 2-foot drop-off on the left. It continues on generally level compacted gravel and 5 feet wide, except for a couple places where the trail is pinched to 3 feet wide by brush and roots.

The trail below Ceremonial Rock

At 0.7 mile you reach a fork; go left on the Rim Trail (Lookout Rock Campground is to the right). The trail takes a 2% decline for about 50 feet. Go right at the next fork, following the Rim Trail signs marked with an accessibility symbol. There is a trail access information sign that gives data about the Rim Trail. Continue on the compacted gravel trail on a 5–8% incline for about 50 feet. The trail forks again. Rocky Point is on the right—this trail is narrow with a lot of tall stairs to an overlook of the ocean.

Go left on the Rim Trail. The trail takes a 5% incline for about 50 feet as you follow the cliff with nice views of the ocean. At 0.9 mile there is a bench on the left. This is a nice spot for whale watching or just to take a break. The trail starts to get a bit uneven with some alternating cross slopes beyond this point, but it is supposed to be accessible to the Campground Center past Abalone Campground. I decided to turn around and, luckily, the view on the way back is even better! Whether you continue or turn around, retrace your route, going right past the fork for Rocky Point, then left above the campground, following signs for the Rim Trail.

There are nice views of the rocky coastline, then you come to Lookout Rock towering above you. Some steep steps lead up the rock. Continue straight ahead on the 3-foot-wide compacted gravel trail. Take an 8% incline for about 20 feet as you curve slightly right next to a large boulder. This is part of the face of Lookout Rock, and there is a cool cave in it that does resemble a face.

At 1.1 miles the trail forks. Go left to the Patrick's Point Overlook. It takes a 5% incline for a few feet, then levels out and passes a small overlook on the left. Continue ahead through a forest of knotted and contorted trees. You reach the overlook in a couple hundred feet—the right side is wheelchair accessible and there are a couple benches. It overlooks Wedding Rock and is a great place to watch waves crashing along the cliffs.

The trail through the meadow with Ceremonial Rock rising through the trees

For a shorter option, park at the Wedding Rock parking area, which has one accessible parking spot, and take the Rim Trail to the left and then turn right to the overlook.

RETURNING TO THE VISITOR CENTER

Continuing past the turn to the overlook, you almost immediately reach the Wedding Rock parking area. The Rim Trail continues towards the left, but there are many stairs and then it continues narrow and steep. The most accessible route is to turn around and make this an out-and-back. But if you can, I recommend continuing through the parking area and going left on Wedding Rock Road. Walk along the road on a 3% incline for a little over 0.1 mile. At the next parking lot on the left, where there are accessible toilets, go right on a mown path through a meadow. It is slightly uneven but level for about 20 feet then crosses Park Entrance Road. Continue straight through another meadow on the level and even mown path. You will notice Ceremonial Rock ahead of you. This is a great place for birding and wildflowers.

After 0.2 mile you reenter the forest to the right of Ceremonial Rock. There are some exposed roots rising up to 3 inches, but they are easy to bypass. Take an 8% incline for

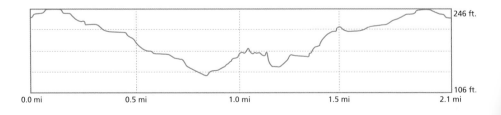

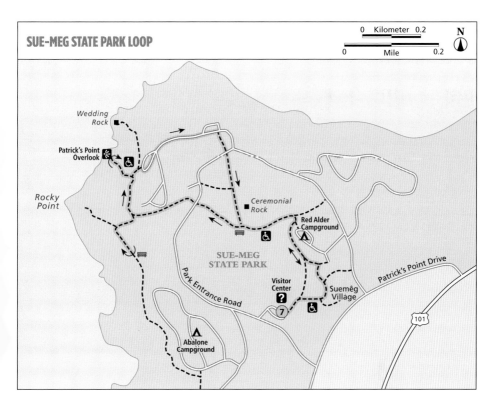

SUE-MEG STATE PARK LOOP

about 30 feet and then return to the intersection with the Ceremonial Rock Trail—go left, retracing your route back to the visitor center (right at Red Alder Campground, left towards Suemêg Village, then right past the village).

MILES AND DIRECTIONS

0.0   Start at the Suemêg Village trailhead.

0.2   Reach Suemêg Village. Go right from the village to the Ceremonial Rock Trail.

0.3   Go right on the Ceremonial Rock Trail.

0.5   Reach Ceremonial Rock. Continue straight on the Ceremonial Rock Trail.

0.6   Cross Park Entrance Road and continue straight on the Rim Trail.

0.7   Go left on the Rim Trail.

0.9   Turn around at the bench.

1.1   Go left to Patrick's Point Overlook. Turn around and go left to the parking area.

1.2   Go left on Wedding Rock Road.

1.4   Go right on the trail through the meadow. Cross Park Entrance Road and continue straight.

1.5   Reach Ceremonial Rock. Go left to return to the trailhead.

2.1   Arrive back at the trailhead.

8 MOONSTONE BEACH

WHY GO?
Moonstone Beach County Park is a 0.5-mile-long strip of beach at the mouth of the Little River. It is one of the easiest beaches to access in the area and the most interesting. There are tide pools and sea caves to explore at low tide, and many interesting rocks and sea stacks. The river's current slows as it reaches the ocean, making it a pleasant place to swim. It is a popular place with local families and can be busy, especially on summer weekends.

THE RUNDOWN

Spoon rating: 1 spoon. Wheelchair access will vary depending on conditions; if the sand is built up to the parking area, it may be possible to navigate a beach wheelchair onto the beach.
Type: Scenic viewpoint
Distance: Up to 1.0 mile
Elevation: 0 feet
Elevation gain: 0 feet
Max grade: 10%
Max cross slope: None
Typical surface: Sand
Trail users: Beach walkers, surfers, rock climbers
Season/schedule: Open year-round, 5 a.m. to midnight
Water availability: None
Sun exposure: Full sun

Amenities: Portable toilet
Pet-friendly: Yes, allowed off-leash on the wave slope (the sloped area of the beach closest to the water)
Cell phone reception: Yes
Nearest town: Trinidad
Land manager: Humboldt County Parks, (707) 445-7651
Pass/entry fee: None
Land acknowledgment: Tsurai Village, the largest southernmost village of the Yurok Tribe, encompassed over 65,000 acres in what is now known as Trinidad. The land was named Trinidad by Spanish explorers in 1775, but Tsurai remained occupied by Yurok people until 1916.

FINDING THE TRAILHEAD
Getting there: From Trinidad, take US 101 south for 2 miles. Take exit 726 for Westhaven. Turn left on Sixth Avenue, right on S. Westhaven Drive, and left on Scenic Drive. Turn right onto Moonstone Beach Road in 0.2 mile and follow it to the end of the road. **GPS:** 41.029304, -124.111170

Parking: Gravel parking area with space for about 30 cars. There is 1 designated accessible parking spot directly in front of the beach, but it is likely to be covered in sand. There may be some large potholes.

Public transit: From the Trinidad Park and Ride, take the Redwood Transit System Scotia or Fortuna route for 2 stops south to Moonstone Beach Road. Walk 0.2 mile down Moonstone Beach Road. The road is fairly steep and there is no sidewalk, so be careful of cars.

THE HIKE
Moonstone Beach stretches 0.5 mile north of the mouth of the Little River. There are many rocks and sea stacks here. Camel Rock, a large two-humped island, is visible to the

Rocks at Moonstone Beach

Looking across the cliffs from Moonstone Beach

The path to the beach from
the accessible parking spot

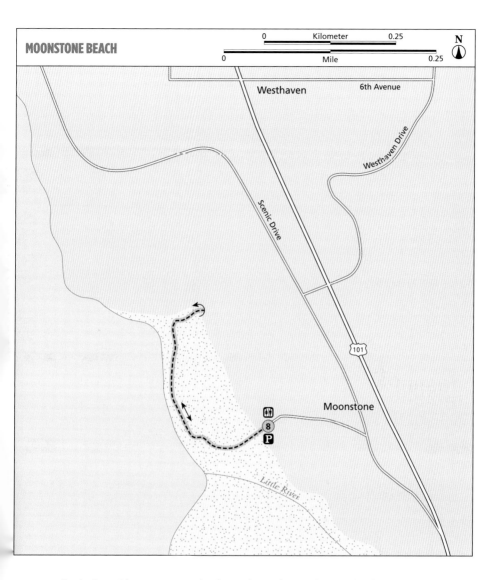

north. At low tide, sea caves and tide pools can be reached at the far end of the beach. The mouth of the Little River is a great place for birding, as is a small stream to the north.

The view from the parking area is limited, but access to the beach is short and direct. There are a couple cuts through shrubs at the edge of the parking lot. Depending on the condition of the sand, there could be a 6-inch step down and an 8% decline for about 10 feet to reach the beach. The beach is flat, but the sand may be a little soft. You can sit and enjoy the experience as soon as you get onto the beach or hike up to 0.5 mile north depending on the tide.

9 ARCATA MARSH

WHY GO?
Arcata Marsh and Wildlife Sanctuary is a naturalized wastewater treatment facility—but don't let that turn you off. It is a unique place that includes freshwater, saltwater, and brackish marsh, tidal sloughs, and grasslands on Arcata Bay at the northern end of Humboldt Bay. The sanctuary is home to thousands of birds, with well over 300 species visiting throughout the year. Over 5 miles of generally accessible trails travel throughout the marsh, and it connects with the Humboldt Bay Trail for an even longer outing. This loop, which offers a sample of everything that makes this place unique, is one of my favorites. It is spectacular at sunset.

THE RUNDOWN

Spoon rating: 2 spoons. Wheelchair accessible on firm packed gravel with one 12% grade for a few feet that can be avoided.
Type: Loop
Distance: 0.93 mile
Elevation: 7 feet
Elevation gain: None
Max grade: 12%
Max cross slope: 2%
Typical width: 6 feet, minimum 3 feet
Typical surface: Compact gravel
Trail users: Hikers, bikers
Season/schedule: Open year-round
Water availability: Water fountains at the interpretive center

Sun exposure: Full sun
Amenities: Picnic tables, benches, toilets
Pet-friendly: Yes, on leash
Cell phone reception: Yes
Nearest town: Arcata
Land manager: City of Arcata. Contact the interpretive center for questions: (707) 826-2359.
Pass/entry fee: None
Land acknowledgment: A Wiyot settlement, Kori, existed in what is now called Arcata. Arcata comes from the Yurok word *oket'oh*, referencing Humboldt Bay as a lagoon.

FINDING THE TRAILHEAD

Getting there: From Samoa Boulevard and I Street in Arcata, head south on I Street for 1 mile. The road curves sharply right and then left. Continue to the parking lot at the end of I Street. **GPS:** 40.855630, -124.098229
Parking: Large paved parking lot with no designated ADA spots.
Public transit: The nearest bus stop is at G Street and Fifth Street.
Start: The trailhead at the end of the parking lot.

THE HIKE
The parking area has several picnic tables, benches, and trash cans; it is a popular spot to gather and can be busy with people hanging out. There is frequent boat and car traffic, so be careful as you go towards the end of the parking lot and continue straight ahead on the 6-foot-wide gravel path. You are traveling on a constructed berm with a human-made lake, Klopp Lake, on the left and Humboldt Bay on the right. It is an excellent

The wide gravel trail along the berm

A bird blind

place for birding, and I always find walking between two bodies of water to be a unique experience. The berm is about 8 feet wide, with a 6-foot compacted gravel trail and a foot or so of grass on either side. It is built up with rocks that generally serve as edge barriers. Blackberry vines line a few sections of the trail on the lake side. There are a couple places with stairs leading down to benches on the lake, but no benches directly on this part of the trail.

At 0.2 mile an interpretive sign on the left identifies the shorebirds that can be found here. At 0.4 mile the trail curves left, continuing to circle the lake. At 0.5 mile there is a bench and trash can and the trail forks at No Name Pond. Go left to continue around Klopp Lake. (**Note:** If you continue straight ahead, the trail connects with the paved

Overlooking Klopp Lake

Klopp Lake and the ocean at sunset

Humboldt Bay Trail. You can go left on the Bay Trail and then left at the four-way trail intersection to avoid the incline below.) The trail narrows to 3 feet and rolls slightly but is firm packed gravel. It inclines at 12% for 10 feet, then meets another fork at 0.6 mile. The trail on the right leads to the Humboldt Bay Trail and Allen Marsh. Continue straight. The trail rolls slightly a couple times and then there is a bird blind on the left—it is a level transition to the blind, and one side is low enough for viewing from sitting height.

The trail continues 4 feet wide and level. There is another bench at 0.7 mile. At 0.8 mile go left at the trail intersection. Pass another bench at the edge of the lake. At 0.9 mile you return to the picnic area at the parking lot; continue straight towards the trailhead to avoid some steps.

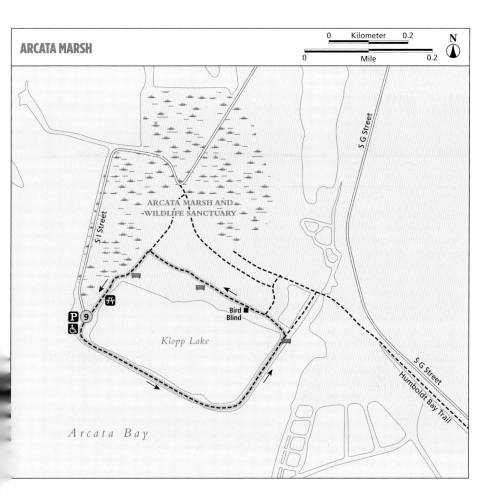

MILES AND DIRECTIONS

0.0 Begin at the trailhead at the end of the parking lot.

0.5 Go left at the fork.

0.8 Go left at the fork.

0.93 Arrive back at the parking lot.

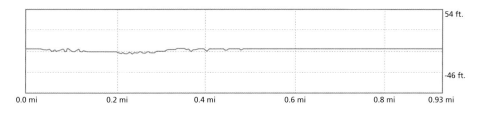

10 ELK RIVER TRAIL

WHY GO?

The 7,472-acre Headwaters Forest Reserve protects some of the only remaining old-growth redwood forest in the area. The old-growth redwoods are deep in the reserve and not easily accessible, but it is a beautiful place to visit. The Elk River Trail follows the South Fork Elk River; there are beautiful redwoods and river views along the way and remnants of an old mill town. The first mile is paved, and several picnic tables provide a spot to enjoy some time here. There is no access to the river in order to protect this sensitive habitat, which is home to many threatened species, including coho salmon, northern spotted owl, and marbled murrelet.

THE RUNDOWN

Spoon rating: 4 spoons due to prolonged grades. Wheelchair hikeable for the first mile but recommended only for power chair and four-wheel scooter riders or strong manual wheelchair users. There are areas of collapsed asphalt towards the end.
Type: Out-and-back
Distance: 3.0 miles
Elevation: 80 feet
Elevation gain: 180 feet gain, 180 feet loss
Max grade: 12%
Max cross slope: 5%
Typical width: 6 feet
Typical surface: Asphalt
Trail users: Hikers, bikers
Season/schedule: Open year-round, sunrise to sunset

Water availability: None
Sun exposure: Shaded
Amenities: Accessible vault toilet, picnic tables, trash cans
Pet-friendly: Yes, allowed on and off leash on the first 3 miles of the Elk River Trail
Cell phone reception: None
Nearest town: Eureka
Land manager: Bureau of Land Management, Arcata Field Office, (707) 825-2300
Pass/entry fee: None
Land acknowledgment: Long before the battle to preserve Headwaters Reserve, this was Wiyot land. Several Wiyot villages existed along the Elk River, including Iksori at the mouth of the river.

FINDING THE TRAILHEAD

Getting there: From Eureka, head south on US 101 for 3 miles. Take exit 702 for Herrick Road and Elk River Road. Turn left on Herrick Road, then right on Elk River Road. Stay on Elk River Road for approximately 6 miles, until it ends at the parking area. **GPS:** 40.692074, -124.140921

Parking: The parking lot is surfaced in pavers for drainage along the outer edge; it is paved in the center. One designated accessible spot but the paint is faded; it is not van accessible but there is a small usable space beside it.

Start: Elk River trailhead on the left side of the parking lot.

A bench along the trail beneath redwoods

THE HIKE

The trail follows the river on an old logging road. It is paved for the first mile and considered accessible, but there are long sections of prolonged grades and areas of cross slope that may be a challenge.

The trail begins on a 5% decline with a 2% cross slope for a few feet, then continues on a 2% incline for about 0.1 mile, with a 2% cross slope towards the end. It levels out briefly and then continues on a 2% incline as you travel through a young mixed forest of redwoods, red alders, maples, and Douglas firs. Pass a sign on the left dedicated to the activists who fought to protect the reserve. There are several large redwoods as you continue up the river, and low interpretive signs provide information about the forest. The trail continues on a generally 2% incline.

At 0.3 mile there is a sign on the left about osoberry (previously known as Indian plum). The trail then takes a 5% incline with a 2% cross slope for about 30 feet, reducing to a 2% incline with a 2% cross slope for a short distance and then inclining at 5–8% for another 30 feet. You then come to an interpretive sign about the caretakers of the headwaters since settlement—there is no information about the Wiyot and Nongati who have been caretakers of these lands for millennia. A footpath on the right leads to the site of a former caretaker's house—the structure's footings, plumbing, and some stairs remain. There is a bench and a nice view of the river.

The paved trail continues on a short 2% decline, then you come to another printed interpretive sign at the base of a large, interesting redwood. Multiple trunks grow out from the base of a cut and burned stump, and the hillside is eroded beneath it so that you can see some of the roots. The trail continues generally level for a few hundred feet.

The trail curving uphill at a rough patch

Passing old stumps on the trail

At 0.5 mile take a 5% incline, increasing to 8% for about 30 feet. You then reach the Headwaters Education Center. There is a bench on the right side of the trail. An accessible route around the historic site on the left, just past the main building, leads to interpretive signs about the history of milling and mining. Continuing past the education center, the trail rises slightly and then declines at 5% for about 50 feet before leveling out again. There are a couple places to watch for salmon in the river. The trail levels out for a short distance, and then takes another 2% incline for about 100 feet, increasing to 5% for the last 50 feet. There are a few mature redwoods along the trail, but it is generally young mixed forest around you.

At 0.7 mile the trail has a 2% cross slope as it curves to the left. You then come to a picnic table set about 20 feet off the trail on the right. The path to it is gravel and grass, and the table sits on a slightly raised gravel pad. It overlooks the river and is a nice, relaxing

ELK RIVER TRAIL

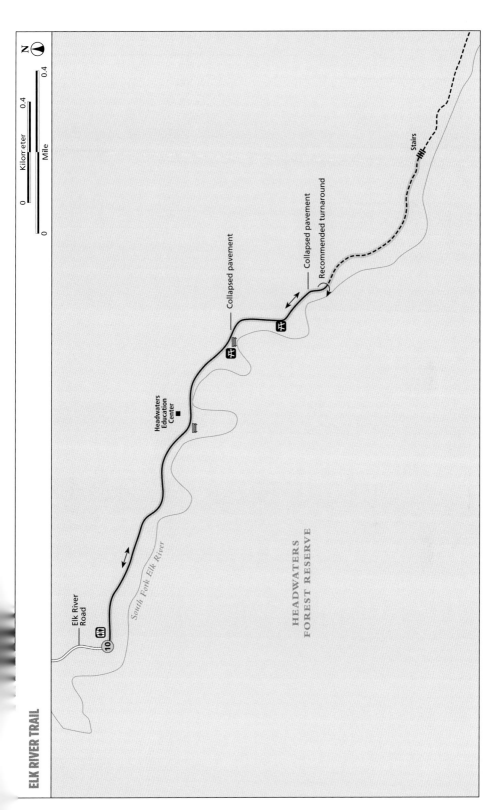

South Fork Elk River

Elk River Road

10

Headwaters Education Center

Collapsed pavement

Collapsed pavement

Recommended turnaround

Stairs

HEADWATERS FOREST RESERVE

N

0   0.4
Kilometer

0   0.4
Mile

spot to enjoy a picnic. Just beyond the picnic table, a backless bench set a few feet off the trail overlooks the river. The trail continues on a slight incline.

At 0.8 mile the pavement has slipped on the right side. There's a large crack with a steep cross slope on the right edge where the asphalt collapsed. The level section on the left is about 3 feet wide and has a narrow vertical crack, but it is passable with caution, especially if additional slippage occurs. The forest here is lush, and there are several seasonal streams and drainage areas. The trail curves right and takes a 5% incline for about 40 feet, then levels out. The surface continues with sections of cracked and uneven asphalt. You enter a more mature redwood forest, with large trees and old stumps along the side of the trail. You may notice the sweet water smell of the river, and lots of mossy maples glow in the sunlight. At 0.9 mile the surface gets a little uneven again as the trail curves left. There is another picnic table set several feet off the trail, accessible by a gravel path. It is another sweet spot to enjoy some time in the forest, and the best place to turn around if you are on wheels. You then pass the fork for the South Side Trail. That trail is closed in winter and available only by reservation. The trail then declines at 5% for a few feet. There are a couple rough log benches on the right with another interpretive sign about salmon in the redwood forest. You are traveling above the river with a nice view across the canyon. Take another incline, then come to an area of collapsed pavement—it has collapsed across the width of the trail and is about 3 feet wide, with a 10% grade to broken pavement in the center. It is passable with caution. The trail then generally levels out.

At 1.0 mile the pavement ends. There is a 2-inch lip at the transition point to natural river silt surface. I recommend turning around here—the trail gets increasingly steep for the next 0.5 mile before reaching a steep set of stairs (which is where I turned around). If you do continue, the trail gains about 75 feet in 0.25 mile, then loses 30 feet in less than 0.1 mile. Several sections have 10–15% grades for up to 200 feet and alternating cross slopes of 5%. You'll pass several large redwoods, but there are no benches or good places to sit.

MILES AND DIRECTIONS

0.0 Begin at the trailhead on the east side of the parking lot.

0.5 Pass the Headwaters Education Center on the left.

0.8 Cross a section of collapsed pavement.

0.9 Reach a picnic table and the recommended turnaround spot if you are using a wheelchair or scooter.

1.0 Reach the end of the pavement and the recommended turnaround if you want to avoid steep sections of trail.

1.5 Reach a set of steep wooden stairs. Turn around to return to the trailhead.

3.0 Arrive back at the trailhead.

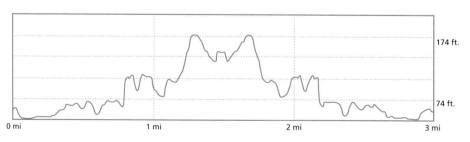

11 DRURY-CHANEY TRAIL

WHY GO?

There are many beautiful trails in Humboldt Redwoods State Park, but this one is unique in the amount of redwood sorrel creating a lush carpet beneath towering old-growth redwoods. Birdsong may create a fantastic soundtrack to your hike, and there is limited evidence of logging, making this feel like a truly magical place. Picnic tables in a clearing at the trailhead offer a place to take a break. However, while the trail is designated as wheelchair accessible, there are many areas of steep cross slopes and obstacles along the way, making it inadvisable for wheelchair users.

THE RUNDOWN

Spoon rating: 2 spoons. A generally level trail with areas of steep cross slope and exposed roots. Not recommended for wheelchair users.
Type: Lollipop loop
Distance: 2.1 miles
Elevation: 125 feet
Elevation gain: 26 feet gain, 26 feet loss
Max grade: 5%
Max cross slope: 12%
Typical width: 3 feet
Typical surface: Compact gravel covered in redwood needles
Trail users: Hikers
Season/schedule: Open year-round
Water availability: None
Sun exposure: Shaded

Amenities: Picnic tables, benches, trash cans
Pet-friendly: No
Cell phone reception: None
Special notes: Some highway noise on the trail
Nearest town: Rio Dell
Land manager: California State Parks, Humboldt Redwoods State Park, (707) 946-2409
Pass/entry fee: None
Land acknowledgment: Lolangkok Sinkyone. Sinkyone territory extends from the ocean to the main stem of the Eel River and the South Fork Eel River and south past present-day Leggett.

FINDING THE TRAILHEAD

Getting there: From Rio Dell, travel south on US 101 for 9 miles. Take exit 671 for Redcrest and turn left, then left onto the Avenue of the Giants. Continue 0.5 mile, passing Shively Flat Road. The trailhead is on the left. **GPS:** 40.443111, -123.986247

Parking: Gravel pullouts with space for about 10 cars on both sides of the road. No designated accessible parking.

Start: The trailhead on the west side of the Avenue of the Giants.

THE HIKE

The trail begins on compact gravel. There are two picnic tables and a bench at the trailhead; the table on the left is accessible on gravel, but it may be partially surrounded by stinging nettles and thimbleberry plants. Stinging nettles grow in abundance along the beginning of the trail, so watch your hands. The trail surface is a little uneven and

The Drury-Chaney Trail through redwoods

becomes compacted soil as you enter the redwoods, curving left and then right on a steep cross slope with an unprotected drop-off. You immediately enter a lush redwood forest—the ground is carpeted in redwood sorrel, a three-leaved plant that vaguely resembles clover, and sword ferns.

At 0.06 mile there is a 10% cross slope for a few feet as the trail curves right. It then takes a 5% incline and continues on a slightly rolling grade. Curve right and left again, passing between two large old blowdowns—there is a slight drop-off on the right. At 0.18 mile the trail passes narrowly between a cut-out blowdown, and the surface becomes a little uneven.

At 0.25 mile the trail narrows to 3 feet as it passes between another old cut-out log. This section may be difficult to traverse with mobility aids—there is a tight curve and old log rounds along the edge of the trail. Beyond this point, the trail widens back out to 4 feet and you are surrounded by more old-growth redwoods. Take another 5% decline with an 8% cross slope for about 10 feet, then another short curve right with a 5% cross slope next to a large redwood.

At 0.3 mile a California bay laurel curves over the trail and pinches the trail width to less than 3 feet. You may have to duck under or around it. A couple hundred feet further, there are two sections of steep alternating cross slopes and then the trail rolls slightly. At 0.4 mile an old log on the left has been 1/4 cut out to make a low bench and there is a sign that says Drury Chaney Trail on it. The trail rolls slightly uphill on 2–5% grades with some small roots and rocks.

At 0.5 mile there is a 15-foot-long section of exposed roots that are up to 6 inches wide and 2 inches high—these would be difficult to navigate using a wheelchair or mobility aids. Immediately following that you reach an old blowdown with more exposed roots rising a few inches above the surface of the trail. You can pass between the blowdown and a large standing tree, or go to the right of the standing tree—it is a little more level and there are no roots, but it's a bit narrow. The trail then curves left with a steep cross slope—the level section is about 2 feet wide with a 10% cross slope on the edge. Take a 2% incline, passing between two large old-growth redwoods with some exposed roots.

At 0.67 mile you come to what looks like a trail intersection at a dirt road—just follow the sign pointing straight ahead. You'll pass a few old burned-out redwoods with open trunks; these are called goosepens. There are lots of signs of fire on the trees and a beautiful mix of old-growth redwoods, younger trees, and sorrel and ferns. The trail curves left and right on a slightly rolling surface with a few small, exposed roots. Pass a fallen old-growth tree with a huge root base. You then take a slight incline, and at 0.75 mile a footpath on the left leads to a small ephemeral stream.

At 0.8 mile you reach the beginning of the loop. Going right, the trail starts on a slight cross slope with level areas on the top and bottom. Pass a slight dip in the trail that may be muddy in winter, and then the trail curves left and gets a little uneven. At 0.88 mile there is an old stump on the left with evidence of logging—the horizontal holes in the trunk are for the planks that loggers put into the tree for sawing. Take a 10% cross slope as the trail curves left, then pass between a cut-out fallen tree with about 3 feet of clearance.

At 1.0 mile there is a sturdy wooden bench on the right beneath a large redwood, with a sign indicating the Harry Irving and Norma Irving Redwood Grove. You may start to hear some highway noise. Past the bench, there is a steep 10% cross slope with no level area for about 8 feet.

At 1.23 miles you pass another old blowdown on the right and the trail curves slightly left. A sign on the right indicates another grove. The trail then curves sharply left at the

Left: The Drury-Chaney Trail curving around a large redwood on a steep cross slope
Right: An area of roots on the trail

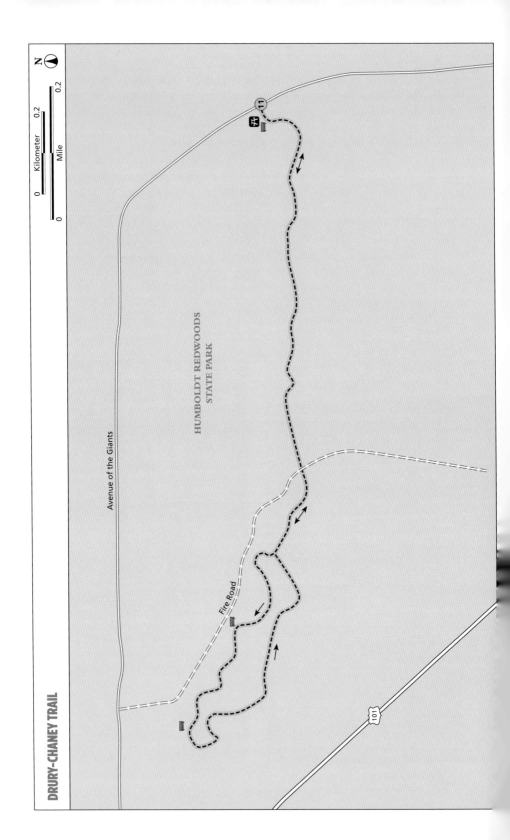

DRURY-CHANEY TRAIL

N

Kilometer
0   0.2   0.2
Mile
0   0.2

Avenue of the Giants

HUMBOLDT REDWOODS
STATE PARK

Fire Road

11

101

View of an old blowdown and a redwood with a goosepen

top of the loop and continues on a steep cross slope for a few feet. You're now on the opposite side of the loop, parallel to US 101—which you are likely to hear and may see through the trees—but there are lots of big old-growth trees in this part of the grove. At 1.3 miles pass narrowly between a large standing tree and a tree that has fallen parallel to the trail—you can easily reach out and touch both.

At 1.45 miles take a 5% incline and then cross a bridge made of bumpy boards with a handrail. The transition is even on either side. The trail curves left and right. Take a slight incline for about 30 feet at 1.6 miles. The trail splits around a blowdown—the right side has some exposed roots on the right, the left has no obstacles but does have a cross slope. At 1.7 miles continue straight past what looks like another trail intersection. At 1.75 miles you reach another footbridge—it is also made of bumpy boards with a level transition on either side. You then reach the end of the loop; go right to return to the parking area.

MILES AND DIRECTIONS

0.0 Begin at the trailhead on the west side of Avenue of the Giants.

0.67 Continue straight past the intersection with an old dirt road.

0.8 Reach the beginning of the loop. Go right.

1.45 Cross a bridge.

1.75 Cross a bridge and then reach the end of the loop. Go right.

2.1 Arrive back at the trailhead.

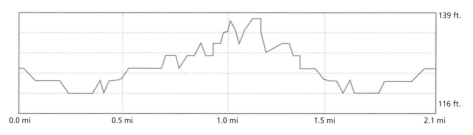

12 FOUNDERS GROVE

WHY GO?
Founders Grove is one of the largest groves in Humboldt Redwoods State Park. It is also one of the most accessible and popular. The highlights of the trail are the giant Founders Tree and the fallen Dyerville Giant, but the entire grove features huge old growth almost as far as you can see. While it is generally wheelchair accessible, you will need to use caution and be prepared to turn around past the Dyerville tree. Huge old-growth redwoods greet you at the trailhead, and the picnic tables scattered around the parking area make it a worthwhile stop even if you don't take the trail.

THE RUNDOWN

Spoon rating: 2 spoons. Partially wheelchair accessible, with a couple sections of steep cross slopes.
Type: Loop, out-and-back for wheelchair users
Distance: 0.5 mile, 0.6 mile for wheelchair users
Elevation: 150 feet
Elevation gain: 33 feet gain, 30 feet loss
Max grade: 5%
Max cross slope: 12%
Typical width: 6 feet, minimum 2 feet
Typical surface: Compacted gravel and soil
Trail users: Hikers
Season/schedule: Open year-round
Water availability: None
Sun exposure: Shaded

Amenities: Gendered restrooms with accessible stall, picnic tables, benches
Pet-friendly: No
Cell phone reception: None
Special notes: Possible highway noise on the trail
Nearest town: Redcrest
Land manager: California State Parks, Humboldt Redwoods State Park, (707) 946-2409
Pass/entry fee: None
Land acknowledgment: Lolangkok Sinkyone. "Sinkyone" is a newly ascribed term for several groups of Indigenous people who spoke the same Athabascan dialect. Many descendants of the Lolangkok are members of the Bear River Band of the Rohnerville Rancheria.

FINDING THE TRAILHEAD

Getting there: From Redcrest, head south on Avenue of the Giants for 4 miles. Stay left at the South Fork Eel River Bridge, then turn left onto Dyerville Loop Road. The parking lot is straight ahead. **GPS:** 40.352474, -123.923599

Parking: Paved circular parking area with space for about 20 cars. One van accessible parking spot.

Public transit: The Southern Humboldt Intercity Route makes a requested rest stop at Founders Grove. Limited schedule; please confirm with the Transit Authority.

Start: The trailhead on the south side of the entrance road.

THE HIKE
A wheelchair-accessible route through the center of the picnic area passes an important interpretive panel about the history of the grove and the founders of the conservation

Founders Grove Trail

movement, including their eugenicist beliefs. The trail then crosses the entrance road and arrives at the trailhead. A trail access information sign lists the typical grade as 2%, the typical width at 6 feet, and the typical surface as compact soil; while this is generally accurate, there are a couple steep grades and cross slopes that may be difficult for wheelchair users.

Continuing past the trailhead sign, there is a short section with a dip in the trail on the left and a 10% cross slope—the level section is about 2 feet wide. You almost immediately come to the Founders Tree and the beginning of the loop. A wood board ramp leads to a small platform at the base of the tree, which rises over 346 feet above you with a trunk circumference of 40 feet—it is not the biggest tree in the park but certainly still impressive. There is an old 3/4 log bench here as well.

Go right on the loop, following a wooden barrier on the left that widely circles the Founders Tree. The trail curves slightly left on a 5% incline, then right on a 6-foot-wide gravel and soil surface. Pass a huge redwood with a big goosepen in its base—it is worth checking out, but please don't climb inside. The trail narrows to about 4 feet as it curves around another large redwood and continues along a large old blowdown. There is a big drop-off in front of the blowdown, so take care as you approach. A 2–5% cross slope and a slightly crowned section are just beyond the blowdown, then the trail widens back out to about 6 feet. There are lots of foot traffic trails—stay on the wide main trail. Curve around a huge old-growth redwood with a slight cross slope in the trail close to its base— the trail is 4 feet wide here, and you can reach out and touch the trunk.

The trail widens to more than 6 feet and continues generally level to slightly rolling through this large grove of giant redwoods. You'll pass an old, burned-out tree with only the outer bark of two sections of its base still standing. You then pass between the trunk of a large blowdown that has been cut out with 5 feet of distance in between. The trunk

The trail approaching a large blowdown

is over 6 feet high and a neat opportunity to experience the inside of a redwood—you can follow the growth rings with your fingers. The trail curves right and left, then passes a small interpretive sign. You are surrounded by towering redwoods. The trail then gets slightly crowned and uneven and takes a 5–8% incline with a slight cross slope as you pass between two trees.

At 0.25 mile you reach the Dyerville Giant. This massive redwood was 362 feet tall before it fell in 1991. It now rests along the trail, the bulk of its base splintered into hundreds of pieces, the trunk still towering above you and providing a home for ferns and other plants to grow. There is a bench beneath a tree on the left. Carefully follow the trail as it travels along and around this and other giant fallen trees. You'll pass between a cut-out log and continue along the trunk of the tree to its base. After you pass the base of the fallen trees, the trail widens out to over 10 feet and there are a couple sections of roots rising up to 4 inches above the surface of the trail; they can be bypassed with care but wheelchair users may want to turn around here, as the other side of the loop has a couple narrow sections with a steep cross slope.

At 0.4 mile another root rises 2 inches down the center of the trail, with about 3 feet of level space to bypass it. The trail then curves slightly right past another blowdown's root system. There's an unprotected drop-off due to people going off trail, with up to a 15% cross slope. The level section is about 4 feet wide. The trail then splits around a small redwood. The left side is about 3 feet wide, but a few roots rise up to 2 inches above the

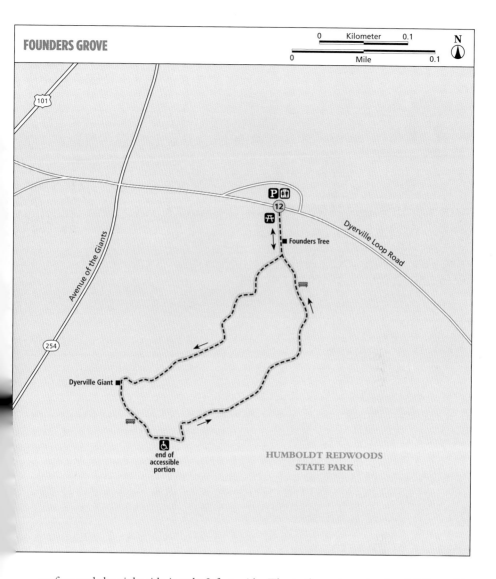

FOUNDERS GROVE

0   Kilometer   0.1

0   Mile   0.1

N

101

254

Avenue of the Giants

Dyerville Loop Road

P

Founders Tree

Dyerville Giant

end of
accessible
portion

HUMBOLDT REDWOODS
STATE PARK

surface and the right side is only 2 feet wide. The trail continues level and 5 feet wide on the other side, becoming slightly uneven. The trail then narrows to 3 feet and curves right with a 10–12% cross slope at the curve and a sharp drop-off—I don't recommend it for wheelchair users.

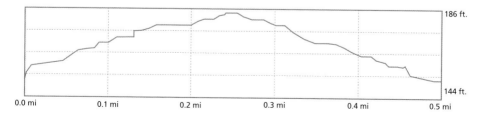

186 ft.

144 ft.

0.0 mi   0.1 mi   0.2 mi   0.3 mi   0.4 mi   0.5 mi

Trail along the Dyerville Giant

The trail widens back out and continues generally level. You'll come to another large tree with a burned-out section in its base. Pass a low bench on the right, and then continue straight ahead towards the Founders Tree. Go right at the tree to return to the parking area.

MILES AND DIRECTIONS

0.0 Begin at the trailhead across the road from the parking area. Go right on the loop.

0.25 Reach the Dyerville Giant.

0.3 Wheelchair users should turn around here.

0.5 Reach the end of the loop. Go right to return to the parking area.

13 POINT CABRILLO LIGHT STATION

WHY GO?

Point Cabrillo is a beautiful headland between Fort Bragg and Mendocino. The trails travel across the grassy headland and along the cliff, with incredible ocean views and wildlife opportunities. The trails aren't very accessible, but you can drive out to the light station if you have a disabled parking placard. It's a great place for a picnic while whale watching and listening to the waves.

THE RUNDOWN

Spoon rating: 4 spoons for the hike; narrow, uneven footpaths with an elevation loss and gain of 135 feet in 0.7 mile. 1 spoon, wheelchair accessible for the viewpoint.
Type: Loop, scenic viewpoint
Distance: 2.3 miles (loop)
Elevation: 170 feet
Elevation gain: 135 feet gain, 135 feet loss
Max grade: 10%
Max cross slope: 2%
Typical width: 2 feet
Typical surface: Compact soil
Trail users: Hikers
Season/schedule: Open year-round, dawn to dusk

Water availability: None
Sun exposure: Full sun
Amenities: Single-stall accessible restroom, picnic tables, EV charging, museum and gift shop
Pet-friendly: Yes, on leash
Cell phone reception: None
Special notes: Lots of ticks on the grassy trail.
Nearest town: Mendocino
Land manager: California State Parks, (707) 937-6122
Pass/entry fee: None
Land acknowledgment: Northern Pomo had seasonal villages along the headlands and fished and gathered here in the summer.

FINDING THE TRAILHEAD

Getting there: From Mendocino, head north on CA 1 for 1.5 miles. Turn left on Brest Road just past Russian Gulch State Park, then right on Point Cabrillo Drive. Continue 1.2 miles and turn left at the park sign onto Lighthouse Road. Turn immediately into the parking lot. **GPS:** 39.350139, -123.813055

Parking: Paved parking lot at the entrance with space for approximately 30 cars. People with a disabled parking placard can drive down Lighthouse Road to accessible parking near the lighthouse.

Public transit: From Main and Lansing Streets in Mendocino, take Fort Bragg route 60 north (weekdays only). Get off at the next stop for Caspar Beach, and walk 1 mile south on Point Cabrillo Drive. The road is a bit steep and curvy with no sidewalk, so be very cautious if you go this route.

Start: Lighthouse Road on the south side of the parking area.

THE HIKE

The historic Kearn Farmhouse is located at the main entrance. There are picnic tables, restrooms, and a printed map of the park, including locations of the accessible parking spots.

The Point Cabrillo Light Station

Begin your hike on Lighthouse Road—go through the parking lot and make a right at the sign. The road is paved with a grassy gravel shoulder and starts on a 2% decline for about 100 feet. There are some signs along the way about gray whales, but otherwise it's not particularly interesting as you head downhill. The decline increases to about 5% for approximately 75 feet, then increases to an 8% decline for about 50 feet before generally leveling out. At approximately 0.25 mile you reach a picnic table on the left in a clearing beneath some trees. From here you start to get a view towards sand dunes and the ocean. The road continues to decline, increasing to 5% then 8–10% for about 40 feet. It levels out briefly as you pass between wooden barriers. The road then becomes rough, with 0.25 mile of steady 3–5% decline.

As you approach the bottom of the road, there is a grove of cypress trees on the right with signs pointing towards the vacation rentals, parking, and restrooms. Continue straight ahead on the paved road. At 0.6 mile you'll pass the Lightkeeper's House museum entrance on the right. There are restrooms behind the house and picnic tables on the grass. If you drive down, park in one of the two van-accessible parking spots on the left. Picnic tables and benches are located near the parking area.

The road transitions to gravel, but there is a sidewalk on the right side. You pass many charming old buildings that have been restored to vacation rentals. Continue on a 2–5% decline as you approach the light station at 0.7 mile. A wooden fence on the left protects the edge of a cove, with signs about the whales. On the right is a building with a marine science exhibit, but there is a 3-inch threshold to enter. Continue straight ahead to the light station, which is accessible on the lower floor; the entrance faces the ocean. Picnic tables are scattered in the grass, with one accessible table on gravel at the left side of the light station. Narrow footpaths lead out to the point, and there are nice views out to some sea caves and rocks. This is a great place to enjoy some time by the ocean and to watch whales, birds, and other wildlife.

To continue the loop, go right past the lighthouse, heading north on a narrow dirt footpath with grass on either side. The surface is uneven and rolling. Pass between two wooden poles with two pieces of exposed wood across the trail. You're now traveling along the cliff with incredible views of the coastline, including some sea caves. But there are many unprotected drop-offs and it can be a bit dizzying, so take care. Continue along the headlands on a narrow double-track footpath through the grass. The trail declines slightly, curves left, and crosses a footbridge with barriers. It may be a little muddy on either side, but the bridge is stable with closely placed boards. The trail widens to 2 feet on a 2–5% incline, then curves right along the headlands. You'll pass closely above another cove, and there are beautiful views along the coastline.

At 1.1 miles you come to a wide grassy area with a faint fork in the trail. The North Trail on the right loops back to the trailhead. If you want to enjoy the coastline some more, you can continue straight ahead for another 0.2 mile. It continues on a narrow, uneven footpath, occasionally dividing into two paths. Depending on the tides, huge waves crash onto the rocks below you, or you may spot some tide pools from above.

At 1.2 miles cross another footbridge with barriers on a slight cross slope. You'll start to notice houses along the rocky coastline ahead of you. The trail curves right along a cove, and there is a sharp drop-off along the edge. You may spot a natural rock arch. The trail starts to get brushier as you travel through tall grass on a narrow footpath. You then reach an interpretive sign on the right about a shipwreck. I recommend turning around here, as the trail gets increasingly brushy before ending.

You'll arrive back at the fork at 1.5 miles. Go left. There is an old wooden pole that vaguely reads Trail. The footpath takes an 8% incline for about 15 feet. You then enter an enclosed corridor—the trail is surrounded by low-growing trees and shrubs, including California bay laurel. It feels a bit like entering a secret passageway, but it is narrow and the footpath is uneven. It opens a bit after about 15 feet, then you pass under a

Overlooking the sea cliffs at Point Cabrillo

The trail through coastal chaparral

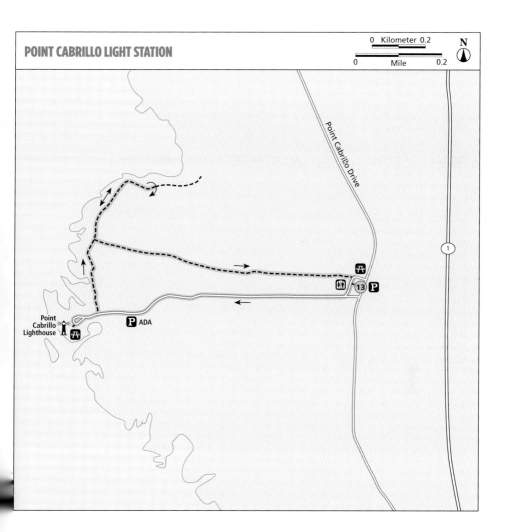

low-growing cypress. I encourage you to stop and smell it, if you can, by gently rubbing the needles. Across the trail are a few small roots. The trail corridor then opens up again as you continue along the grassy headlands. This is a great place to notice hawks and coyotes; I watched a hawk hunting over the grass for a long time!

You'll pass a sign that reads Tick Infested Area, pointing into the grass, and To Ocean and Lighthouse, pointing behind you—there are ticks here most of the year, so check yourself and your dogs. The trail widens to 2 to 3 feet and continues on a generally 2% incline, slightly uneven on a natural surface with tufts of grass. The trail then inclines at 5%, crosses a deep washout down the center, and curves to the right at another old sign that reads Trail. The trail continues slightly eroded down the center, then eventually widens to approximately 4 feet on a gradual incline. You may notice signs of deer beds in the grass. Continue to another cypress tree that offers a bit of shade, but nowhere to sit. Pass narrowly through more coastal chaparral shrubs, including coyote brush, which has beautiful, profuse white flowers that bloom in winter. Birds frequent the shrubs here. The trail is generally loose gravel on a narrow footpath between the shrubs. You then cross a slightly eroded area down the center with some exposed rocks, then pass underneath another low-growing cypress.

At 2.0 miles, or halfway on the return loop, the trail takes an 8–10% incline and is deeply rutted down the middle with exposed rocks—the level section is about 2 feet wide. The incline continues for about 100 feet, then the trail widens and levels out slightly and you curve left, passing next to a cypress offering another shady spot. The trail narrows again and takes another washed-out 5% incline with exposed and loose rocks. It continues like this for a few feet before widening to 3 feet and continuing on a generally 3% incline. You'll pass a couple more low-growing cypress trees along the trail.

At about 2.2 miles the trail inclines at 5–8% with another rut down the center and exposed, loose rocks for a few feet. It continues to be uneven and slightly rutted on a 3% incline. As you approach the end of the trail, you can see the tall Monterey cypress ahead of you and a trail sign. The trail continues eroded and uneven with loose rocks on a 2–5% incline. Pass the trailhead sign and then go right to return to the parking lot.

MILES AND DIRECTIONS

0.0   Start at Lighthouse Road on the south side of the parking area. Go right.

0.7   Reach the light station. Go right on the North Trail.

1.1   Reach a fork in the trail. Continue straight along the cliff.

1.3   Turn around at the interpretive sign about a shipwreck.

1.5   Return to the fork in the trail. Go left on the North Trail.

2.3   Arrive back at the parking area.

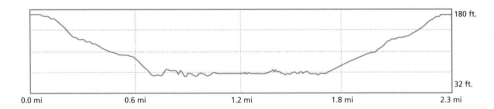

180 ft.

32 ft.

0.0 mi   0.6 mi   1.2 mi   1.8 mi   2.3 mi

14 SHAKOTA TRAIL

WHY GO?

The Shakota Trail is a 3-mile-long trail that follows the west side of Lake Mendocino. It is surprisingly beautiful, especially in the fall when the oaks change color and then drop their leaves, revealing incredible views of the lake. The entire length of the trail has a lot of ups and downs with some very steep short grades. This guide follows only the northern half, which is less steep than the southern half. It ends at the historic remains of a winery, which is now a site of graffiti art. There is also lake access from the day-use area at the trailhead.

THE RUNDOWN

Spoon rating: 4 spoons. Lots of rolling grades and no benches. Few obstacles, but many potentially slick areas.
Type: Out-and-back
Distance: 2.7 miles
Elevation: 790 feet
Elevation gain: 210 feet gain, 210 feet loss
Max grade: 25%
Max cross slope: 5%
Typical width: 2 feet
Typical surface: Firm soil
Trail users: Hikers, bikers
Season/schedule: Open year-round, sunrise to sunset
Water availability: None
Sun exposure: Mostly shaded

Amenities: Picnic tables and shelters, restrooms, playground, swimming beach
Pet-friendly: Yes, allowed on leash on the trail but not at the Pomo A and B Day Use Areas
Cell phone reception: None
Special notes: This is a popular mountain biking trail, with few places to step aside. There is a building that may emit a loud electric hum near the end.
Nearest town: Ukiah
Land manager: US Army Corps of Engineers, San Francisco District, (707) 467-4200
Pass/entry fee: None
Land acknowledgment: Northern Pomo. Shakota means "rabbit" in the Pomo language.

FINDING THE TRAILHEAD

Getting there: From Ukiah, travel north on US 101 for 6 miles. Take exit 555A for Calpella. Turn right on Moore Street, right on Eastside Calpella Road, then left on Marina Drive. Turn right into the day-use area. **GPS:** 39.234136, -123.183366

Parking: Paved parking with 3 designated accessible spaces at the Pomo Cultural Center. Paved parking with no accessible spaces at the other day-use areas.

Start: The trailhead on the southwest corner of the Pomo Cultural Center parking lot.

THE HIKE

This area is recovering from a fire, and the first 0.5 mile of the trail was closed for almost two years. It has reopened with some improvements and is in much better shape. There are a couple points from which to start your hike—from the end of the parking area next to the Pomo Cultural Center, which is where this guide begins, or if the gate is open

Left: The Shakota Trail through oak and madrone woods
Right: The Shakota Trail along the top of the hill

you can continue down the road to the last day-use area. This will shave about a mile round-trip off your hike.

To start, find the trail board on the far-right side of the parking area next to the cultural center. Go left onto the Shakota Trail. The trail starts 3 feet wide on natural surface, briefly level and then inclining at 6–8% for about 100 feet. Continue on generally rolling grades of 3–8% as the trail travels along the hill above the road. At 0.3 mile you curve slightly downhill, moving closer to the road and then parallel to the last parking area at 0.4 mile. At 0.5 mile a short path on a 10% grade connects with the end of the parking lot. This is where you will begin the hike if you park in this lot.

The fire did not burn past this point. The trail continues about 2 feet wide through manzanita and madrone on a 10% incline, then increases to 15% for a few feet and curves slightly left and right. The trail is natural surface and may be slightly muddy in the rainy season. It takes a 5% incline, briefly widening out to 4 feet, then narrowing to 2 to 3 feet. As you approach a Douglas fir on the left side of the trail, take a 20% decline for about 15 feet. There are some roots across the trail that you can use as a step-down, but it is generally a grade that may be slick with fallen leaves and mud, so I definitely recommend using hiking poles. The trail then levels out for a few feet and inclines at 20% again for about 10 feet. Cross over a lush stream area. It is really beautiful, with oaks and madrones lining the trail. The incline then decreases to approximately 15% for another 10 feet and then levels out.

Traversing the hillside, a park building is below you on the left. There is a bit of an unprotected drop-off, so watch your footing. Take a short 5% decline as you continue through a canopy of madrone and oak, then take a 10% incline for almost 50 feet. The trees are mossy here, and there are some cool rocks. The incline increases to 15% for another 50 feet, then declines at about 12% for nearly 15 feet. The trail levels out as it crosses over another culverted stream, then inclines again at 10–12% for close to 10 feet before leveling out and curving right along the hillside. There are nice views of the surrounding hills and the lake to the left. The trail continues level for about 100 feet, then takes a slight decline with a washed-out rut down the center for a couple feet. It then declines again at about 8–10%, rutted down the center and slightly uneven for about 50 feet. The decline increases to 20% for about 10 feet and then generally levels out and continues curving right and left along the hillside.

At 0.8 mile the trail splits around a big madrone. It then generally inclines at 8%, rolling a few times. You eventually pass over a metal culvert that is about 8 inches wide. The hillside curves and rises steeply above you. You then continue through the beautiful manzanita grove, the red and black trunks twisting and arching over the trail. Cross over a 4-foot-long bridge. The trail curves right along the hill; below you is a stream gully that may be lined with flowers depending on the time of year. You cross another bridge over the stream, and then the trail curves left on a 12% incline for a few feet, levels out, and continues 3 feet wide with a few roots and rocks in the surface.

At 1.1 miles you cross another bridge. Take a 20–25% incline on the other side for about 15 feet, decreasing to 10% for another 30 feet, and then curving right to another 20% incline. There are a few exposed roots. Take a 20% decline for a few feet, followed by a short 15% incline. The trail continues on a slight incline for a few more feet, then levels out and curves to the right. You continue to be surrounded by lots of manzanitas and madrones. The trail rolls on a slight grade a few times and passes an old road on the

Overlooking Lake Mendocino from the Shakota Trail

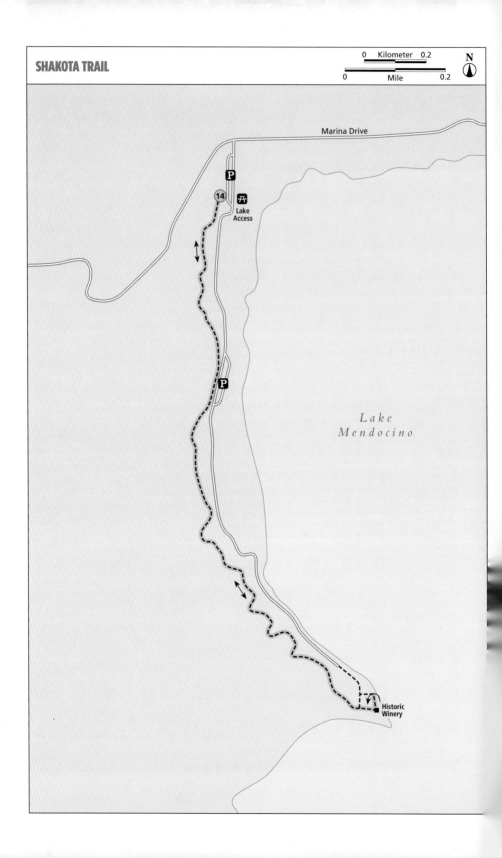

SHAKOTA TRAIL

0 Kilometer 0.2

0 Mile 0.2

N

Marina Drive

P

14

Lake Access

P

Lake Mendocino

Historic Winery

Manzanita arching over the Shakota Trail

left—there is a building below you that may emit a loud electric buzz. You are now near the top of the hill and the trail widens to 4 feet.

At 1.2 miles, just as you pass the buzzing building, the trail forks. The trail on the left leads to the remains of the historic winery, the end point of this hike. Take a slight decline on an uneven surface for a few feet, and then come out to a nice overlook of the lake. Continue to the left.

Continue straight at the next fork, where the trail is level and wide. The land juts into the lake here, so there is water on both sides. Go right at a spray-painted metal pole, then come to some concrete footings that are all spray-painted. Take three steps down, coming out on the footings of an old concrete building, with more nice views of the lake. You can explore this area as much as you are comfortable—there are some steps and an unprotected drop-off to the lake with a low barbed-wire fence. Historic equipment is scattered about, and there is a large building with lots of graffiti art inside. There are no benches, but you can sit on some of the concrete structures to rest up for the hike back.

MILES AND DIRECTIONS

0.0   Start at the trailhead on the southwest side of the cultural center parking area.

0.5   The trail connects with the last parking area and inclines uphill.

1.2   Go left at the fork to the historic winery.

1.25 Reach the winery. Turn around.

2.5   Arrive back at the trailhead.

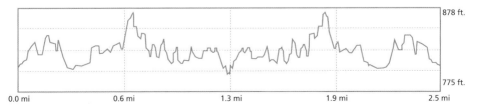

BAY AREA

The Bay Area is defined in different ways depending on the designations someone uses, but for the purposes of this guide I have included hikes from Sonoma County south to Santa Clara County, including San Francisco and the East Bay. These are all within a reasonable distance of the major population centers of the area. But this region also shares important geological, ecological, and cultural factors. It is defined by several ranges in the Coastal Mountain Ranges, which include the Santa Cruz Mountains, Sonoma Mountains, and Mayacamas Mountains, the Diablo Range, and many ranges of hills. Four peaks define what is most commonly considered the Bay Area—Mount Tamalpais, Mount Diablo, Mount Umunhum, and Mount Hamilton (the highest peak among the four).

The Bay Area is currently home to over 7.76 million people, and development has certainly had an impact on the river valleys, estuaries, marshes, and other ecosystems that once covered the region. But these rich lands have always been one of the most populated regions on the West Coast. Indigenous people have lived in the region for at least 10,000 years. At the time of European contact, an estimated 50,000 people lived in the area of the San Francisco and San Pablo Bays and south to the Carmel River. Thousands more lived in the areas of present-day Marin and Sonoma Counties.

Coast Miwok territory includes Bodega Bay in the west across the Petaluma Plain to the Sonoma Valley, and south to the Golden Gate. Five bands, which included many tribal groups, lived in the area (www.coastmiwokofmarin.org/our-history.html). Coast Miwok is a distinct language in the Miwokan language family. Southern Pomo territory includes most of present-day Sonoma County. Southern Pomo lived in the area now known as Sebastopol, and includes the area south of the Russian River to the southern Santa Rosa area. Kashia Pomo lived along coastal Sonoma County. Their traditional territory extends from the Gualala River to south of the Russian River and 30 miles inland to the confluence of Warm Springs Creek and Dry Creek.

The San Francisco Bay area to the Monterey Bay area is Ohlone territory, which includes at least eight distinct language groups and many independent tribal groups at the time of contact. The Costanoan-speaking people speak three different dialects in the Bay Area: Chochenyo, Tamien, and Ramaytush. The San Francisco Peninsula is Ramaytush Ohlone territory (www.ramaytush.org/terminology.html), which includes the entire land base of the peninsula to the south near the mouth of Stevens Creek on the bay side and Bean Hollow on the coast side. Several local tribes and communities lived within this area, including the Yelamu who lived in present-day San Francisco County. Yelamu is used as the native name for the City and County of San Francisco. The East Bay is Chochenyo Ohlone territory, which extends from the Berkeley Hills to the bay and encompasses the present-day cities of Berkeley, Alameda, Emeryville, El Cerrito, and much of Oakland. Xučyun (Huichin) is the native name for this area.

The history of Native California in the Bay Area is complex. Dozens of bands lived as independent tribal groups throughout the area and spoke related and unrelated languages. Through the genocidal violence of the mission era, land theft during the gold rush and logging eras, and the continued erasure and termination of Native communities by the federal government, entire bands were lost and tribal languages went dormant. As a result, there is a lot of misinformation about the Indigenous people of the Bay Area. I encourage you to refer to the websites noted in parentheses for more research.

There is also a long history of resistance by Native people to the theft of land and erasure of the people. Many individuals, tribes, and organizations are actively engaged in resistance and revitalization, including language programs, land-back efforts, and protecting and restoring places that are essential to the ecological well-being of the area.

15 RIVERFRONT REGIONAL PARK LAKE TRAIL

WHY GO?

This pleasant trail packs a lot of scenery into a short distance. The two lakes are reclaimed gravel pits, now home to numerous birds and popular destinations for fishing, canoeing, and picnicking. There are views of the Russian River, and mature redwoods, oaks, and California bay laurel line the trail. Best of all, the trail is virtually flat and partially wheelchair hikeable. The park does flood periodically, closing the western end of the loop, so this guide is written as a Y-shaped out-and-back.

THE RUNDOWN

Spoon rating: 2 spoons. Partially wheelchair hikeable with some areas of steep cross slope and exposed rocks.
Type: Y-shaped out-and-back, or a lollipop loop if not flooded
Distance: 4.0-mile out-and-back, 2.1-mile loop
Elevation: 79 feet
Elevation gain: 79 feet gain, 75 feet loss
Max grade: 8%
Max cross slope: 8%
Typical width: 6 feet
Typical surface: Compacted soil and gravel

Trail users: Hikers, bikers, equestrians
Season/schedule: Open year-round, dawn to dusk
Water availability: Water fountain
Sun exposure: Partial shade
Amenities: Picnic tables, accessible restrooms, benches
Pet-friendly: Yes, on leash
Cell phone reception: Yes
Nearest town: Windsor
Land manager: Sonoma County Regional Parks, (707) 433-1625
Pass/entry fee: Day-use fee or Sonoma Regional Parks pass
Land acknowledgment: Central Wappo and Southern Pomo

FINDING THE TRAILHEAD

Getting there: From Windsor, take Windsor River Road west to Eastside Road. Turn left and continue 1.8 miles to the signed entrance road for the park. Turn right and continue to the parking lot at the end. **GPS:** 38.518810, -122.854470

Parking: Large gravel parking lot with 2 ADA paved parking spots with access aisles.

Start: The trailhead is on the north side of the parking lot, to the right of the picnic area.

THE HIKE

There's a large picnic area in a grove of redwoods to the north of the parking area, but the paths are covered in loose woodchips and redwood leaves and there are no accessible tables. There are gendered restrooms with an accessible stall adjacent to the parking area. The trail around the lake starts at the entrance to the parking area on the right. It starts on pavement and then transitions level onto compact gravel, passing between vertical

A bench beneath redwoods overlooking Lake Benoist

poles with a minimum of 3 feet clearance. The surface is uneven and bumpy, with rocks embedded. The trail takes a 5% decline for the first 20 feet and then levels out along Lake Wilson. It is 8 to 10 feet wide, becoming a more natural surface that may be muddy.

Two benches overlook the lake with areas of shade, and a nice viewing deck is on the right at 0.2 mile—the deck has a 2-inch lip onto the platform. A hill rises above you on the left, with a beautiful forest of redwoods, oaks, and other native trees. The trail surface continues as natural soil with some large gravel embedded in the surface. There are areas of medium-size loose gravel and some dips in the trail, making it slightly uneven and unsteady.

At 0.3 mile the Lake Trail forks for the loop around Lake Benoist. The right (northern) side of the lake is less shaded and has some nice views of the Russian River but may have flooded areas. The left (southern) side of the lake is more shaded with lots of redwoods and bay laurel, but it is a little rougher.

Go right at the fork. The trail passes between Lake Wilson and Lake Benoist. You almost immediately come to a small picnic area with six tables and a couple grills, but none of them are wheelchair accessible. Another bench overlooks the lake. The trail continues about 8 feet wide on firmly packed soil with some ruts down the center or along the side of the trail and some rocks protruding up to 1 inch above the surface. Take a rolling 5% decline to a spillway—there may be water across the trail here, and the surface is uneven on a steep cross slope. On the other side, it takes an uneven 5% incline for about 20 feet, increasing to 8% for a total of 50 feet. The trail then levels out, continuing on a slightly uneven surface.

At 0.6 mile take another 2–5% incline for a few feet. There appears to be a fork here, but the trail on the right is closed to the public, so continue straight ahead. You then reach

Lake Benoist at flood stage

Overlooking Lake Benoist

a spur trail on the right that leads to the river. There are five steep steps down and then a nice bench under some beautiful oaks overlooking the river.

Continue on the Lake Trail as it curves left around Lake Benoist. A pedestrian-only trail on the left travels more closely along the lakeshore, but it is narrow and may be damaged or flooded. The main trail continues level on an elevated berm between the lake and the river. It is 8 to 10 feet wide, compacted river silt, and may have some ruts. Oaks and other small trees line the trail, and birds frequent the area.

At 0.9 mile the trail becomes a little more uneven but still level on compacted surface. At 0.95 mile another forked path leads down to the pedestrian trail along the lake. The trail then takes a 2% incline for a few feet, becoming slightly uneven. There is a double-track section with patchy grass along one side; the level section is about 3 feet wide. It then widens back out to 8 feet, but the trail is mostly covered in low grass for about 30 feet.

The trail on the south side of the lake

At 1.1 miles the trail forks, with one side going slightly uphill. There are a couple benches on the uphill trail. It leads to a rocky area where you may be able to scramble across the lake if it is flooded, but I don't recommend it. The main trail continues on compacted gravel for a few feet, then reaches the area that is likely to be flooded. These lakes are reclaimed gravel pits, and the trail is in the floodplain at an elbow bend in the river, so it floods in heavy rain. But it makes for a fantastic birding spot.

Turn around and arrive back at the fork for the Lake Trail at 2.0 miles. Go right, curving around the lake. Take a slight decline for a few feet. The trail surface is somewhat uneven, hard-packed soil. At 2.1 miles the trail has a 5% cross slope with a level area on the right side. Pass a sign pointing straight ahead for the Lake Trail. Cross another drainage area with a slight dip and a 5% cross slope. Large redwoods grow on the hill above you, providing some shade on a sunny day.

At 2.25 miles there is another 5–8% cross slope with a slightly level area on the left side. You then reach a bench on the right overlooking the lake, next to a grove of redwoods encircled by a wooden fence. It's a nice, tucked-away spot. The trail continues slightly uneven on a 5–8% cross slope. A few large rocks protrude up to 2 inches above the trail. Continue on areas of alternating steep cross slopes with level and rolling sections. Some more medium-size rocks protruding out of the surface make the trail a little rough. At 2.4 miles the trail inclines at 5% for about 10 feet, then levels out and continues generally rolling with areas of 2–5% cross slopes.

At 2.5 miles there is a rocky and uneven section with a dip in the trail—it is passable but would be difficult in a wheelchair. You then reach a 4-foot-wide armored crossing that is not passable in a wheelchair. Uneven rocks cover the trail with gaps in between them. There is about 12 inches of clearance on the right that has only a couple of low rocks that are easier to walk across. The opposite side has a slight incline with more protruding rocks. At 2.6 miles there is a dip in the trail. The surface is mostly compacted soil and silt, but it can be very muddy in the rainy season. There are some surprisingly large redwoods and lots of large California bay laurel.

At 2.75 miles a couple benches overlook the lake with nice views of the Sonoma Mountains. At 2.9 miles you arrive at the other end of the area that is likely to be flooded. Turn around and head back to the parking lot.

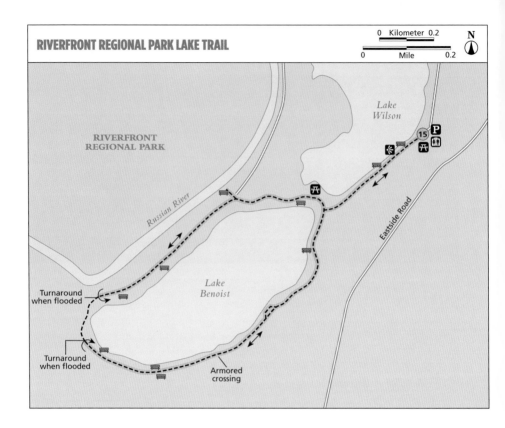

RIVERFRONT REGIONAL PARK LAKE TRAIL

MILES AND DIRECTIONS

0.0 Begin at the trailhead on the north side of the parking lot, to the right of the picnic area.

0.3 Reach the beginning of the loop. Go right.

0.6 A short spur trail on the right leads to an overlook of the Russian River.

1.1 Reach the northwest side of the lake and an area that is likely to flood. Turn around.

2.0 Arrive back at the beginning of the loop. Go right.

2.5 Reach an armored crossing. This is the end of the accessible portion.

2.9 Reach the southwest side of the lake and an area that is likely to flood. Turn around.

3.7 Arrive back at the beginning of the loop. Go right.

4.0 Arrive back at the trailhead. Go right to return to the parking lot.

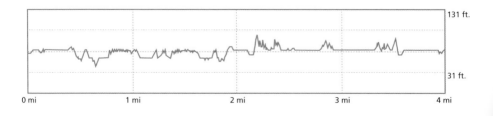

16 SONOMA COUNTY SCENIC DRIVE

WHY GO?

This 54-mile loop drive takes you through some of the nicest scenery in Sonoma County. It starts in the foothills of Sebastopol, climbs the coastal hills, and then descends to the Sonoma coast and heads north to the Russian River. Many people take Bodega Highway straight to the coast, but this route offers beautiful views and some interesting stops along the way. You even bypass the traffic in Bodega and Bodega Bay.

THE RUNDOWN

Type: Scenic drive
Distance: 54 miles round-trip. Allow at least two hours to complete the drive.
Elevation: 1,000 feet to 50 feet
Typical width and surface: Two-lane paved roads. Drivable in a standard passenger car and most RVs, except on Fitzpatrick Lane.
Pet-friendly: Pets allowed at all recommended stops except Goat Rock Beach
Cell phone reception: Spotty

Nearest town: Services in Sebastopol, Occidental, and Monte Rio
Land acknowledgment: This route travels through the ancestral lands of the Southern Pomo and Coast Miwok. Southern Pomo inhabited the town now known as Sebastopol for thousands of years. Kashia Pomo lived on the coast from the mouth of the Gulala River to south of the Russian River and inland to the confluence of Warm Springs Creek and Dry Creek.

FINDING THE TRAILHEAD

Getting there: To begin this loop, start in downtown Sebastopol.
GPS: 38.402087, -122.824294
Start: Main Street and Bodega Avenue in Sebastopol.

THE DRIVE

From Main Street in downtown Sebastopol, take Bodega Avenue west. It is a two-lane residential road with speed bumps and traffic lights. The speed limit is 25 mph. In about 2 miles you reach the outskirts of Sebastopol and start traveling through farmland and vineyards on a two-lane, somewhat curvy road. There are a few farm stands along the way. The speed limit increases to 35 mph and you start climbing through rolling hills.

Turn right onto Bohemian Highway at 5.7 miles. You then enter the town of Freestone, with some historic buildings and farm shops, followed by more rolling hills with views of open pastureland. Continue on the slightly curvy two-lane road, following a creek on the right with lots of pretty forested hills. At 9.5 miles you enter Occidental; there are shops and restaurants here. Make a left at the stop sign onto Coleman Valley Road.

You start climbing up a hill on a curvy two-lane road. This is a popular route for bicyclists, so keep an eye out. There are great views of the mountains off to the right. The road gets pretty bumpy, and some places have a steep drop-off. At 11.4 miles Coleman Valley Road curves sharply left and then turns right. I recommend continuing straight instead onto Joy Road for a short detour to the Grove of the Old Trees.

Continue for 0.2 mile on Joy Road, then turn right on Fitzpatrick Lane. This is a 1.5-mile-long, one-lane residential road that travels past houses. There are some low-hanging power lines, so it's not recommended for large or tall vehicles, and no real pullouts except for some driveways and places where the road is slightly wider, so drive carefully. The speed limit is 15 mph. It's very pretty, with lots of redwoods and hills and nice views. At 12.7 miles cross over a cattle guard and climb a short hill into redwoods. Continue past a sign that says "Grove of the Old Trees parking lot 400 yards ahead on the right." Park in the gravel pullout on the right. There is no cell service here.

GROVE OF THE OLD TREES

This 0.75-mile loop trail winds through a mix of old-growth redwoods, oaks, and California bay laurel. There are a couple benches and picnic tables to rest and enjoy the forest. The trail is almost flat, with a few short sections of 5–8% grades. Some roots rise up to 2 inches across the trail, and the surface is compact soil covered in redwood leaves. Wheelchair users may be able to enjoy the trail with some assistance, but it is most accessible for people who use walkers, canes, or poles. It is a peaceful walk that makes for a nice place to stretch your legs or stop for a picnic.

Leaving the grove, head back on Fitzpatrick Lane. Make a left back onto Joy Road. At 14.7 miles turn left on Coleman Valley Road, a paved, narrow, two-lane road traveling along a creek surrounded by pretty farmland and forests. There are some bumpy sections with patched potholes as you wind between hills. At 17.7 miles you leave the forest and reach the top of a hill. There are some incredible expansive views across rolling hills all the way to the ocean on the left and lots of interesting geological features, including large rocks, and you can see the coastal headlands.

At 18.8 miles cross over a cattle guard and then at 19 miles reach a nearly 180-degree view of the ocean ahead of you, with rolling hills all around you. At 20 miles you cross another cattle guard and may start to pick up some cell reception again. Cross another cattle guard at 20.9 miles, and pass some cool rock formations with nice views of the valley. At 21.8 miles the road gets a little rough; cross another cattle guard, continuing with beautiful views of the coast. At 22.1 miles there are a couple very small pullouts on the right and then a sign indicating a winding one-lane road for the next half mile. You start heading downhill on a wide one-lane road, passing under Monterey cypress and eucalyptus. At 22.6 miles cross another cattle guard.

At 23 miles turn right onto CA 1. Your next stop is Arched Rock Vista Point, located almost immediately on the left at the top of the hill.

ARCHED ROCK VISTA POINT

A large, paved pullout parking area is on the left. Incredible views can be had from the car, but if you can, I recommend getting out of the car and going out onto the grassy bluff that juts out from the parking area. You'll spot Arched Rock off on the right (north) side, just beyond the beach. The view up the coastline is expansive. You should have cell service again as well.

A picnic table in Grove of the Old Trees

View of the ocean from Coleman Valley Road

From the overlook, continue north on CA 1. Pass a couple beaches that have steep stairs down. At 24.2 miles you pass Portuguese Beach, which has a couple picnic tables at the overlook. At 25.7 miles there's a pullout on the left for Duncan's Cove—go just past it to the sign for Duncan's Landing, making a left onto the road.

DUNCAN'S LANDING OVERLOOK

There is a paved parking area with no designated accessible parking. This used to be a road that circled the head, but it has been decommissioned and is now a nice, paved loop. It circles an interesting rocky bluff covered in ice plants (an invasive species) with incredible views of the coast. Evidence of the dangerous surf here is obvious—the waves often

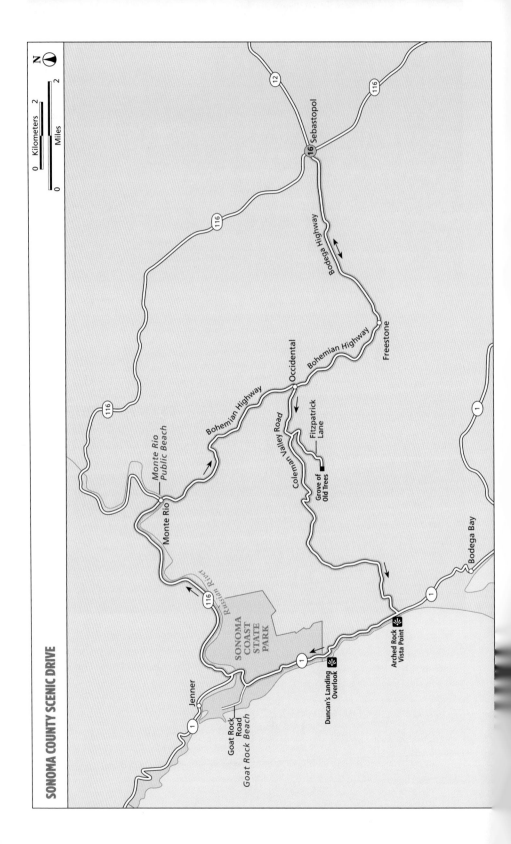

SONOMA COUNTY SCENIC DRIVE

Duncan's Landing Overlook

crash high on the cliff, washing out plants and damaging the road, so stay back from the edge. The road takes a 2–5% grade as it loops around, and wheelchair accessibility will vary depending on washout conditions.

Leaving the overlook, go left on CA 1. Continue approximately 4 miles. An optional detour not included in the mileage of this guide is Goat Rock Road on the left, just before the highway curves right. Goat Rock Road is a wide, one-lane, paved road that travels north along the coastline at the mouth of the Russian River with incredible views. There are many beaches along the way, but the most popular and most accessible is Goat Rock Beach at the end of the road, which has accessible vault toilets and picnic tables at the paved parking areas. It is fairly level onto the beach, though the sand is deep and soft. Seals frequent the beach (always stay at least 50 yards away), and pets are not allowed.

Continuing on CA 1, the road curves sharply right and crosses the Russian River on a bridge. Go right on CA 116. You're now following the river on a paved two-lane highway, traveling through rolling hills. There are a few pullouts with river views. At 36.8 miles the road starts to get curvy and a little narrow and the speed limit drops to 30 mph as you reach the town of Monte Rio, with a nice public beach on the Russian River. Turn right just before the stop sign in the center of Monte Rio, then right again at the sign for the public beach.

MONTE RIO PUBLIC BEACH

The large, paved parking lot has several accessible parking spots. There are accessible restrooms and picnic tables, and a concession stand operates during the summer. Access to the beach is pretty level on sand and would be accessible with an appropriate wheelchair.

Continuing from the public beach, turn right onto Bohemian Highway and cross the Russian River on a historic bridge, then turn right onto Main Street. Continue on the paved two-lane road, taking a pretty drive through large redwoods along a creek winding between cliffs. You'll pass a trailhead on the right for the new Monte Rio Redwoods Open Space, and then Main Street merges onto Bohemian Highway.

At 44.4 miles you arrive back in Occidental. Go straight at the stop sign in Occidental and continue on Bohemian Highway, making a right onto Bodega Highway. At 54.2 miles you arrive back in Sebastopol.

17 DORAN REGIONAL PARK

WHY GO?

Doran Regional Park is one of the most popular parks on the Sonoma coast. It features a flat, wide, 2-mile-long beach on Bodega Bay. The tidal marshes offer some of the best birding locations in the area, and there are many accessible features including picnic areas, campsites, and beach wheelchairs. The primary trail in the park is the Bird Walk Coastal Access Trail, which is wheelchair accessible. I've also included an overview of many of the day-use areas.

THE RUNDOWN

Spoon rating: 1 spoon. Wheelchair accessible on the Bird Walk Coastal Trail. Beach wheelchairs are available to borrow.
Type: Lollipop loop, scenic viewpoint
Distance: 1.3 miles (lollipop loop)
Elevation: 7 feet
Elevation gain: 30 feet gain, 30 feet loss
Max grade: 8%
Max cross slope: 2%
Typical width: 5 feet
Typical surface: Gravel
Trail users: Hikers, bicyclists, equestrians
Season/schedule: Open year-round, sunrise to sunset
Water availability: Water fountains
Sun exposure: Full sun
Amenities: Accessible restrooms, picnic tables, showers, campground, beach wheelchairs

Pet-friendly: Yes, on leash
Cell phone reception: Yes
Special notes: Beach wheelchairs are available from the campground host at site 59; ask at the entrance kiosk or any park staff (the chairs are currently described as all-terrain chairs on the website, but they are not). The campground has several ADA spots with electricity, and there are accessible showers.
Nearest town: Bodega Bay
Land manager: Sonoma County Regional Parks, (707) 875-3540
Pass/entry fee: Day-use fee or Sonoma Regional Parks annual pass
Land acknowledgment: Olamentko (Bodega Miwok) lived in the area of Bodega Bay in several villages, including Helapattai, Hime-takala, and Ho-takala.

FINDING THE TRAILHEAD

Getting there: From Bodega Bay, head south on CA 1 for 1 mile. Turn right on Doran Park Road and then right on Doran Beach Road. Continue to the entrance station. **GPS:** 38.314111, -123.033634

Parking: The most accessible lots are at the Jetty Day Use Area at the end of Doran Beach Road and the Bird Walk Coastal Access Area on CA 1 just north of Doran Park Road. The other day-use areas have accessible parking but may be covered in sand.

Start: For the Bird Walk Coastal Access Trail, start at the trailhead on Doran Beach Road across from the equestrian parking lot.

THE HIKE
JETTY DAY USE AREA

The Jetty day-use parking area is located at the end of Doran Beach Road. It has four paved ADA spots. There are gendered restrooms with an accessible stall. Paved paths lead to accessible picnic tables with grills, and a few benches have paved access next to them for companion seating. This is a nice spot for a picnic while enjoying Bodega Bay and watching boats coming in and out of the harbor.

DORAN VISITOR CENTER

There is a large parking area at the Doran Visitor Center with two accessible spots; however, the parking lot is frequently covered with sand. The short boardwalk along the beach has an accessible picnic table, but is also frequently covered in sand. A ramp leads down to the beach. If you are using a wheelchair that can't travel on sand, borrow a beach wheelchair from the campground host at site 59. There are day-use showers on the east end of the parking lot.

CYPRESS DAY USE AREA

The Cypress Day Use Area has three designated accessible spots, but they are often covered in sand. There is level beach access here, and it is the nearest day-use lot to the campground where you pick up a beach wheelchair. Several picnic tables are located in the sand around the parking area, and there are gendered restrooms with an accessible stall.

SANDY DUNE TRAIL

A 1.3-mile-long unnamed trail travels along the south side of the road above the beach—I'm calling it the Sandy Dune Trail. It connects the day-use areas, parking lots, and tent sites and offers some nice views of the sand dunes and the beach. However, it is typically 2 to 3 feet wide with deep, loose sand, so it is not the easiest walk and would be a challenge in a wheelchair.

Jetty Day Use Area

View of Cheney Creek from the Bird Walk Coastal Access Trail

Great blue herons in the marsh

BIRD WALK COASTAL ACCESS TRAIL

There are two starting points for this trail—across from the rocky gravel equestrian lot just past the entrance station, and from a paved parking lot with one accessible spot off of CA 1, north of Doran Park Road. This guide starts from the equestrian lot, but the most wheelchair-accessible route begins from the parking lot on CA 1.

Cross Doran Beach Road to the trailhead sign for the Bird Walk Coastal Access Trail. There is some loose gravel at the trailhead, and it starts on a 5% decline of about 50 feet then continues level. The trail is generally 4 feet wide, and the ground is firm, compact surface with small loose gravel on top. You are traveling on a levee with Cheney Creek

The beach at Doran Regional Park

on the left and surrounded by tidal marshland. Numerous benches along the way provide an opportunity to sit and appreciate birds, otters, and other wildlife, although some of the benches are difficult to reach. There are a couple places with steep drop-offs on the levee, so be cautious with wheels and children. The area is generally quiet, with beautiful views of the bay and surrounding hills.

At 0.3 mile you reach a bridge over the creek. As you approach, there is a 10% incline for about 40 feet and a 2- to 3-inch lip onto the concrete platform. The bridge is on a slight incline. On the opposite side, it is level off of the bridge. The trail curves right and continues on the same compact gravel surface. The creek is now on your right, and the trail takes a 5% incline, increasing to 8% for about 30 feet. At the top, you reach the loop around the seasonal ponds. Continue straight ahead.

At 0.4 mile the trail curves left above the parking lot on CA 1. If you need access to a restroom, take the gravel path that curves downhill on 3–5% grades to the parking lot, where there is a toilet. The trail continues 4 feet wide with some small loose gravel. The highway is on your right, so it's not very quiet. At 0.5 mile the trail curves left again away from the highway. The bay is on your right, and you are continuing on an elevated path around the ponds. Pass a couple of the numerous benches, then at 0.6 mile you reach a fork. The left trail bisects the loop to travel between the two ponds. It is another good birding spot, but the trail is a grassy double track. Continue straight ahead on the main loop, traveling between the tidal marsh and the ponds. I noticed many birds during my visit, including great blue herons, ducks, an eagle, vultures, and more. You may hear waves crashing in the distance.

At 0.7 mile there is a picnic table down in the sand along the pond and the trail curves left. This section of the trail has some afternoon shade. It's about 5 feet wide, with a compact dirt and gravel surface. At 0.8 mile the trail curves left again. There is a lovely overlook of the creek and the trail below you. You then reach a sign that says "Welcome to Cheney Creek Bridge and Trail." At 0.9 mile make a sharp right, following the trail back towards the bridge then returning the way you came.

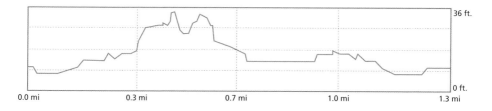

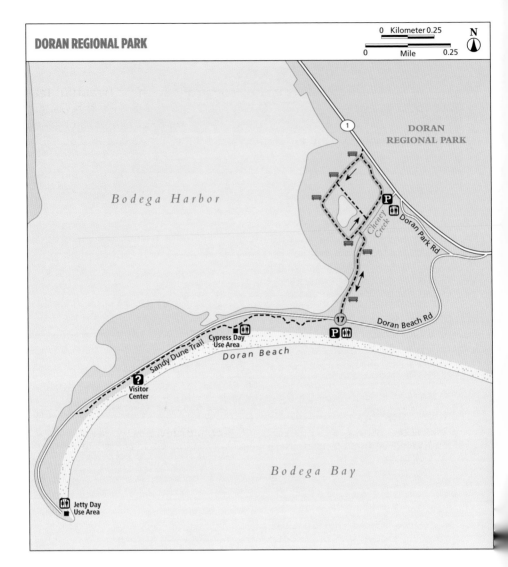

0   Kilometer 0.25

0   Mile   0.25

N

DORAN
REGIONAL PARK

1

Bodega Harbor

Cheney Creek

P

Doran Park Rd

17

P

Cypress Day
Use Area

Sandy Dune Trail

Doran Beach

Doran Beach Rd

Visitor
Center

Bodega Bay

Jetty Day
Use Area

MILES AND DIRECTIONS

0.0   Begin at the trailhead on Doran Beach Road across from the equestrian parking lot.

0.3   Cross the Cheney Creek bridge. Continue straight ahead to the loop.

0.35 Reach the start of the loop. Go right.

0.4   Reach the accessible parking lot on CA 1. Continue left on the loop trail.

0.6   Reach a fork in the trail. Continue straight ahead.

0.95 Reach the end of the loop. Go right and return to the trailhead.

1.3   Arrive back at the trailhead.

18 VALLEY OF THE MOON TRAIL

WHY GO?

Sonoma Valley Regional Park has some of the most beautiful features of Sonoma County. The woodlands are filled with the unique blue oak, and poppies, lupines, and other wildflowers bloom in the spring. The Valley of the Moon Trail is a paved, wheelchair-accessible trail that travels through a canopy of blue oak and along a seasonal creek, with at least ten benches and picnic tables along the way. This is a great place to visit at any time of year, and there is rare summer shade.

THE RUNDOWN

Spoon rating: 1 spoon. Paved trail with lots of benches. Wheelchair accessible, but there are a couple short grades up to 8% and cross slopes up to 5%.
Type: Out-and-back
Distance: 2.7 miles
Elevation: 340 feet
Elevation gain: 164 feet
Max grade: 8%
Max cross slope: 5%
Typical width: 6 feet
Typical surface: Asphalt
Trail users: Hikers, bikers, equestrians

Season/schedule: Open year-round, sunrise to sunset
Water availability: Water fountain
Sun exposure: Mostly shaded in summer
Amenities: Portable toilets, picnic tables, benches, trash cans
Pet-friendly: Yes, on leash
Cell phone reception: Yes
Nearest town: Glen Ellen
Land manager: Sonoma County Regional Parks, (707) 539-8092
Pass/entry fee: Day-use fee or Sonoma Regional Parks annual pass
Land acknowledgment: Southern Pomo and Miwok

FINDING THE TRAILHEAD

Getting there: From Glen Ellen, head north on Arnold Street. Turn right on CA 12 E / Sonoma Highway. Continue 0.4 mile to the entrance road for the park on the right. **GPS:** 38.364128, -122.512324

Parking: Paved parking lot with 2 accessible parking spots and 30 additional parking spots, including pull-through trailer parking.

Start: The paved trail behind the gate at the end of the parking lot.

THE HIKE

The trail begins at the end of the parking area. A metal gate blocks vehicle access, but there is a 3-foot-wide paved path around it on the left. The trail curves right, following a hill with water tanks at the top, and then declines at 8% for a few feet. The pavement is slightly cracked, with a couple cracks up to 2 inches wide, but they can be bypassed. At 0.1 mile you pass the first of many picnic tables. The trail levels out, following the seasonal creek and traveling below a canopy of blue oaks. These trees are pretty rare in this area and put on an especially spectacular show in the spring when their new leaves

Top: Blue oaks along the paved Valley of the Moon Trail
Bottom: The Valley of the Moon Trail curving downhill from the trailhead

are a bright bluish green. The trail continues level and even, passing a couple benches and picnic tables along the creek.

At 0.5 mile the trail takes a 5% decline for about 70 feet. You pass the Milkmaid Trail on the left and the Black Canyon Creek Trail—both of these rise steeply uphill. Continue through the valley, winding along the seasonal creek and passing a few more benches and picnic tables. At 0.8 mile the trail starts curving left around the hill at the west end of the park. There are houses far below you, but you can't see them from here.

The pavement gets a little rough with some areas of steep cross slope as you continue along the edge of the hill. Between 1.0 mile and 1.15 miles there are three sections of 5% cross slope, each about 30 feet long with some cracked pavement. At 1.2 miles take an 8%

Valley of the Moon Trail

decline. The trail surface is cracked and slightly crowned. At 1.35 miles there is a picnic table on the left. The trail then takes a 15% decline before ending at Arnold Street, so I recommend turning around at the picnic table.

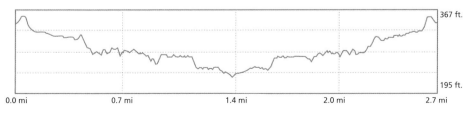

367 ft.

195 ft.

0.0 mi   0.7 mi   1.4 mi   2.0 mi   2.7 mi

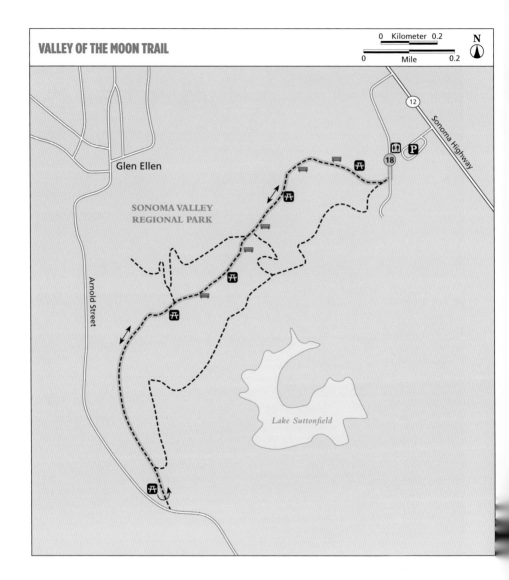

0   Kilometer 0.2

N

0   Mile   0.2

Glen Ellen

SONOMA VALLEY
REGIONAL PARK

Arnold Street

12

18

P

Sonoma Highway

Lake Suttonfield

MILES AND DIRECTIONS

0.0   Begin at the trailhead behind the metal gate.

1.0   Cross a few sections of cracked trail on a steep cross slope.

1.35 Reach the end of the trail. Turn around at the top of the hill.

2.7   Arrive back at the trailhead.

19 BEAR VALLEY TRAIL

WHY GO?

This pleasant trail travels through Bear Valley on a service road. You follow Bear Valley Creek most of the way, and trees, wildflowers, and ferns create a lush and shady landscape. The entire length is about 4 miles one way, ending at the Coast Trail in the Phillip Burton Wilderness. This hike takes you to the halfway point at Divide Meadow, a wonderful grassy meadow that makes a perfect turnaround spot for an easier hike. Stop for a picnic here or have one at the visitor center picnic area.

THE RUNDOWN

Spoon rating: 3 spoons. The trail averages a 3% grade with short sections up to 10%. It may be wheelchair hikeable with an all-terrain chair and some assistance. No benches along the trail.
Type: Out-and-back
Distance: 3.4 miles
Elevation: 108 feet
Elevation gain: 276 feet
Max grade: 10%
Max cross slope: 5%
Typical width: 8 feet
Typical surface: Firm soil and gravel
Trail users: Hikers, bikers, equestrians
Season/schedule: Open year-round, 6 a.m. to midnight
Water availability: Bottle filling station at the visitor center

Sun exposure: Mostly shaded
Amenities: Accessible restrooms at the visitor center, picnic tables, trash cans
Pet-friendly: No
Cell phone reception: Yes
Special notes: The visitor center is generally accessible, but the front doors are heavy and do not have automatic openers.
Nearest town: Point Reyes Station
Land manager: Point Reyes National Seashore, (415) 464-5135
Pass/entry fee: None
Land acknowledgment: Kule Loklo means "Bear Valley" in the Coast Miwok language. A re-created village is located at the visitor center.

FINDING THE TRAILHEAD

Getting there: From Sir Francis Drake Boulevard and CA 1, head south on CA 1 for 1.8 miles. Turn right on Bear Valley Road and then left at the sign for the visitor center. Continue 0.2 mile to the visitor center. **GPS:** 38.040572, -122.799731

Parking: A gravel parking lot at the trailhead at the end of the road has 2 designated accessible spots, but they are not paved or van accessible. There is a paved parking lot at the visitor center with ADA parking.

Start: Bear Valley trailhead at the end of the Bear Valley visitor center access road.

THE HIKE

The trail begins on compact gravel behind the Bear Valley trailhead sign at the end of the road. Pass between a fence and a round vertical pole with 3 feet of clearance in between. The path then transitions to the service road, and there may be some ruts and potholes

Two views of Bear Valley Trail

in the firm soil and compacted gravel surface. It starts at 8 feet wide on a 2% incline with a slight cross slope. At 0.15 mile the trail inclines at 8%, passing beneath an oak and continuing on an 8–10% incline for about 50 feet. You may have to navigate around some ruts caused by water flowing down the trail. The trail then declines slightly and levels out.

At 0.25 mile the Mount Wittenberg Trail forks to the right—continue straight ahead on the wide natural surface and sand service road. The trail continues generally level and shaded by Douglas fir, California bay laurel, and coast live oak. At 0.37 mile take a 2–5% incline. The trail curves left, then takes a 5–8% incline for a few feet and passes a small stream on the left flowing down to the creek. The trail then curves right on a 5% cross slope; you are traveling along the creek on the left.

At 0.5 mile there is another 5% incline for 30 feet and the trail curves slightly. At 0.6 mile the trail curves sharply left on a 3% cross slope, passing a large bay laurel. The creek rushes by on the left, and the corridor is lushly lined with grass and flowers. The trail then curves right and left a few more times. The creek crosses below the service road as you take a generally 5% incline. You then come to two steel plates in the surface as you cross over the creek again—the plates are level on either side but may be slippery. Continue on a gradual incline.

At 0.9 mile the Meadow Trail forks to the right—continue straight on the gravel road. The trail levels out for approximately 200 feet and is lined with Pacific trillium, nettles, and other spring wildflowers. It then inclines at 8% and there may be a deep rut down the center. The trail continues to incline for about 50 feet as you travel along the creek on the right. It then generally levels out for a few feet before inclining again at 8% with a 2–5% cross slope for about 100 feet.

At 1.0 mile the trail generally levels out again. You may notice evidence of fire with burn marks on the Douglas firs along the trail. At approximately 1.1 miles the trail inclines at 5% for a few feet before generally leveling out until 1.2 miles, where it begins a steady 5% incline. At 1.3 miles the trail opens up as you leave the forest. It levels out briefly at 1.5 miles, then you come to several steep humps across the road—they are similar to speed bumps. The humps are approximately 10% grade; some of them are a couple feet tall, others are less than a foot. There is no way to bypass them.

At 1.6 miles there's a 5% cross slope in the trail as it continues on a 5% incline. It then takes a 10% incline on a 5% cross slope and curves left to another hump. The incline decreases to 8% on the other side of the hump and the trail continues curving left, crossing another hump, and then curves right on an 8% incline.

At 1.7 miles the trail levels out as you reach Divide Meadow. There are accessible vault toilets up a short, steep slope and trash cans. A rustic log bench is on the left, and a mowed and compacted path leads to a couple secluded spots. This is a great place for a picnic, but please do not enter the meadows because it will damage the sensitive landscape. Turn around when you are ready to return.

The Bear Valley Trail along the creek

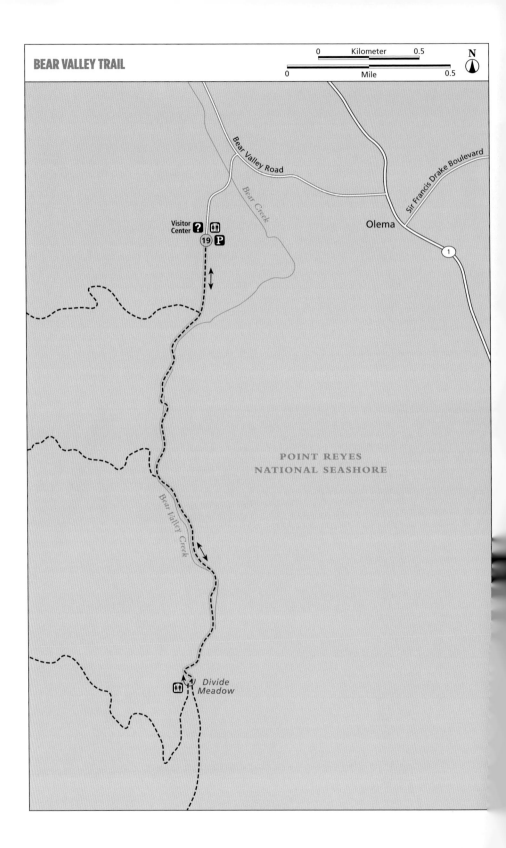

BEAR VALLEY TRAIL

0   Kilometer   0.5
0   Mile   0.5

N

Bear Valley Road

Sir Francis Drake Boulevard

Bear Creek

Visitor Center

19

Olema

1

POINT REYES NATIONAL SEASHORE

Bear Valley Creek

Divide Meadow

Overlooking Divide Meadow

MILES AND DIRECTIONS

0.0   Begin at the Bear Valley trailhead at the end of the visitor center access road.

0.25 Continue straight past the Mount Wittenberg Trail.

0.9   Continue straight past the Meadow Trail.

1.7   Reach Divide Meadow. Turn around.

3.4   Arrive back at the trailhead.

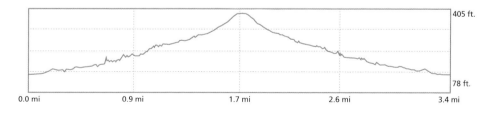

405 ft.

78 ft.

0.0 mi   0.9 mi   1.7 mi   2.6 mi   3.4 mi

20 POINT REYES NATIONAL SEASHORE BEACHES

WHY GO?

Point Reyes is an unparalleled experience along the California coast. Rocky headlands, expansive beaches, open grasslands, and lush forests draw over 2.25 million visitors per year. But long before this area became a recreation hot spot, and long before settlers came to the area, it was home to thousands of species of plants, birds, and other animals, including the tule elk. It has also been home to the Coast Miwok since time immemorial. This guide takes you on a 50-mile-long trip to the most accessible beaches in Point Reyes, plus the lighthouse. It would be difficult to visit all of these in a single day—it takes over two hours just to travel in between them—so I recommend picking a couple that work for you and saving the rest for another trip.

THE RUNDOWN

Spoon rating: 2 spoons for the beaches—most require crossing sand dunes. 4 spoons for the hike to the lighthouse, 1 spoon if you drive up.
Type: Scenic viewpoint, out-and-back
Season/schedule: Open year-round, 6 a.m. to midnight
Water availability: Fountains at Drakes Beach and South Beach
Sun exposure: Full sun
Amenities: Accessible restrooms at Drakes Beach, South Beach, and the lighthouse; non-accessible restrooms at North Beach; vault toilets at Limantour Beach and Kehoe Beach; picnic tables at most locations

Pet-friendly: Yes, on leash at Limantour Beach, Kehoe Beach, North Beach, and South Beach
Cell phone reception: Spotty
Special notes: A beach wheelchair is available for use at Drakes Beach. Online reservations are required at https://www.nps.gov/pore/plan yourvisit/beach-wheelchairs.htm.
Nearest town: Point Reyes Station
Land manager: Point Reyes National Seashore, (415) 464-5100, ext. 2
Pass/entry fee: None
Land acknowledgment: Coast Miwok. The land was stolen from Coast Miwok during settlement and continues through the legacy of ranching.

LIMANTOUR BEACH

Getting there: From Point Reyes Station, take Sir Francis Drake Boulevard and turn left on Bear Valley Road, then right on Limantour Road. Continue 8 miles to the end.
Parking: Large gravel parking lot. Two designated accessible spots with narrow access aisles are located down the hill by the vault toilets.

THE HIKE

A wide gravel trail goes around to the right behind the vault toilets. There are trash cans and a couple picnic tables. Continue through coastal chaparral on the level but slightly uneven trail. Pass some interpretive signage in English and Spanish, and then cross over a bridge that spans a small creek. There is a 0.5- to 1.5-inch lip onto the bridge, and then a

Overlooking a creek at Limantour Beach

Sand dunes at Limantour Beach

2- to 3-inch lip on the other side depending on the amount of sand. The trail transitions to sand with some small bits of gravel mixed in, up to 2 inches deep, and inclines slightly as you approach the dunes. The sand is very deep and loose as you cross over the dunes on an 8% or greater grade. Once you're on the beach, the sand is generally pretty firm and level.

DRAKES BEACH

Getting there: From Bear Valley Road and Sir Francis Drake Boulevard, head north on Sir Francis Drake Boulevard for 7.7 miles. Turn left on Drake Beach Road and continue 1.6 miles to the end.

Parking: One of the largest paved parking lots in the park is located here, with RV parking and several ADA accessible spots.

THE HIKE

The visitor center is accessible by a wooden ramp. Access to the beach is short and level, but may be blocked by sand, driftwood, or plant growth. Contact the visitor center at the phone number above to inquire about current conditions. Beach wheelchairs are available by online reservation.

Tule elk at Point Reyes

Overlooking Drakes Beach

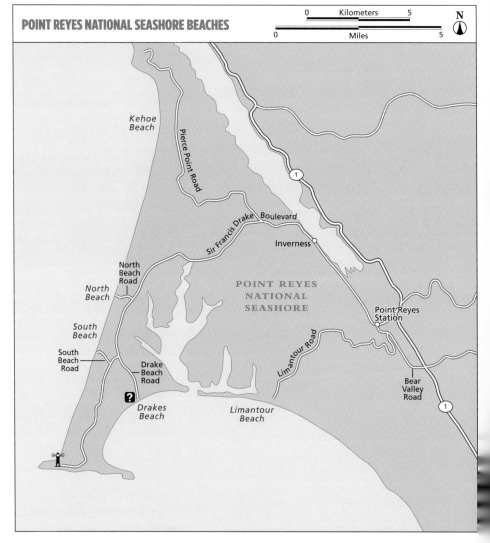

POINT REYES NATIONAL SEASHORE BEACHES

0   Kilometers   5
0   Miles   5

N

Kehoe Beach

Pierce Point Road

Sir Francis Drake Boulevard

Inverness

North Beach Road

North Beach

POINT REYES NATIONAL SEASHORE

South Beach

Point Reyes Station

South Beach Road

Drake Beach Road

Limantour Road

Drakes Beach

Limantour Beach

Bear Valley Road

1

SOUTH BEACH

Getting there: From Drake Beach Road, head south on Sir Francis Drake Boulevard for 0.5 mile. Turn right on South Beach Road and continue 0.7 mile to the end.
Parking: Large paved parking lot with 6 designated accessible spots; none are van accessible but may be usable by a van.

THE HIKE

A short paved pathway leads to a couple interpretive signs, restrooms, showers, and water fountains. There are some nice views of expansive sand dunes from the parking lot. Access to the beach is short but steep down the dunes. The beach is generally firm and level sand.

LIGHTHOUSE

Getting there: From South Beach, continue south 7.8 miles on Sir Francis Drake Boulevard until it ends.
Parking: Paved parking lot with 2 designated accessible parking spots at the end of the road. If you have a disabled parking placard, you can drive up to the visitor center at the lighthouse. You have to open a chain that blocks the gate; it is clipped on with a large carabiner and quite heavy. There are 2 ADA accessible spots, 1 van accessible, at the top.

THE HIKE

The hike up to the lighthouse and the viewing area is steep. It is 0.45 mile one way on a generally 8% grade. The viewing area around the visitor center is ADA accessible, with concrete sidewalks and handrails, but getting to the lighthouse requires taking 313 stairs over 0.2 mile. There are incredible views of the point and the entire peninsula from the road and the observation deck.

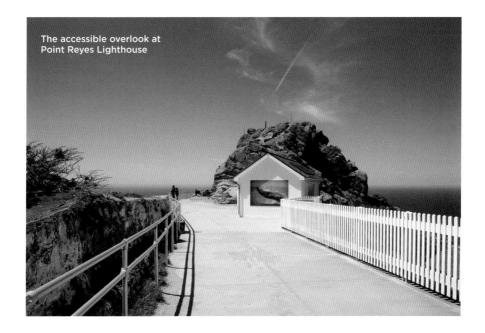

The accessible overlook at Point Reyes Lighthouse

NORTH BEACH

Getting there: From Sir Francis Drake Boulevard at Pierce Point Road, continue south on Sir Francis Drake Boulevard for 5.6 miles. Turn right on North Beach Road and continue 0.6 mile to the end.

Parking: Paved parking lot with 4 designated accessible parking spots.

THE HIKE

An accessible paved path leads up through the sand dunes and to the restrooms, but there is a 3-inch lip onto a wooden platform to get into the restrooms and the sinks don't meet current accessibility guidelines. The easiest path onto the beach is from the end of the parking lot. There is a slight step down from pavement and a short, slight decline on sand to get to the beach. The beach is firm and level sand.

Access to North Beach

Paved path through dunes covered in ice plants at North Beach

KEHOE BEACH

Getting there: Take Sir Francis Drake Boulevard north to Pierce Point Road and turn right. Continue 5.6 miles to the signed trailhead.

Parking: Gravel pullouts on both sides of the road with space for about 6 cars.

THE HIKE

I saved the best for last—this is my favorite beach. The 0.5 mile trail to the beach is generally level and 3 feet wide on hard-packed gravel. There's a couple short grades at 5–8%, short slight cross slopes, and a couple uneven sections with divided double track. You'll travel down a beautiful creek drainage and wetland—there are lots of birds and wildflowers and views of the hills all around you. Cross the dunes to get to the beach. They're not too steep, but the sand is deep—it is the most difficult part of the trail. Once you are on the beach, the sand is generally firm. Incredible cliffs tower above you, and there are tide pools at low tide.

Kehoe Beach

Trail to Kehoe Beach

21 VERNA DUNSHEE TRAIL

WHY GO?

This paved, wheelchair-accessible loop circles the East Peak of Mount Tamalpais. On a clear day, it offers incredible views all the way across the Bay Area to the Pacific Ocean. There are restrooms, water fountains, and picnic tables at the trailhead. The visitor center is open irregular hours as volunteer staffing allows.

THE RUNDOWN

Spoon rating: 1 spoon. Wheelchair accessible with some caution due to cracked pavement, drop-offs and prolonged grades. Not recommended if you have trouble with heights.
Type: Loop
Distance: 0.75 mile
Elevation: 2,350 feet
Elevation gain: 49 feet gain, 56 feet loss
Max grade: 8%
Max cross slope: 5%
Typical width: 5 feet, minimum 32 inches
Typical surface: Pavement
Trail users: Hikers

Season/schedule: Open year-round, 7 a.m. to sunset
Water availability: Water fountain
Sun exposure: Full sun
Amenities: Accessible restrooms, picnic tables
Pet-friendly: Yes, on leash
Cell phone reception: Yes
Nearest town: Tamalpais Valley
Land manager: Mount Tamalpais State Park, (415) 388-2070
Pass/entry fee: Day-use fee or California State Parks annual pass
Land acknowledgment: Coast Miwok. Tamalpais (tam-al-pie-us) roughly translates to "bay mountain" or "coast mountain" in the Miwok language.

FINDING THE TRAILHEAD

Getting there: From US 101 and CA 1 in Manzanita, head west on CA 1 for 3 miles. Turn right on Panoramic Highway and continue for a very windy 5.3 miles. Turn right on Pantoll Road, then right on E. Ridgecrest Boulevard. Continue 3 miles on a curvy uphill drive to the parking lot at the end. **GPS:** 37.927325, -122.580293

Parking: Large paved parking lot at the East Peak Visitor Center with 4 designated accessible spots, 1 van accessible.

Start: Follow the ramp along the parking lot to the signed trailhead to the right of the restrooms.

THE HIKE

The trail begins on a slight incline with a 6-inch-wide raised crack on the right and 21 inches of level clearance on the left, so proceed with caution. The trail switchbacks right and left a couple of times; there are several cracks in the pavement up to an inch and a half wide on a general 8% decline. At the bottom of the switchbacks, a pullout and overlook offers views of the mountains and the ocean. The trail then generally levels out. There is a dip in the trail on the right with a 15% cross slope as you pass an old snag; the level section is about 4 feet wide.

Left: Overlooking the Bay Area from the trail
Right: The Verna Dunshee Trail traveling around the peak

A bench is on the left at 0.1 mile. Pass a low rock wall barrier on the right with a dip in the pavement—there is still about 5 feet of clearance. The paved trail continues on a 5% incline, passing under manzanita and oak with beautiful views across the hills to the water. Be mindful of a few edges with a sharp, unprotected drop-off up to 6 inches high. At 0.2 mile the trail continues on a 3% incline. A metal handrail and rock barriers provide a bit of protection along the right as you pass next to a rock outcropping on the left—there is a long, steep drop below you with expansive views. I found it to be pretty dizzying, so take care if you have vertigo or can't manage heights.

At 0.25 mile the trail is pinched to 3 feet next to a boulder and exposed rock face, with 32 inches of pavement and a couple extra inches of dirt next to the rock. It would be difficult to pass for large wheelchairs. The trail curves left on a 5% incline, and you reach an accessible overlook with metal handrails that goes out above the cliff. The trail continues with a metal handrail on the right and then crosses a wooden bridge beneath a low overhanging rock. Take an 8% incline, curving slightly left and right. There are generally low rock barriers on the outer edge, but they are missing in a few places where there is a steep drop-off.

At 0.3 mile the trail levels out briefly and there is a narrow pullout. It then continues on an 8% incline for a couple hundred feet, leveling out at 0.38 mile with a bench on the left. The trail then continues on a generally 3% incline, rounding the peak. Some loose rocks may be scattered across the trail from washouts. Cross another bridge with handrails and closely placed, rough horizontal boards. Continue on a 5% incline with level areas

Top: The Verna Dunshee Trail winding around the peak
Bottom: The Verna Dunshee Trail traveling through a shaded section

every 30 feet or so. At 0.45 mile there's a bench on the left with an armrest in the center. You then enter a shadier area on the north side of the peak as the trail curves left.

At 0.5 mile the trail rolls slightly on 5% grades for a few feet, then levels out at another bench with a pullout. At 0.6 mile there's a 2–5% cross slope for a few feet, sloping into the cliffside. The trail then curves left and continues 5 feet wide with a wooden handrail on the right. You then start a general 5% decline, traveling along the west side of the peak and back down towards the parking area. At 0.7 mile you close the loop behind the barn. Continue straight ahead to return to the parking area. There's a picnic table on the left and a few more picnic tables set off the path in the gravel, but none of them

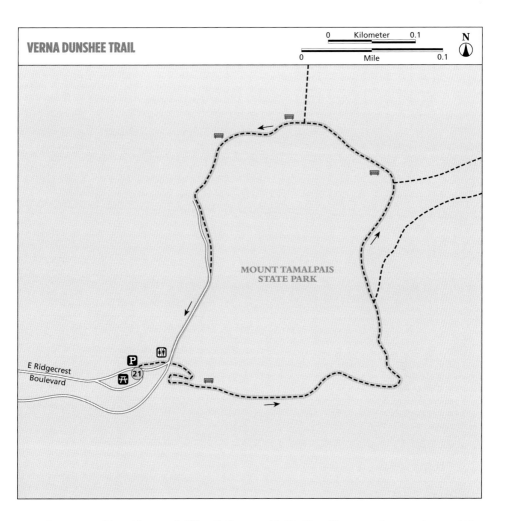

have accessible tabletops. A 3D relief map with Braille offers a tactile experience of the mountains and watershed.

MILES AND DIRECTIONS

0.0 Begin at the trailhead to the right of the restrooms.

0.75 Reach the end of the loop. Continue straight ahead to return to the parking area.

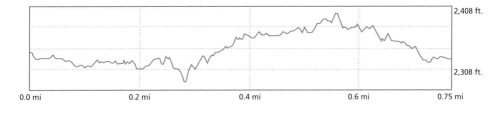

22 FORT FUNSTON

WHY GO?

Fort Funston is perhaps best known as a dog lover's paradise; it is one of the largest off-leash dog spaces in the Bay Area. It is also a premier hang gliding destination, and there are ample opportunities to watch them from the 200-foot-high bluffs. A former military fort, the park contains the San Francisco peninsula's largest remaining sand dune field and is home to threatened bank swallows. A paved trail along the top of the bluffs provides a wheelchair-accessible spot for you to enjoy time outdoors with furry friends.

THE RUNDOWN

Spoon rating: 1 spoon. Wheelchair accessible with all-terrain tires—there may be areas of sand across the trail.
Type: Out-and-back
Distance: 0.66 mile
Elevation: 178 feet
Elevation gain: 20 feet
Max grade: 5%
Max cross slope: 3%
Typical width: 6 feet
Typical surface: Pavement
Trail users: Hikers
Season/schedule: Open year-round, dawn to dusk
Water availability: Water spigot for dogs
Sun exposure: Full sun

Amenities: Portable toilets, benches, picnic tables, trash cans, dog watering station
Pet-friendly: Yes, allowed on and off leash
Cell phone reception: Yes
Special notes: Lots of off-leash dogs. Some foxtails grow along the edge of the trail.
Nearest town: San Francisco
Land manager: Golden Gate National Recreation Area, (415) 561-4700
Pass/entry fee: None
Land acknowledgment: Yelamu Ohlone. Yelamu lands encompass the north end of the peninsula, including Fort Funston.

FINDING THE TRAILHEAD

Getting there: From 19th Avenue and Sloat Boulevard in San Francisco, head west on Sloat Boulevard and make a left on CA 35 / Skyline Boulevard. Continue 1.6 miles, then make a right on Fort Funston Road. Continue to the parking lot at the end. **GPS:** 37.714626, -122.502603

Parking: Large paved parking lot with 4 accessible parking spots.

Public transit: The nearest bus stop is at John Muir Drive and Skyline Boulevard. There is a crosswalk and bike lane, but the road is steep.

Start: Northwest corner of the parking lot behind the trailhead sign.

THE HIKE

Golden Gate National Recreation Area is the only park in the National Park Service with designated areas for off-leash dog walking, including Fort Funston. It is a fantastic spot to watch for hang gliders, birds, and perhaps even whales. Eucalyptus and Monterey cypress grow along the top of the bluffs, and much of the dunes are carpeted in the pretty but invasive ice plant. There are a few remnants of the location's military history,

Above: The boardwalk to the overlook at Fort Funston
Below: Paved trail across the dunes at Fort Funston

including tunnels under Battery Davis. It is often very windy and foggy when the rest of the city is bathed in sunlight, so prepare accordingly.

From the two ADA accessible parking spots at the end of the parking lot, an accessible boardwalk with edge guards and handrails leads less than 0.1 mile to an overlook with

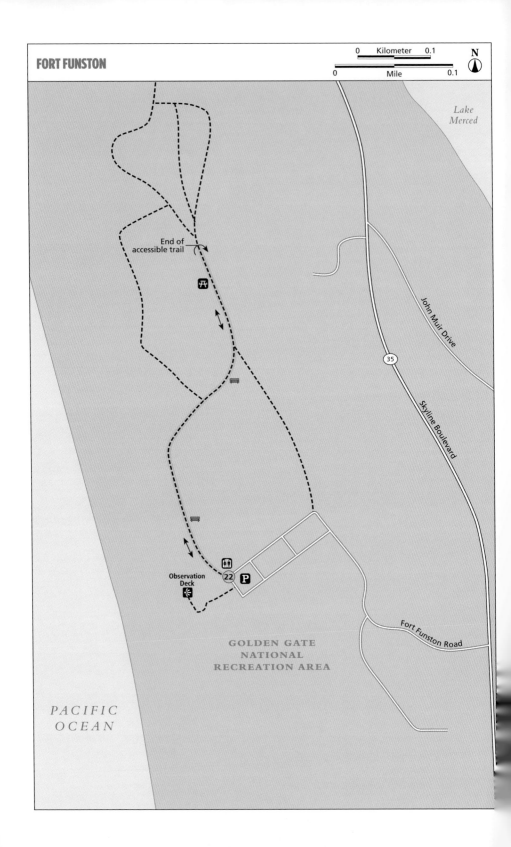

FORT FUNSTON

0   Kilometer   0.1
0   Mile   0.1

N

Lake
Merced

End of
accessible trail

John Muir Drive

35

Skyline Boulevard

Observation
Deck

22

P

GOLDEN GATE
NATIONAL
RECREATION AREA

Fort Funston Road

PACIFIC
OCEAN

several benches. Tucked away behind trees along the edge of the bluff, it is a great spot to enjoy the ocean and watch for birds and hang gliders. I highly recommend it at sunset.

The paved Sunset Trail starts at the northwest corner of the parking lot, to the right of a trailhead sign and map with Braille that describes the trails and historic and natural features of the park. The trail starts out level with some rocks in the sand as barriers along the edge. You almost immediately pass two benches with a pullout on the right. The trail begins a 2–5% incline for about 50 feet, increasing to 6% as it curves right then levels out. At 0.18 mile the trail declines briefly at 2% then levels out—there may be some sand across the trail here, blown or tracked in from the dune above; it usually disperses quickly, but can be 0.5 inch deep or more.

At 0.2 mile the trail inclines at about 3% and there are two more benches with a pull-out on the right. It then levels out and curves left around a tall dune with lots of eucalyptus trees. At 0.25 mile you reach the other side of the dune—which actually covers Battery Davis. The trail is likely to be covered in 0.25 to 0.5 inch of sand. Pass the Battery Davis tunnel on the left. There are nice views of Lake Merced on the right.

At 0.33 mile you reach two accessible picnic tables set off on the left and then a dog watering station on the right (this is often a busy spot of dogs crowding the water bowls). I recommend turning around here. The trail gets increasingly rough and steep beyond this point, with sections of badly damaged and collapsed pavement.

MILES AND DIRECTIONS

0.0 Begin at the trailhead.

0.33 Reach the dog watering station. Turn around.

0.66 Arrive back at the trailhead.

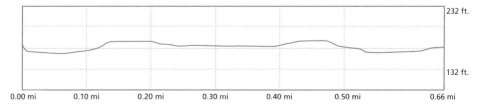

232 ft.

132 ft.

0.00 mi   0.10 mi   0.20 mi   0.30 mi   0.40 mi   0.50 mi   0.66 mi

23 MORI POINT

WHY GO?

Mori Point has recently increased in popularity for the spectacular spring wildflower displays. But it is equally beautiful the rest of the year, and visiting outside of wildflower season should ensure a less crowded experience. The Old Mori Trail is a gentle stroll or roll through wildflowers, wetlands, and grasslands with views of the hills. The Coastal Trail continues along the bluff with expansive ocean views. The route is generally wheelchair hikeable with caution, and there is relatively easy access to the beach.

THE RUNDOWN

Spoon rating: 2 spoons. Wheelchair accessible on the Old Mori Trail; wheelchair hikeable with some caution on the Coastal Trail due to ruts and uneven surface. Elevation change is at the beginning of the trail.
Type: Out-and-back
Distance: 2.5 miles
Elevation: 59 feet
Elevation gain: 70 feet
Max grade: 5%
Max cross slope: 5%
Typical width: 8 feet
Typical surface: Firm soil, gravel

Trail users: Hikers, bikers
Season/schedule: Open year-round; busiest in spring
Water availability: None
Sun exposure: Full sun
Amenities: Vault toilet with handwashing sink
Pet-friendly: Yes, on leash
Cell phone reception: Yes
Nearest town: Pacifica
Land manager: Golden Gate National Recreation Area, (415) 561-4700
Pass/entry fee: None
Land acknowledgment: Aramai Ohlone

FINDING THE TRAILHEAD

Getting there: From Pacifica, head south on CA 1 to the exit for Mori Point Road. Follow Mori Point Road to the right. The trailhead is on the left at a sharp right curve where Mori Point turns into Bradford Way. **GPS:** 37.619232, -122.486483

Parking: Parking is very limited. There is a small gravel parking area at the trailhead with 2 paved accessible spots—neither are really van accessible but you could use the pad in front of the vault toilet. Some roadside parking is available but take care not to impede traffic.

Public transit: Take SamTrans Route 110 to CA 1 and Westport Drive. Walk 1 block west on Westport Drive to Bradford Way and turn left. Go approximately 1 block to the trailhead on the right.

Start: The trailhead behind the gate.

THE HIKE

Mori Point has undergone extensive habitat restoration to support red-legged frogs, San Francisco garter snakes, and many other species, so please be respectful during your visit by staying on the trails.

The boardwalk at Mori Point

Overlooking the meadow at Mori Point

The trail begins behind a gate with an accessible route through the gate. It immediately transitions from pavement to gravel with a 1-inch lip at the transition point, narrows to about 5 feet wide, and becomes a little rough with some loose gravel. Start on a 2% decline as you travel along a fence with houses to the right. There are some trees to provide a little shade and lots of foxtails and other sticker plants along the edge, so be careful with your furry friends. The decline increases to about 4% for a few feet and then generally levels out.

At 0.3 mile you enter Mori Point recreation area and reach a trail intersection—on the left is the Lishumsha (an Ohlone word for the endangered resident garter snake) Trail. Continue straight ahead on the Old Mori Trail. There are beautiful views of the hills above you, and this area erupts with wildflowers in spring and summer. Pass between two vertical barriers with 5 feet of clearance in between. The trail surface gets a little rough with some exposed rocks up to 0.5 inch high, and then transitions to boardwalk with a

The Coastal Trail along the beach at Mori Point

0.5-inch lip. The boardwalk is 8 feet wide, with tightly placed boards and a few metal grates in the center. There are a few benches and pullouts with overlooks and interpretive signs.

At 0.37 mile the trail transitions briefly back to gravel with some exposed rocks up to 1 inch above the surface, then transitions back onto boardwalk. The first couple boards are a little rough. At 0.4 mile the boardwalk ends and you transition back to gravel, with an 8-foot-long section that is rough with some exposed rocks. Continue on a 2% incline, increasing to 5% for 40 feet.

At 0.5 mile you reach a wide trail intersection. Follow the 8-foot-wide gravel path that curves to the right on a slight incline. There are some low, rough exposed rocks but they can be avoided. You then arrive at the top of the bluff with a beautiful view of the beach and rocky cliffs. Trash cans, a low-positioned doggy bag station, and a bike rack are on the right. A big Monterey cypress arches above the cliff on the left with a large flat area beneath—there is no bench here, but there are some logs you can sit on and it's a nice spot to spread a blanket.

Follow the trail to the right—it becomes the Coastal Trail and continues 8 to 10 feet wide on firm packed soil and gravel. This is a popular multiuse trail, and it will likely have rough and rutted areas with tire damage that may be difficult to navigate in a wheelchair. You are traveling along a levee above Sharp Park Beach, which is covered in black sand. The restored Laguna Salada is on the right; this lagoon is habitat for the threatened red-legged frog and numerous birds.

At 0.9 mile there is a flat area up a slight rise on the right with a few large concrete blocks that you can sit on. It overlooks the lagoon and has interpretive signs about the coastal ecosystem, a trash can, and a 4-foot-high doggy bag station. Across the trail, eight steps lead down to the beach.

Beyond this point, there is a long section that may be deeply rutted with vehicle tire tracks. A more even section is along the edge, but it may be difficult to navigate with a wheelchair. The ruts end at 1.0 mile, but the trail continues to be a bit rough. Pass a ramp down to the beach that is covered in deep sand at 1.15 miles. The trail reaches a

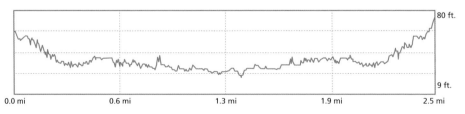

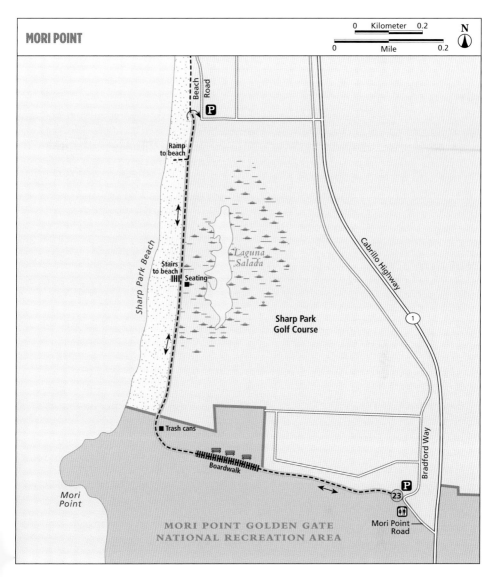

parking lot on Beach Road at 1.2 miles (a good parking alternative to the small lot on Mori Point Road)—the access path to the parking area is level with deep sand and could be accessible with a beach wheelchair. The Coastal Trail continues along a promenade that follows Beach Road out to a pier, but I recommend turning around here.

MILES AND DIRECTIONS

0.0   Begin at the trailhead on Bradford Way.

0.5   Reach a trail intersection. Curve right, following the wide gravel trail.

1.2   Reach the end of the trail on Beach Road. Turn around.

2.5   Arrive back at the trailhead.

24 POINT PINOLE REGIONAL SHORELINE

WHY GO?
Point Pinole feels like a remote escape even though it's within a couple miles of several major cities. The 2,315-acre park features miles of trails, over a hundred species of birds, and multiple ecosystems including salt marsh, meadows, and eucalyptus forest. Picnic areas and other amenities dot the park, and the off-leash trails make it a popular family and pet destination. This loop circles the point, passing through all of the major ecosystems in the park and offering incredible views of San Pablo Bay.

THE RUNDOWN

Spoon rating: 3 spoons. Generally level and even, with one section of up to 15% grades and rutted areas. Wheelchair accessible on the first and last third of this loop, or take an optional more accessible loop.
Type: Loop
Distance: 3.9 miles
Elevation: 50 feet
Elevation gain: 144 feet
Max grade: 15%
Max cross slope: 10%
Typical width: 6 feet
Typical surface: Compact gravel, firm sand
Trail users: Hikers, bikers, equestrians
Season/schedule: Open year-round starting at 8 a.m. Closing hours vary between 4 p.m. and 7 p.m. depending on the season.
Water availability: Water fountains
Sun exposure: Partial shade

Amenities: Accessible restrooms, picnic tables with shade, trash cans
Pet-friendly: Yes, on leash on paved trails and in developed areas, allowed off leash on other trails and undeveloped areas. No dogs allowed in the marsh. The park is full of foxtails in summer.
Cell phone reception: Spotty (East Bay Parks has a cellular coverage map on their website)
Nearest town: Richmond
Land manager: East Bay Regional Parks, (888) 327-2757, option 3, ext. 4551
Pass/entry fee: Parking fee (charged April–October only when the kiosk is open); additional fee for pets (service animals are free)
Land acknowledgment: Point Pinole was the site of several Ohlone coastal villages.

FINDING THE TRAILHEAD

Getting there: From Richmond, take Richmond Parkway approximately 1.5 miles to Atlas Road. Follow Atlas Road for 1 mile to the park entrance, and continue to the parking area at the end. **GPS:** 37.999778, -122.356415

Parking: Large gravel parking lot with 4 paved ADA accessible spots.

Public transit: AC Transit route 71 stops at Giant Highway and Atlas Road. Walk 0.5 mile north on Atlas Road to the park entrance.

Start: The trailhead on the left side of the parking area behind the picnic area and restrooms.

Top: A bench overlooking the marsh at Pinole Point
Bottom: The Cooks Point Trail at Pinole Point

THE HIKE

Begin your hike on the 10-foot-wide gravel trail behind the picnic area, heading left (southwest). Pass beneath some large eucalyptus trees, then at 0.1 mile reach a fork with the Cooks Point Trail on the left and the Giant Station Trail on the right. Go left on the Cooks Point Trail. Continue on a 6-foot-wide gravel trail with some loose gravel on the surface, taking a 5–8% incline for about 30 feet, then declining at the same grade as you round the top of the hill.

The Bay View Trail through eucalyptus forest

At 0.3 mile you reach an intersection with the Pinole Point Trail. (**Option:** This paved trail travels the length of the point and is generally wheelchair accessible; if you go right here, it travels 2 miles to the picnic area at mile 2.5 of this guide, and then out to the pier. You could then return on Owl Alley Way for a more wheelchair-accessible loop.) For this loop, go left on the Pinole Point Trail and take a 5% incline with a 5% cross slope. There are a few picnic areas beneath large eucalyptus trees and a playground overlooking San Pablo Bay; a couple picnic tables can be accessed on a paved and gravel path, but most are on firm sand. Continue on a 5% incline for 50 feet as you pass the picnic area and approach the toilets.

At 0.55 mile you reach another fork. The bridge straight ahead leads to the Giant Highway parking area. Continue to the right on the paved trail, and curve left down a 6% decline. Reach a trail intersection at 0.6 mile. Continue straight ahead and then make a right onto the Bay View Trail. Take a slight decline and almost immediately the pavement ends with a slight dip onto compact gravel. The Bay View Trail continues generally 5 feet wide. There is some medium-size loose gravel as the trail continues on a 2–5% incline for a few feet. The trail has some slight rolls and divots in it, but it is generally level and even. You are now traveling along the shoreline with views of the marsh and San Pablo Bay.

At 0.8 mile there is a bench under large eucalyptus trees overlooking the marsh. As you pass under the eucalyptus trees, the surface is more sand than gravel for about 50 feet, and there may be some sticks and bark on the trail. The trail then returns to gravel, some loose.

At 1.0 mile take a 2–5% incline, passing under another grove of eucalyptus. The trail generally continues on 2% inclines interspersed with level areas. At 1.2 miles the trail levels out. There's a bench on the left that's accessed over grass, then the trail inclines at 5% for about 30 feet. The surface becomes slightly uneven with some loose gravel as you continue on a 2% incline. There may be California poppies and other wildflowers on the hillside to your right. At 1.3 miles an outhouse-style chemical toilet is on the right. This is a good turnaround spot if you are using a wheelchair.

You then reach an intersection with beach access going down steeply on the left and a closed trail straight ahead. Stay on the Bay View Trail as it curves right and heads uphill on a 12% incline with a 5–10% cross slope for about 100 feet. This entire section, from the beach access point to the top of the hill, is likely to be deeply rutted with some exposed rocks. The park continues to work on this section, so you may want to call for current conditions. Continue left on the Bay View Trail at the top of the hill. You are now in a eucalyptus forest above the bay. The trail widens to 8 feet and there may be some deep ruts running vertical along the trail, but otherwise it is compact gravel and firm sand.

At 1.5 miles take a 5–8% incline for about 50 feet. You may have to cross over a deep rut at the top, and then the trail continues level but rutted through a eucalyptus forest, with slopes rising on either side. Numerous bike trails fork off into the woods.

At 1.65 miles take a 15% decline for 30 feet, then cross over a dip in the trail with a rut down the center and take a 5% incline for a few feet, increasing to 8% for 50 feet. At 1.7 miles you reach the intersection with the Packhouse Trail on the right and the remnants of a bunker. Continue straight ahead. The trail narrows to 5 feet, takes a 5% incline for a few feet, and then leaves the forest, hugging the hillside above the bay. It is now mostly compact gravel with some sand.

At 1.8 miles a bench on the left overlooks the water. The trail curves right on a slight incline, and then there's some exposed roots rising up to 4 inches across the trail with a 2-foot-wide level section you can pass on. Continue on an 8% incline with some ruts down the side. At 1.9 miles the trail curves slightly right, passing along some nice eucalyptus trees. Take an 8% incline for a few feet. Continue straight ahead between large eucalyptus trees, passing a footpath on the left that winds down to a small bluff. You then enter an open grassy area.

At 2.0 miles take a 5–8% incline for about 50 feet. There's a bench set off the trail on the left overlooking the bay—this is a nice place to take a break. Continue on a slight incline. Pass another bench at 2.2 miles and continue on a 5–8% cross slope with loose gravel for a few feet, then the trail curves sharply right. You are now at Pinole Point. A rutted, steep footpath leads down to an overlook on the left—I don't recommend going down there. Continue straight on the Bay View Trail. It takes an 8–10% decline with some loose gravel for a couple hundred feet.

You reach the east side of the point at 2.4 miles. Go right on the paved Pinole Point Trail. There are picnic tables, water fountains, and accessible vault toilets. At 2.5 miles go left on the Owl Alley Trail. The trail is 8 feet wide, level, and compact gravel and passes through another eucalyptus grove before opening up along a marsh on the left. This is a very pretty area. I noticed bald eagles, hummingbirds, and lots of other birds, and poppies and other wildflowers in the grassy areas. At 2.75 miles you pass the China Cove Trail—a fairly level footpath that goes down to the beach.

At 3.0 miles there's a bench that is set off on the right along a footpath that circles a pond. You then reach a fork with the Marsh Trail on the left. The Owl Alley Trail continues straight ahead—it is flat and the most direct route back to the parking area. But if

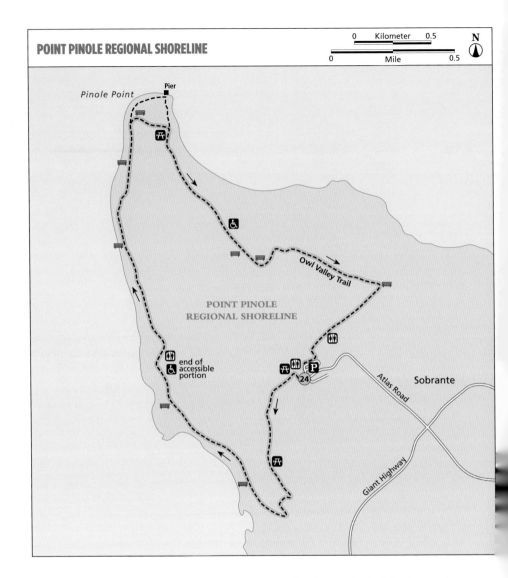

0   Kilometer   0.5

0   Mile   0.5

N

Pinole Point

Pier

Owl Valley Trail

POINT PINOLE
REGIONAL SHORELINE

end of
accessible
portion

24

Atlas Road

Sobrante

Giant Highway

you want to extend the hike a little longer, you can take the Marsh Trail for better views of the salt marsh. There's a low bench on the left and an interpretive sign about the salt marsh. The trail curves left to a 15% cross slope with a narrow level section on the inside for about 30 feet. It then levels out, with eucalyptus trees on the right and the salt marsh on the left. The trail inclines slightly and curves right.

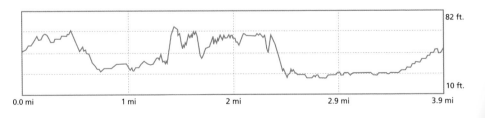

82 ft.

10 ft.

0.0 mi   1 mi   2 mi   2.9 mi   3.9 mi

At 3.25 miles the trail becomes mostly compact sand, inclines at 10% for a few feet, levels out, and then takes an 8% incline for a few feet. You'll pass a couple vernal pools and then reenter the woods. The trail returns to compact gravel and continues level but is a little rough.

At 3.5 miles you reach a trail intersection with a bench and trash can. Go right on the Cooks Point Trail—it continues on level compacted gravel and sand through the eucalyptus forest, with tall, densely growing trees surrounding you. At 3.7 miles the trail inclines slightly and gets a little rutted, then you pass the park office and maintenance shed. Continue straight on a long, slight incline. Arrive back at the picnic area at the trailhead at 3.9 miles and go left to the parking lot.

MILES AND DIRECTIONS

0.0 Begin at the trailhead at the picnic area.

0.1 Go left on the Cooks Point Trail.

0.3 Go left on the Pinole Point Trail.

0.6 Go right on the Bay View Trail.

1.3 Reach a toilet and the recommended turnaround spot if you are using a wheelchair.

1.4 Stay right on the Bay View Trail, then left at the top of the hill.

2.4 Go right on the Pinole Point Trail.

2.5 Go left on the Owl Alley Trail.

3.5 Go right on the Cooks Point Trail.

3.9 Arrive back at the picnic area. Go left to the parking lot.

25 NIMITZ WAY

WHY GO?

This hike in Tilden Regional Park follows the ridge of the East Bay hills with incredible views across the Bay Area. There are lots of benches along the way, and several vantage points to watch the fog rolling in from the Pacific Ocean to envelop San Francisco and the bay. Wildflowers grow along the hillside in the spring. While it is considered wheelchair accessible, there are a lot of ups and downs on this trail and little shade. It is worth the hike, but be prepared with plenty of water and sun protection.

THE RUNDOWN

Spoon rating: 4 spoons. Lots of inclines and declines on up to 10% grades, a prolonged 8% grade, and areas of cracked pavement. Most accessible for power chair users or strong manual chair users.
Type: Out-and-back
Distance: 3.8 miles
Elevation: 1,036 feet
Elevation gain: 269 feet
Max grade: 10%
Max cross slope: 5%
Typical width: 6 feet
Typical surface: Pavement
Trail users: Hikers, bikers, equestrians

Season/schedule: Open year-round, 5 a.m. to 10 p.m.
Water availability: None
Sun exposure: Full sun
Amenities: Benches, picnic tables, trash cans, vault toilets
Pet-friendly: Yes, on leash
Cell phone reception: Yes
Nearest town: Berkeley
Land manager: East Bay Regional Parks, (888) 327-2757, option 3, ext. 4562
Pass/entry fee: None
Land acknowledgment: This is in Xučyun (Huichin), the ancestral and unceded land of the Chochenyo Ohlone people.

FINDING THE TRAILHEAD

Getting there: From Berkeley, take Grizzly Peak Boulevard to Shasta Road and turn east towards Tilden Regional Park. Follow Shasta Road until it turns right and becomes Wildcat Canyon Road. Continue 1.4 miles, then turn left into the Inspiration Point parking area. **GPS:** 37.90548, -122.24432

Parking: Paved parking area with space for about 30 cars and 2 designated accessible parking spots.

Start: The trailhead is on the right at the exit of the parking lot.

THE HIKE

There are stunning views from the parking area—this is called Inspiration Point for a reason—and the drive up here is beautiful as well. There are also a couple benches and picnic tables if you'd like to take a break before beginning your hike.

Start at the southwest corner of the parking lot. A brick structure with a concrete sign reading East Bay Regional Park District "Nimitz Way" marks the trailhead. Pass between metal poles with 3 feet of clearance and continue on the 6-foot-wide paved trail. It

Overlooking the reservoir from the Nimitz Way trail

A bench overlooking the hills and foggy bay from the Nimitz Way trail

begins on a 5% incline and curves right on a 5% cross slope. At 0.2 mile the trail curves sharply right; a bench offers a nice view across the bay. Take a 5% decline as you curve right, then it generally levels out.

At 0.35 mile the trail inclines at 5% for about 50 feet. The surface is slightly cracked—one or two gaps could catch a wheel but can be bypassed. At the top of the hill there are two benches set off the trail in the grass with a nice view overlooking the San Pablo Reservoir. The trail descends slightly, then inclines at 5% and curves right. A bench on the left overlooks the hills. Continue on a slight incline with some cracked and uneven sections with a steep cross slope on the left where the pavement has slipped.

At 0.5 mile the trail curves right on a 2% cross slope, continuing on a 2–5% incline with a few more sections of slightly cracked and uneven pavement. At 0.65 mile the trail levels out below the ridgeline. There are expansive views of the bay and the Berkeley Hills, and the grassy hills around you may have lots of wildflowers in spring. The trail curves

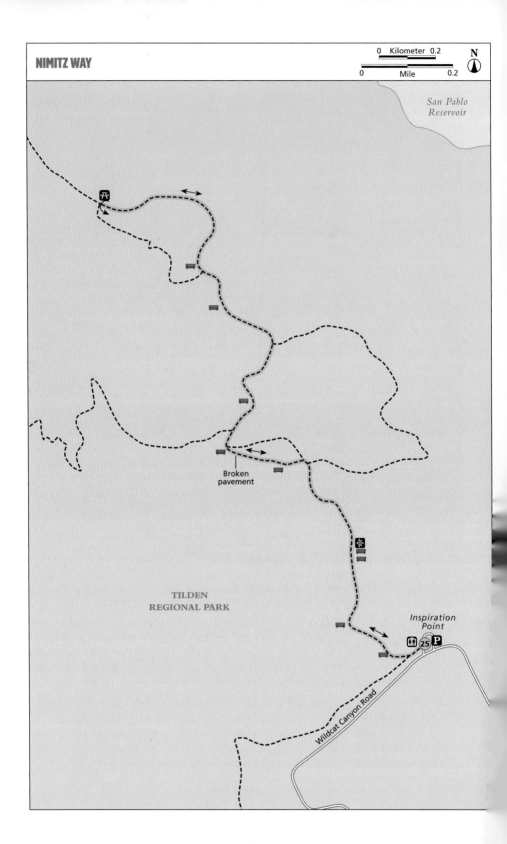

San Pablo
Reservoir

Broken
pavement

TILDEN
REGIONAL PARK

Inspiration
Point

25

Wildcat Canyon Road

0   Kilometer 0.2
0   Mile   0.2

N

left and takes another slight incline as it curves right around a hill. There is another the bench on the left overlooking the canyon and the bay. The trail continues generally level until 0.9 mile, where it curves sharply right with a 5% cross slope for about 15 feet and then levels out again.

At 1.0 mile the trail rolls and then dips. It then curves and banks left; there's some lifted sections of pavement followed by a large pothole with about 3 feet of clearance on the right—navigate this carefully if it hasn't been repaired. Pass another bench and then curve right on a 5% incline with an 8% cross slope as you start heading uphill.

Reach the top of the hill at 1.1 miles and then take a long 5–8% decline, level out briefly, then decline again. At 1.25 miles the trail inclines at 8%, reducing to 5% with some uneven sections for about 100 feet. At 1.3 miles the trail levels out and there is a bench under an oak on the left—your first shady spot. A pretty vernal pool is on the right. The trail then curves left on an uneven 5–8% cross slope.

The Nimitz Way trail through eucalyptus forest

At 1.4 miles you start another long, steep incline of 5–8% for a couple hundred feet. You then pass a trail on the left that leads down to the Tilden Nature Area. Continue straight ahead on the paved trail, taking a 5% incline with a slight cross slope as the trail curves right. A bench on the left overlooks the bay. At 1.5 miles the trail inclines at 8–10% and curves left on an uneven cross slope. At 1.6 miles it levels out and you enter eucalyptus forest. The trail surface gets a little uneven in some spots and may be covered with leaves and bark from the eucalyptus. This is a shady and refreshing spot, with eucalyptus growing high above you, its scent perfuming the air.

At 1.9 miles take an 8–10% incline, then pass a trail on the left for the Rotary Club Peace Grove. Just beyond that trail fork, there's a picnic table up on a hill under the eucalyptus. It's a short, steep incline to get up there, so if that isn't possible for you, some logs may be available to sit on closer to the trail. The trail continues for a few more miles, but this marks a good turnaround spot.

MILES AND DIRECTIONS

0.0 Begin at the trailhead.

1.9 Reach a picnic table in a eucalyptus grove. Turn around.

3.8 Arrive back at the trailhead.

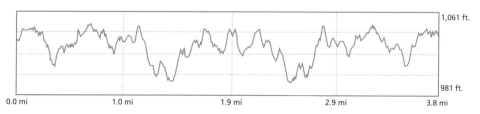

26 STREAM TRAIL

WHY GO?

This trail in Reinhardt Redwood Regional Park is one of the most accessible places to experience redwoods in the Bay Area. The trees are not as large as the ones in Muir Woods or the North Coast parks, but they are impressive. It is a wonderful place to pack a picnic and spend the afternoon, especially on a warm summer day. The park is popular, and parking can be a challenge, but the crowds usually disperse on the trail. The first mile is paved and generally accessible.

THE RUNDOWN

Spoon rating: 2 spoons. Partially wheelchair accessible with some caution due to a prolonged grade. Lots of rest areas.
Type: Out-and-back
Distance: 3.0 miles, 2.0 miles accessible portion
Elevation: 580 feet
Elevation gain: 174 feet, 100 feet accessible portion
Max grade: 10%
Max cross slope: 8%
Typical width: 8 feet
Typical surface: Pavement
Trail users: Hikers, equestrians
Season/schedule: Open year-round, 5 a.m. to 10 p.m.

Water availability: Water fountains
Sun exposure: Mostly shaded
Amenities: Accessible restroom, vault toilet, picnic tables, benches
Pet-friendly: Yes, on leash
Cell phone reception: None
Nearest town: Oakland
Land manager: East Bay Regional Park District, (888) 327-2757, option 3, ext. 4553
Pass/entry fee: Parking fee (charged April–October on weekends and holidays); additional fee for pets (service animals are free)
Land acknowledgment: Lisjan Ohlone

FINDING THE TRAILHEAD

Getting there: From CA 13 in Oakland, take the Redwood Road exit and head east. Continue on Redwood Road. Cross Skyline Boulevard and continue another 2 miles to the Redwood Gate park entrance. Make a left and continue to the Canyon Meadow staging area at the end of the road. **GPS:** 37.806529, -122.147804

Parking: Paved parking lot with 4 designated accessible spots.
Start: The end of the parking area, past the gate.

THE HIKE

The Stream Trail begins at the end of the parking area, past a metal gate with 4 feet of clearance on the side. It is paved and 8 feet wide. Pass a trailhead sign with a large map and printed brochures, then take a slight incline for a few feet. Three all-gender restrooms are on the right—one is accessible with a sliding barn-style door—with an accessible outdoor sink and water fountain. A path leads through a grassy area with lots of picnic tables.

Continue past the restrooms on a 5% cross slope, then the trail inclines at 5–8% with a 5% cross slope for about 50 feet and levels out. There is interpretive signage in English

The Stream Trail through redwoods

A steep hill on the Stream Trail

and Spanish, but no Braille. Take another 8% incline for 30 feet, then arrive at the Orchard picnic area, with a playground, picnic tables in the grass, benches, a water fountain, trash cans, grills, and a restroom.

The trail takes a 5% incline as it passes the playground area and continues curving towards the left. It then declines at 5% and you cross over a shallow crack across the pavement. Cross over the creek on the wide paved trail and then continue past the Ferndale picnic area on the left. The trail passes the sign for Aurelia Henry Reinhardt Grove and takes an 8% incline with a 5% cross slope, curves right, then declines into the redwood grove. You are now surrounded by large redwoods in a lush, creekside environment.

At 0.6 mile you reach the Old Church picnic area. The trail takes a 5% incline, increasing to 8% with a 2–5% cross slope. Cross over a shallow, roughly paved drainage area that crosses the trail. There are a few picnic tables and benches and an interpretive sign about the former church. On the left are two small outhouse-style chemical toilets. Take an 8% decline for a few feet—the pavement is lifted from roots at the bottom with about 2 feet of level space on the left side, so be careful.

At 0.7 mile you reach Big Bend Meadow. This is a pretty place with a couple picnic tables and benches in the grass. There may be wildflowers in the spring. Take a 5% incline for about 30 feet, then the trail declines slightly and rolls a few times. You then incline at 10% with a 5% cross slope for over 50 feet—this may be a challenge for people with mobility limitations, and wheelchair users will need to use caution and may need assistance depending on your wheelchair and strength. The trail then continues on a 2–5% incline for a total of approximately 150 feet. You then level out briefly before taking a slight decline for a few feet.

The Stream Trail as it heads downhill

Group photo at the Trail's End picnic area on the Stream Trail
SEMPERVIRENS FUND / ORENDA RANDUCH

At 0.95 mile the pavement transitions to compact gravel and natural surface. It is firm and level but a little uneven. You then reach the Trail's End picnic area at 1.0 mile. There are a couple picnic tables, a picnic shelter, and a grill set over in a gravel area on the right. This makes a nice spot to hang out for a little while—the creek runs close by, and you are surrounded by big redwoods. Wheelchair users should turn around here, though, as the trail is not very accessible beyond this point.

If you do continue, the trail becomes natural soil surface with occasional rocks and roots rising up to 3 inches and rolling grades up to 8%. It is a pretty section of redwoods, with the creek flowing along the side of the trail. A few benches and picnic tables are scattered along the way. I usually turn around at 1.5 miles, where the trail climbs steeply for several feet and crosses a bridge over the creek, for a 3-mile round-trip hike.

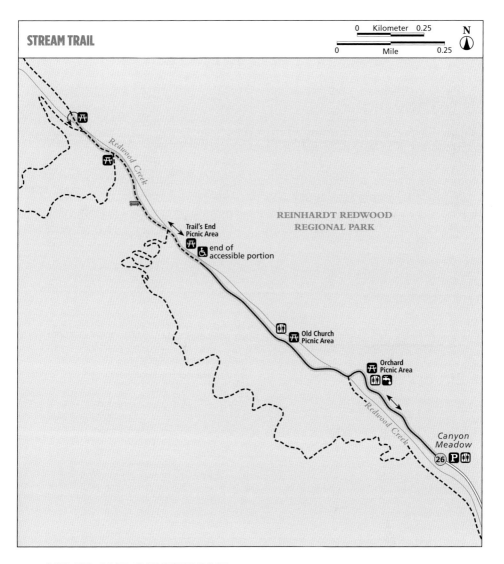

REINHARDT REDWOOD
REGIONAL PARK

Trail's End
Picnic Area

end of
accessible portion

Old Church
Picnic Area

Orchard
Picnic Area

Canyon
Meadow

MILES AND DIRECTIONS

0.0 Begin at the trailhead.

1.0 Reach the Trail's End picnic area. This is the end of the accessible portion.

1.5 Reach a bridge over the creek. Turn around.

3.0 Arrive back at the trailhead.

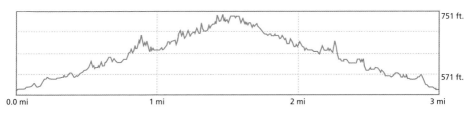

27 MOUNT UMUNHUM SUMMIT OVERLOOK

WHY GO?
Sierra Azul Open Space Preserve encompasses over 19,000 acres of the Santa Cruz Mountains, including the Sierra Azul range and foothills, and offers a sense of remoteness less than an hour from San Jose. You can experience expansive views of the entire Bay Area from the summit, including the three other peaks that surround the area: Mount Tamalpais, Mount Diablo, and Mount Hamilton. The serpentine soils of the rocky summit are home to many unique species of plants and animals. An accessible path travels along the east and west summit with benches and interpretive signage, and an audio tour is available.

THE RUNDOWN

Spoon rating: 1 spoon. Wheelchair-accessible overlook with benches and a paved path.
Type: Scenic viewpoint
Distance: 0.3 mile
Elevation: 3,486 feet
Elevation gain: 20 feet
Max grade: 8%
Max cross slope: 2%
Typical width: 5 feet
Typical surface: Pavement
Trail users: Hikers
Season/schedule: Open year-round, 7 a.m. to sunset
Water availability: None
Sun exposure: Full sun
Amenities: Accessible toilets, benches, shade pavilion, audio tour

Pet-friendly: No
Cell phone reception: Spotty
Nearest town: Almaden
Land manager: Midpeninsula Regional Open Space, (650) 691-1200
Pass/entry fee: None
Land acknowledgment: Mount Umunhum holds great spiritual significance for many local tribal bands. It is within Tamien Ohlone ancestral territory. *Umumhum* translates to "resting place of the hummingbird." The mountain is a part of the creation stories of the Amah Mutsun, who continue to hold ceremonies here.

FINDING THE TRAILHEAD

Getting there: From the Almaden area of San Jose, take Almaden Road south for approximately 4 miles to Hicks Road and turn right. Continue 1.7 miles and turn left on Mount Umunhum Road. Continue 5 miles on this curvy two-lane road to the parking area at the summit. **GPS:** 37.160378, -121.898273

Parking: Paved parking with 54 spaces and 3 ADA spots. A disabled-only parking area with 3 ADA spots is at the end of the road.

Start: The disabled-only parking area at the summit.

THE HIKE
Two parking areas are located at the summit. The first is large, with three ADA spots and accessible vault toilets, but you have to hike several sets of stairs to reach the overlook.

The paved trail to the Mount
Umunhum summit overlook

At the end of the road is a visitor drop-off and turnaround area with three ADA parking spots; one is van accessible and all three have access aisles.

There is a shade pavilion with interpretive signs in English; an audiovisual tour is available online at tinyurl.com/UmunhumAudioTour. A large deck protected by a metal fence with vertical poles stretches over the cliff and provides a nice 180-degree view to the west, north, and east. A paved path encircles the radio tower with several benches

MOUNT UMUNHUM SUMMIT OVERLOOK

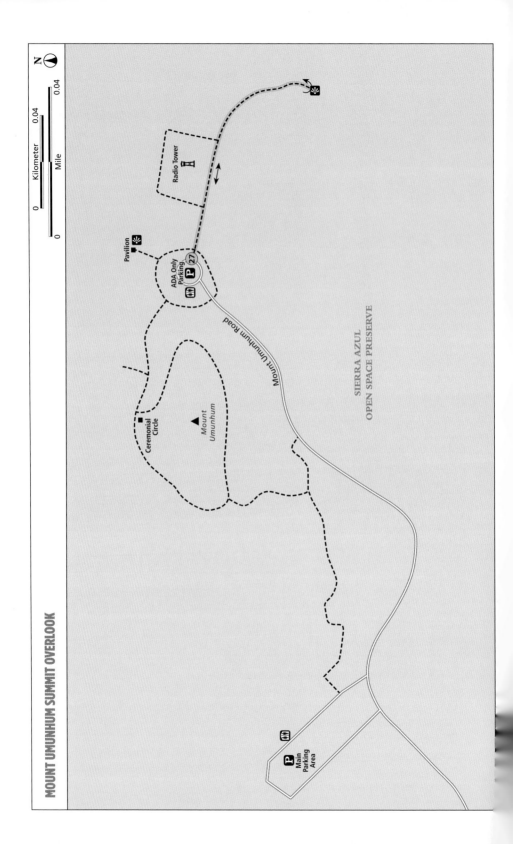

surrounding it, providing an opportunity to rest and take in the experience. To the right of the radio tower, a short paved trail takes a maximum 8% grade to an overlook on the east summit. The viewpoint is encircled by a low rock wall and offers views to the east and south across the mountains. Some areas of the concrete around the radio tower are a bit rough, and there may be some gravel across the trail to the overlook, but it is generally navigable.

On the west side of the turnaround area, a paved path leads to a ceremonial circle. Take a short 8% grade and then reach a large circle bordered by a low rock wall and surfaced in firm, fine gravel on the left. An interpretive sign explains the spiritual significance of this area and welcomes visitors to use the circle for contemplation and prayer. The trail continues beyond the circle to the main parking lot.

MONTEREY BAY

The Monterey Bay area represents the northernmost region of California's Central Coast. It extends roughly from Año Nuevo Bay to Ragged Point on the coast and inland across the Southern Coast Ranges to San Joaquin Valley. It includes Santa Cruz, Monterey, Big Sur, and the Salinas Valley, which is one of the most productive agricultural areas in the state. The landscape is incredibly diverse and features rugged coastlines, abundant estuaries, and the southernmost range of coast redwoods. Numerous parks and conserved areas are located throughout the region, making it both a recreational hotspot and an important place for conservation efforts. The hikes in this guide are located around Monterey Bay.

Monterey Bay is the second-largest bay in California at 45 miles long. It is entirely protected within the Monterey Bay National Marine Sanctuary, which stretches 276 miles from the Golden Gate to Cambria. The abundance of the bay has supported Indigenous peoples in the area since time immemorial. While the ancestors of the Indigenous peoples of this region are collectively referred to as Ohlone, there were numerous tribal bands and villages throughout the Monterey Bay area who spoke related languages and held distinct territories.

The Awaswas included six tribes: the Quiroste, Cotoni, Uypi, Aptos, Sayante, and Chaloctaca. Their ancestral territory stretches from the northern edge of the Santa Cruz Mountains to Aptos Creek and the northern tip of Monterey Bay. Amah Mutsun ancestral territory includes the area between the Pajaro and San Benito Rivers and Monterey Bay. Twenty to thirty villages existed throughout the territory, known as Popeloutchom (https://amahmutsun.org/history). The Tribe continues stewardship and restoration practices through a land trust. Rumsen people are indigenous to the lower Carmel River Valley, Monterey, and the Point Lobos area; five villages existed along Carmel Bay and into the Carmel Valley (https://www.rumsenohlone.com/who-we-are). The Esselen Tribe speaks Hokan, a language distinct from the Ohlone languages. Esselen ancestral lands include the Big Sur coast and Santa Lucia Mountains.

View across the sand hills

28 HENRY COWELL HIGHLIGHTS LOOP

WHY GO?

This loop is a "best of" tour of Henry Cowell Redwoods State Park—you'll experience redwood forest, the San Lorenzo River, oak woodlands, and incredible views across the Santa Cruz Mountains. But most unique of all are the Santa Cruz Sandhills. These hills were once an inland sea, but now rise high above the river valley and are home to rare marine deposits and unique species. It is worth the hike, but it is definitely the most difficult trail in this book. For a shorter route to visit just the sand hills, you could start at the campground.

THE RUNDOWN

Spoon rating: 5 spoons. Long, steep grades, narrow trails, and uneven footing. Limited places to rest.
Type: Lollipop loop
Distance: 5.2 miles
Elevation: 270 feet
Elevation gain: 719 feet
Max grade: 20%
Max cross slope: 10%
Typical width: 6 feet to narrow footpath
Typical surface: Pavement, sand
Trail users: Hikers, bikers, equestrians
Season/schedule: Open year-round, sunrise to sunset

Water availability: None
Sun exposure: Shaded except for the middle portion across the sand hills
Amenities: Benches, picnic tables, accessible restrooms
Pet-friendly: No, allowed only on Pipeline Road
Cell phone reception: None
Nearest town: Felton
Land manager: Henry Cowell Redwoods State Park, (831) 335-4598
Pass/entry fee: Day-use fee or California State Parks annual pass
Land acknowledgment: Sayante Ohlone

FINDING THE TRAILHEAD

Getting there: From Felton, head south on CA 9 for 0.5 mile. Turn left on N. Big Trees Park Road. Continue to the parking lot at the end. **GPS:** 37.039914, -122.063537
Parking: Paved parking lot with designated ADA parking.
Start: The road at the end of the parking lot.

THE HIKE

The park has completed renovations of the day-use area, and there is now ADA parking, accessible restrooms, and improved accessibility to the nature store. The Redwood Grove Loop trail, a wheelchair-accessible loop through the largest redwoods in the park, has also been improved (you can find a trail description at DisabledHikers.com).

You can begin this hike from the Redwood Loop, but for this guide, we'll start on the Pipeline Road trail. Follow the parking lot road to the right, past the trailhead for the Redwood Grove Loop, and take a left onto Pipeline Road. This paved trail begins

View of the San Lorenzo River from the Pipeline Road trail

on a 10–12% decline for about 30 feet and then continues generally level along the San Lorenzo River and large second-growth redwoods and California bay laurel. At 0.5 mile the pavement gets a little rough and you take a slight incline.

At 0.6 mile you reach a trail intersection. The trail on the left is the Redwood Grove Loop (this is where you join the Pipeline Road trail if you took the loop trail). Continue straight ahead on the paved trail, past a bench on the left that sits beneath large redwoods. You are traveling through an impressive grove of coast redwoods.

At 0.7 mile pass a trail map on the left. The trail takes a slight decline heading towards the river, then passes underneath the railroad. The trail gets rough as it descends on an 8–10% decline for about 30 feet, inclining again at 5%, then generally leveling out after 40 feet. This is a pleasant section of trail along the river, but you soon start climbing the hill. Take a 10–12% incline for over 100 feet, then the trail levels out slightly at a fork—continue on the paved trail.

You're hiking up a lush, creek-fed hillside full of redwoods and ferns above the river. The trail continues uneven and cracked, with several dips and rolls. Pass another fork, staying on the paved trail. At 0.9 mile you start inclining again at 8%, increasing to 12–15% for about 30 feet, then continuing on a generally 5–8% incline. The road is rough, with some small cracks and uneven areas.

At 1.1 miles take another steep incline for about 40 feet, leveling out briefly before climbing again at 10%, increasing to 15% with a steep cross slope. The trail continues on a very slight incline for a few more feet, then levels out as it curves left. A soft shoulder is generally along the side if you don't want to walk on the pavement. At 1.2 miles you may notice Eagle Creek down on the right, and you take a 10% decline. You then reach the beginning of the loop. Go right to stay on the paved Pipeline Road trail.

The Pipeline Road trail heading uphill near the ridge

The trail takes another 12–15% incline for about 30 feet, passing a fork with Rincon Fire Road going off to the right. Continue straight on an incline of 10–12% with a steep cross slope for over 100 feet. At 1.3 miles a big log may be on the left side of the trail that you can sit on, but there aren't any benches along this trail so bring a collapsible chair if you need one. The trail continues on an incline, generally 5–10% and increasing to 10–15% for about 50 feet. Curve right and cross over a stream storm drain. Continue on a 15% incline with a steep cross slope, increasing to 20% for about 20 feet, then reducing to 12% then 10% for 100 feet.

At 1.4 miles you start to get a view of the surrounding hills and creek drainage as you curve along the northwest slope of the hill. The trail curves left at a 15% incline with a steep cross slope, increasing to 20% for about 100 feet, then continues on a generally 8% incline. There are lots of small redwoods and other plants—it felt surprisingly peaceful. At 1.5 miles the trail inclines again at 20% for about 20 feet, then reduces to 10% for 100 feet. Continue on a generally 8% incline. At 1.6 miles you curve left around the hill and the incline decreases to 5%. At 1.7 miles the trail finally levels out a bit as you start traveling along a saddle between two peaks. The forest is drier and more open here.

At 1.8 miles you reach the intersection with Ridge Road. I recommend a short detour to a bench with an incredible view—continue straight ahead on the level paved trail. At 1.9 miles it declines at 8% for a few feet, then you approach the overlook with an expansive view across the mountains to Monterey Bay. There is a bench and a low wooden barrier that you could also sit on, and you may pick up a bit of cell service.

Once you've had a rest, turn around and then go right on Ridge Road. This trail is firm sand and soil. You immediately take six steps up; a couple are a foot high, stepping up

Overlook on Pipeline Road

Trail through the Santa Cruz Sandhills

on roots. The trail continues uneven, heading uphill on a 10% incline to ten more eroded steps, with large roots across the trail that you have to weave around a bit.

At 2.2 miles you leave the woods and reach the Santa Cruz Sandhills—this is a place of ancient marine deposits, and you may feel more like you are in the desert than the Santa Cruz Mountains. The trail gets sandy and very narrow, passing between rocks and across uneven sand. It is also exposed with no shade and very hot in the summer. Take another set of three steps with a narrow foothold. There are lots of silver-leaf manzanita and other unique plants, with incredible views across the mountains as you continue up the ridge. Take three more steps up to a foot tall, some with narrow footholds. The trail continues at 1.5 to 2 feet wide.

At 2.3 miles there are six more steps, and then the sand becomes up to 3 inches deep, continuing on a slight incline. The trail narrows and you pass through a deep gully, with sand hills rising over 5 feet high on either side of you. Take several more steps, passing over a couple round barriers in the trail. At 2.4 miles the trail generally widens to 3 feet, with soft sand and beautiful views across the mountains to the ocean. Ponderosa pines and oak trees dot the hills along with manzanita and chaparral. It is an incredibly unique landscape.

At 2.5 miles the trail inclines at 5–8%, with beautiful views on both sides of the surrounding ridges. You may notice lots of acorn woodpeckers and other birds. The sand gets up to 3 to 4 inches deep, and then at 2.6 miles you reach the observation deck. Take twenty-two wood steps to get to the top of the deck, with picnic tables and a view scope. You can see across the Santa Cruz Mountains and Monterey Bay from the top. Just past the observation deck, there is another picnic table beneath a large ponderosa pine that offers a little shade.

From just past the observation deck, go left on the Pine Trail, at a sign that points you to the campground and the Eagle Creek Trail. This trail is sandy and immediately begins heading back downhill—take two steps down, curve left, then continue on a slight decline. At 2.7 miles the trail narrows to a footpath with a steep slope on both sides. It is pretty uneven and difficult to walk on. Curve right, then there is about a 2-foot step down, then another one, but you can bypass it. Take five shorter steps down, then continue straight ahead and reenter the woods, passing some tall manzanita, madrone, and oak. The trail continues generally level and 2 to 3 feet wide.

At 2.9 miles there are a few more steps down. They can be navigated so that they're less than a foot high, but the surface is pretty uneven. You then reach a fork on the right to the campground (you can begin at the campground if you only want to do the observation deck loop, but it is open seasonally). Continue straight on the Pine Trail. The surface continues to be uneven, rooted, and on a generally 5–8% decline. There are several exposed roots and barriers to step down or over up to 4 inches high. But this is a really interesting trail—it feels like you're in a different world from the redwood forest and the sand hills, surrounded by bay laurel, madrone, and other species.

At 3.1 miles continue on a 5% decline and reenter the open sand hill area, with some loose sand up to 3 inches deep. There were lots of hummingbirds and bees even in February, and probably bugs in the summer. At 3.2 miles you reenter the shady woods; the trail is a level and compacted natural surface, and about 3 feet wide. It's cool with lots of oak curving in different directions and some madrone.

At 3.3 miles you reach an intersection with the Eagle Creek Trail. Go left on a 5% decline, passing next to an old blowdown. The trail is uneven and rutted down the center, continuing on an 8% decline, increasing to 10% for about 20 feet. The path then levels out and continues on compacted sand and soil, and 3 feet wide.

At 3.4 miles take a couple steps down. The trail narrows again in a washed-out gully, with no real level area and a deep cross slope on both sides. There's a steep 2-foot step-down, then the trail continues deeply rutted down the center. You may have to weave and cross the rut for a few feet. The trail curves to the right, following a sign to Pipeline Road. Come to a washed-out section with several ruts, uneven areas, exposed roots, and steep steps.

At 3.5 miles you reenter the boundary between the redwood forest and the oak woodlands, taking an 8% decline. Lot of roots cross the trail. The trail curves left and you cross one long section of root mat, then take several steps down. You may start to hear

Left: View on the Eagle Creek Trail
Right: Redwoods and the bridge on the Eagle Creek Trail

the creek again. Take a 15% decline on about a dozen steps down, each of them up to 6 inches high.

You reach Eagle Creek and the bottom of the hill at 3.6 miles. This is another interesting transition point—there is an open hill and the woodlands behind you, and ahead of you it is all redwoods. On the right is an old stump with new redwoods growing next to it. Take a few steps down over roots, and then continue on a 10% decline to a bridge over the creek. Continue on a slight incline with many roots to step up on, traveling through mixed forest. The trail continues 4 to 5 feet wide, uneven and rolling on up to 10% grades.

At 3.7 miles you come to another series of steep steps on the trail. The second one has a lot of exposed roots and two old metal poles, sticking up about 2 inches out of the surface on the left side. The trail becomes more uneven, continuing on a general decline with rolling 5–8% grades on a 2- to 3-foot-wide natural surface.

At 3.8 miles you take a 20% decline with steps, then continue on a 20% grade for about 15 feet, traveling above the creek on the left. You then take a rolling decline up to 12%, increasing to 15% for a few feet. The trail then levels out for a few feet, with some exposed roots. At 3.9 miles there are three more steps with exposed roots in between, then a fallen log that you could sit on. The trail curves sharply right on an uneven 12–15% decline for about 10 feet, then several rolling grades up to 15% and 20 feet long.

At 4.0 miles take eight steep steps down, up to a foot and a half high. Continue a 20% decline, decreasing to 15%. It is very uneven and rutted down the center. After about 100 feet the trail levels out briefly, then takes a 10% decline with several exposed roots up to 3 inches. There may be loose, slick leaves on the trail. Take another 10% decline with some exposed roots. At 4.0 miles you reach the end of the loop. Go right on Pipeline Road and continue 1.2 miles back to the parking lot.

MILES AND DIRECTIONS

0.0 Begin at the parking area and follow the road to the right.

0.1 Go left on the Pipeline Road trail.

0.6 Continue straight at the fork with the Redwood Grove Loop.

1.2 Reach the beginning of the loop. Go right on Pipeline Road.

1.8 Reach the intersection with Ridge Road. Continue straight.

1.9 Arrive at a bench at an overlook. Turn around.

2.1 Go right on Ridge Road.

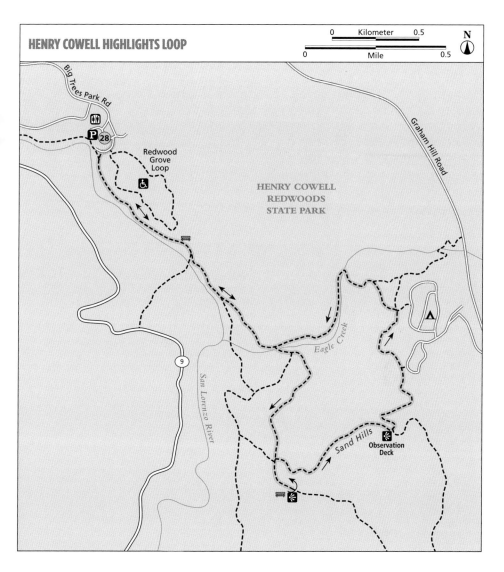

2.6   Arrive at the observation deck. Go left on the Pine Trail.

3.0   Continue past the campground on the right.

3.3   Go left on the Eagle Creek Trail.

4.0   Reach the end of the loop. Go right on Pipeline Road.

5.2   Arrive back at the parking area.

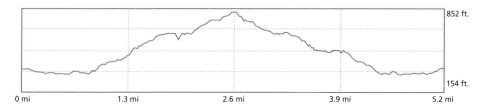

WHY GO?

Striking cliffs, crashing waves, unique coastal plants, and abundant wildlife are the highlights of this generally flat trail along the bluffs at Wilder Ranch State Park. It feels like a remote coastline, but you are only a few miles from Santa Cruz, and the parking area has amenities like restrooms and water fountains. It is a wonderful place to pack a picnic, a chair, and your binoculars for some time by the ocean.

THE RUNDOWN

Spoon rating: 2 spoons. Generally level and firm, but prone to washouts and ruts that make it difficult for wheelchair users to access.
Type: Loop
Distance: 2.6 miles
Elevation: 65 feet
Elevation gain: 120 feet
Max grade: 8%
Max cross slope: 8%
Typical width: 6 feet
Typical surface: Firm sand, gravel
Trail users: Hikers, bikers

Season/schedule: Open year-round, 8 a.m. to sunset
Water availability: Water fountain
Sun exposure: Full sun
Amenities: Accessible restrooms, bench, picnic tables
Pet-friendly: No
Cell phone reception: Yes
Nearest town: Santa Cruz
Land manager: Wilder Ranch State Park, (831) 423-9703
Pass/entry fee: Day-use fee or California State Parks annual pass
Land acknowledgment: Ohlone

FINDING THE TRAILHEAD

Getting there: From Santa Cruz, take CA 1 north for approximately 4 miles. Turn left on Coast Road, at a sign for the park. Continue to the entrance kiosk and the parking lot. **GPS:** 36.959898, -122.085930
Parking: Large paved parking lot with 2 ADA spots.
Start: The trailhead map and sign next to the restrooms.

THE HIKE

The last time I did this hike was in between major winter storms; the trail had significant erosion and washouts but has since been repaired. I recommend calling the park to verify conditions, especially in the winter.

To begin your hike, cross the parking area heading towards the restrooms. There are five individual all-gender restrooms—one is wheelchair accessible—with flush toilets and an outdoor sink. Cross a drainage grate and then pick up the paved trail at a large trail map. Go right, following a sign that points to the coastal bluff trails. The trail transitions to a natural surface of compacted sand. There may be a few holes up to 6 inches wide and 4 inches deep. Go left at the T-intersection on the Old Cove Landing Trail. The trail widens to 10 feet and takes a 3% decline—it may be rough here on an exposed rocky roadbed.

At 0.1 mile you cross the old railroad track; the parallel metal tracks are still there, but the wood braces have been removed and filled in with sand. It is generally level to

Top: Overlooking Wilder Beach and a cove from the Old Cove Landing Trail
Bottom: The Old Cove Landing Trail along the bluffs

cross, but there may be up to a 2-inch lip on either side. The trail narrows to 5 feet and continues on firm sand with some loose gravel and takes a 5% incline for about 20 feet. You are surrounded by coastal chaparral, and the Wilder Beach Natural Preserve is on the left—this is a great spot for birding. There may be some small rocks protruding up to an inch and ruts in the trail from flowing water, especially after it rains. At 0.15 mile the trail gets a little more uneven on slightly rolling grades. You start to get a view out towards the ocean.

At 0.2 mile the trail curves left on a slight decline with a steep cross slope—up to 10% if it has been washed out. The trail continues 6 to 8 feet wide on a prolonged 2% cross slope, then inclines slightly. At 0.4 mile the trail curves right and you have a view of Wilder Creek and the cove off to the left. At 0.5 mile curve left and the trail gets a little more uneven; it is compacted on the outer edges with a raised hump down the middle—the widest level section is about 4 feet. Curve right again, then the trail levels out.

Overlooking the seal beach

At 0.7 mile you reach a beautiful overlook of Wilder Beach and a platform with a bench. The platform is about 16 inches above the ground and there are no steps. This is a nice place to watch and listen to the waves crashing into the cove. The trail curves right and you start traveling along the bluffs with expansive views of the ocean and cliffs. The trail continues generally level but uneven, and there may be areas of sand up to 1 inch deep.

At 0.8 mile a level footpath on the left leads out to the edge of the bluff with another nice view of Wilder Beach and sea caves. The Old Cove Landing Trail continues straight ahead, generally level along the bluff. There is one section with a steep cross slope on the bluff side, but 4 feet of level area on the right.

Another nice viewpoint is at 1.0 mile on a flat, rocky bluff. The waves crash against the cliff below you and may even spray the edge of the bluff. It is a pretty incredible experience, but keep a safe distance from the edge. If you can get down on the ground, the rocks are a decent place to sit and take a break.

The trail then curves right and then left, following the edge of the bluff with beautiful views of sea caves and rocky coastline. Another small footpath on the left at 1.1 miles leads to another overlook of the sea caves. There are lots of wildflowers on the bluffs in the spring and very active ground squirrels. Watch out for holes in the surface of the trail.

At 1.3 miles a bluff-side section of trail previously collapsed, but there was 4 feet of level area on the right when I last visited. At 1.4 miles the trail curves right and you have a view of Fern Grotto Beach down below and the surrounding sea caves. There may be deep ruts from bike tire damage.

At 1.5 miles you pass a trail on the left with a sign for Fern Grotto Beach—this trail is short but very steep and rocky, so I recommend skipping it. Continue on the main trail as

Harbor seals lounging on the beach

it curves left above the cove. As you round the other side of the cove, an uneven section with a steep cross slope is on the right side. The trail then takes a 2–5% incline for about 40 feet, then levels and evens out. There are really cool views of waves crashing against the cliffs. Take another uneven 8% incline for a few feet.

At 1.7 miles you pass above a seal beach—a deep, narrow cove where seals love to haul out and sun themselves. There may be dozens lying across the sand and on the rocks, and it is fun to watch them move around on the beach. The trail continues with a steep cross slope on the outer edge and a dip down the center with some areas of loose sand. It curves left again at 1.8 miles, and there is another nice view down to the seal beach.

At 1.9 miles another overlook on the left offers views of the rocky cliffs and Sand Plant Beach. The trail continues curving slightly right on a 2% decline with about a quarter inch of loose sand. You are now heading away from the coast, with views back towards the hills. Cross a section of 2- to 4-inch-deep sand, about 25 feet long. The trail then continues on compact sand and gravel, with a slight cross slope. I noticed lots of quail, squirrels, and hawks along this section.

At 2.1 miles you reach a farm building and equipment. The trail takes a slight incline and becomes increasingly rutted with some loose medium-size rocks and gravel. Pass the farm building on the right and then the trail curves sharply right then left on an 8–10% cross slope. Continue straight ahead past the Ohlone Bluff Trail, crossing the railroad tracks again at 2.4 miles. You are now on a gravel road—take an 8–10% incline with an 8% cross slope and pass a green park gate on the left as you curve right. The trail levels out. Continue straight, passing park maintenance buildings on the left. You reach the end of the loop at 2.6 miles. Go left towards the parking lot.

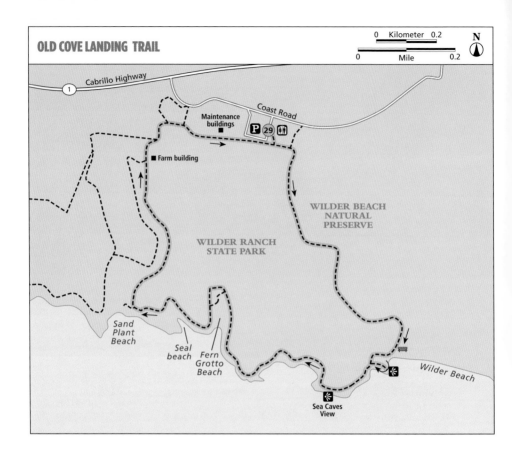

MILES AND DIRECTIONS

0.0 Begin at the trailhead next to the restrooms. Go right towards the bluffs, then left on the Old Cove Landing Trail.

0.1 Cross over railroad tracks.

0.8 A footpath on the left leads to an overlook.

1.5 Continue straight past the fork for Fern Grotto Beach.

2.4 Cross over railroad tracks.

2.6 Arrive back at the trailhead. Go left to the parking area.

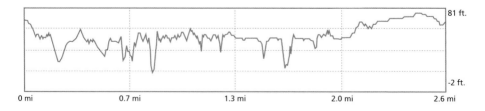

30 ASILOMAR DUNES BOARDWALK

WHY GO?

This lovely boardwalk offers an experience of the only remaining native dune habitat in Pacific Grove. Extensive restoration efforts have brought back critical habitat for several endangered species, including Menzies' wallflower, Tidestrom's lupine, and black legless lizard. The Asilomar Conference Grounds contain some of the only remaining stands of native Monterey pine. The boardwalk also provides access to Asilomar State Beach, and a beach wheelchair and walker are available to borrow.

THE RUNDOWN

Spoon rating: 1 spoon. Wheelchair accessible but be aware of potential sand and rough boards.
Type: Loop
Distance: 0.6 mile
Elevation: 39 feet
Elevation gain: 30 feet
Max grade: 5%
Max cross slope: 2%
Typical width: 5 feet
Typical surface: Composite and wood boards
Trail users: Hikers
Season/schedule: Open year-round
Water availability: Water fountain
Sun exposure: Full sun

Amenities: Restrooms, benches, picnic tables, cafe, audio tour
Pet-friendly: Yes, on leash
Cell phone reception: Yes
Special notes: Beach wheelchair and walker available to borrow from the Asilomar Conference Grounds front desk. Reservations are recommended; call (831) 372-8016.
Nearest town: Pacific Grove
Land manager: Asilomar State Beach and Conference Grounds, (831) 646-6440
Pass/entry fee: None
Land acknowledgment: Rumsen Ohlone

FINDING THE TRAILHEAD

Getting there: From Pacific Grove, take CA 68 / Asilomar Avenue to Sinex Avenue. Turn right into the conference center grounds. **GPS:** 36.618601, -121.937743

Parking: Several large paved parking lots with ADA spaces. Park either at the social hall or in Lot L.

Public transit: Take Monterey-Salinas Transit route 1 or 2 to Asilomar Avenue and Sinex Avenue.

Start: The trailhead at far side of the circle behind the social hall.

THE HIKE

Parking is the most confusing part of this hike; check the map included here and the one in the state park brochure, but the on-site maps are better. Parking along Sunset Drive is a bit of a challenge, and several lots on the conference center grounds have some steep sidewalks in between them. There are multiple trailheads for the boardwalk—one on

Asilomar Dunes boardwalk

Sunset Drive and three on the conference center grounds behind the social hall, the chapel, or the plant nursery, respectively. Lot L near the nursery provides the most direct access to a trailhead. You can also park at the social hall and registration building with a disabled parking placard and head west behind the social hall along the circular driveway.

This description begins from behind the social hall, at the far end of the circle. Travel along a brick paver path to the boardwalk. It is a level transfer onto composite boards with about a quarter-inch gap in between. The boardwalk is 5 feet wide with edge

ASILOMAR DUNES BOARDWALK

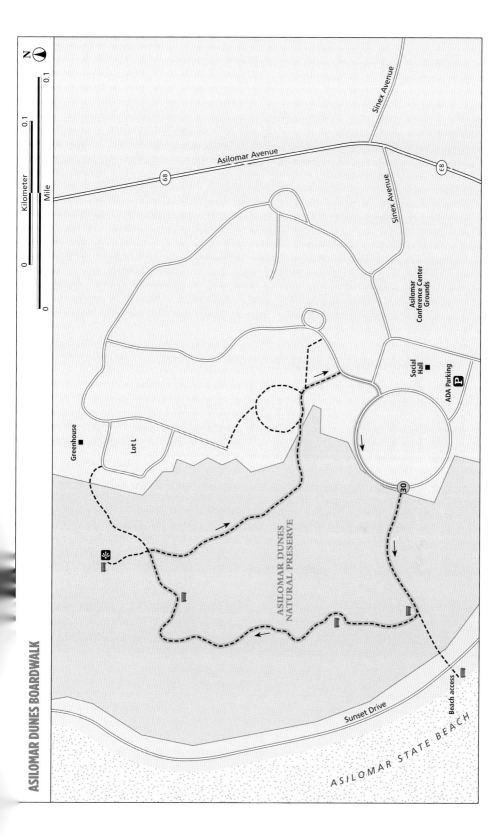

Asilomar Dunes boardwalk

guards. There is a sign with a QR code that you can scan to access an audio tour of the dunes.

To reach the beach, continue straight on the boardwalk past the fork on the right. The boards become a bit rough and rounded, then the boardwalk ends on sand and you cross the street on a crosswalk. Across the street is another short section of boardwalk with a bench on the left that ends at a sandy beach access. The sand may be deep, but it is fairly level and the beach is flat once you are on it. It's a good access point with a beach wheelchair or walker. There are lots of rocks and tide pools to explore.

Back at the main boardwalk, continue on the loop, turning at the fork with two benches. The boards are rough wood, and there may be some sand on the outer edges. You can see the ocean off to the left as you travel through dunes on a very slight incline. After about 0.1 mile, you take a 5% incline. Some of the boards are rough and uneven. Pass a pullout and benches on the left, then take another 5–8% incline for about 30 feet, curving sharply to the right. There are then three raised rounded boards—watch out for small wheels, especially in a manual chair, as they may get caught.

In another 0.1 mile a set of benches is on the right. The boardwalk continues on a 5% incline with some uneven and rounded boards. You then reach a T-intersection with a couple forks. If you go to the left and then the immediate left, there's another set of benches and it ends at an overlook with a nice view of the rocks and the coastline. If you go left and then right, it returns to parking lot L near the greenhouse and nursery. To stay on the loop, go right at the T-intersection. There are a couple more raised and rounded boards and maybe sand on the outer edges. The boardwalk is slightly rolling on a gradual incline.

The boards become more uneven and roughly milled, and you pass more benches on the left. The trail then curves left, and you start passing in front of the lodging. At about 0.5 mile the boardwalk ends behind the chapel. To get back to the circle and social hall, you have to go right down a slightly steep pedestrian-only road with no sidewalk.

MILES AND DIRECTIONS

0.0 Begin at the trailhead behind the social hall.

0.1 Go right to stay on the loop, or detour straight to the beach.

0.3 Go right at the fork.

0.5 Reach the end of the boardwalk. Go right on the road.

0.6 Arrive back at the social hall.

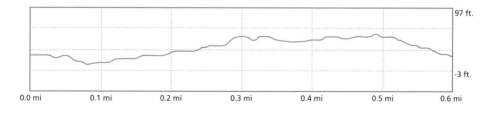

SHASTA CASCADE

The Shasta Cascade region encompasses northeastern and north-central California and includes many of the most popular outdoor recreation areas in the state. It includes the Klamath Mountains, the Cascade Range, the Modoc Plateau, and the most northern parts of the Sierra Nevada range and the Central Valley. It is a land formed by glaciers and volcanic activity, including Mount Shasta, Lassen Peak, and other volcanoes of the region. The area is generally rugged, but that doesn't mean inaccessible. The featured hikes in Klamath National Forest, Mount Shasta, the McCloud River, and Lassen Volcanic National Park provide an opportunity to experience a little bit of everything that makes this region so unique.

The region is the homelands of the Karuk, Klamath, Modoc, Northern Paiute (Nüümü), Shasta, Wintu, and Pit River Tribes, among others. Winnemem Wintu, the Middle Water People, ancestral territory includes Buliyum Puyuuk (Mount Shasta) down Winnemem Waywaket (McCloud River) and the surrounding meadows (www.winnememwintu.us/who-we-are). The Winnemem Wintu have long fought for the removal of the Shasta Dam and the health of the water and salmon in their homelands. They are also fighting for federal re-recognition.

The area surrounding Lassen are the ancestral lands of the Yana, Maidu, Konkow, Nomlaki, Wintu, Atsugewi, and Achumawi, who were forcibly removed to create the national park, national forest, and wilderness areas. Lassen Peak was an important meeting place for four Tribes: Atsugewi, Yana, Yahi, and Maidu. The mountain is known as Waganupa to the Yahi, Kohm Yah-mah-nee to the Maidu, and likely other names. Tribal members continue their traditional ways in the park, and have worked with the National Park Service to document and review cultural exhibits.

31 **TAYLOR LAKE**

WHY GO?

Taylor Lake is the most accessible alpine lake in the Russian Wilderness, but it is not wheelchair accessible (contrary to its current listing on the Klamath National Forest website and many blogs). The trail is 30 inches wide in some sections and has many exposed and loose rocks. If that is not a barrier for you, then the trail is short and relatively level. It provides access to a picturesque lake amidst towering mountains and lots of wildflowers along the way. There are camping spots at the lake for an easier backpacking camp experience.

THE RUNDOWN

Spoon rating: 3 spoons. Short and relatively level trail with some rocks that prevent wheelchair access.
Type: Out-and-back
Distance: 1.3 miles
Elevation: 6,425 feet
Elevation gain: 95 feet
Max grade: 8%
Max cross slope: 5%
Typical width: 32 inches, minimum 30 inches
Typical surface: Sandy packed soil and rock
Trail users: Hikers

Season/schedule: Open year-round, but likely snowed in during winter. Best summer to early fall
Water availability: None
Sun exposure: Partial shade
Amenities: Accessible vault toilet
Pet-friendly: Yes, on leash
Cell phone reception: None
Nearest town: Etna
Land manager: Klamath National Forest, Salmon/Scott River District, (530) 468-5351
Pass/entry fee: None
Land acknowledgment: Shasta

FINDING THE TRAILHEAD

Getting there: From the small town of Etna on CA 3, take Sawyers Bar Road for 10.5 miles, a curvy two-lane paved road. Continue past Etna Summit and in 0.2 mile make a sharp left onto FR 41N18, with a small sign for Taylor Lake. Continue 2 miles to the parking lot at the end. **GPS:** 41.3679, -122.9744

Parking: Paved and gravel with space for about 10 cars. One designated accessible spot at the trailhead.

Start: The trailhead next to the vault toilet.

THE HIKE

The drive to the trailhead is probably the most exhausting part of this hike. The last 2 miles are on a curvy, steep, single-lane road; the first mile is rough dirt road, followed by a half mile of pavement, then another half mile of dirt road, each with rough transitions. I made it in a small passenger car, but you definitely need to be comfortable with narrow roads and steep drop-offs. The views are incredible though.

The trailhead is to the left of the vault toilet. The trail starts 38 inches wide with a crushed gravel surface on an 8% incline for about 10 feet, then levels out. There are a couple rocks rising up to 3 inches in the trail that can be navigated around. The trail then becomes natural soil with some loose sand up to 1.5 inches deep and small, loose rocks

Left: The Taylor Lake Trail along the hillside
Right: The rocky section on the Taylor Lake Trail

on the surface. The outer edge of the trail is generally protected by rocks, but there are a few unprotected drop-offs. You immediately enter the Russian Wilderness and pass some large incense cedars. Pause to appreciate the views of the Russian Mountains, and then continue on the level trail.

At 0.08 mile a few rocks rise up to 2 inches above the surface of the trail. Shortly after, it takes an 8% incline for a few feet, levels out briefly, then takes another 2–5% incline. At 0.1 mile there's another rock in the middle of the trail that is about 3 inches high and 5 inches wide, followed by a couple more shallow rocks. The trail continues on a slight incline, and then there's a couple more rocks rising 3 to 4 inches. The trail surface has 0.5 to 1 inch of loose sand on top. At 0.15 mile the trail inclines at 8% for about 5 feet, then takes a couple short rolling 5% grades. The side of the trail is carpeted in wildflowers, which typically bloom June through July. Pine and fir trees offer some partial shade.

At 0.2 mile a bench made out of a plank of wood sits low across a stump and rocks. The trail then narrows to 32 inches wide but may be pinched to 30 inches in some places by vegetation. There are some loose small rocks and larger exposed rocks rising up to 3 inches in the surface of the trail. At 0.25 mile a large rock crosses the entire trail and is up to 4 inches high as you approach a strip of trees. The trail continues to be a bit rocky, with a few embedded rocks up to 4 inches high.

At 0.27 mile you take a rocky 5% incline for a few feet, and then cross another large rock rising 3 to 4 inches across the trail with lots of small, loose rocks. The trail is rutted and has a washed-out hole on the right side filled with loose rocks. There are more loose rocks up to 6 inches wide across the trail, and then you come to an exposed rock shelf—about a foot of level clearance is on the right, but it is filled with small, loose rocks.

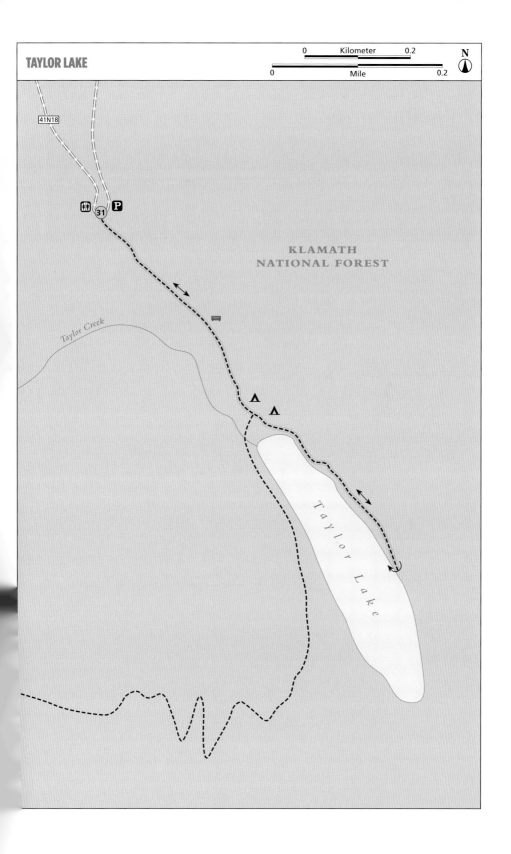

0   Kilometer   0.2

0   Mile   0.2

N

41N18

KLAMATH
NATIONAL FOREST

Taylor Creek

31

T a y l o r   L a k e

Taylor Lake

The exposed rock is about 3 feet long and up to 6 inches high, but it is fairly easy to step across if you can navigate around it. Two more rocks up to 5 inches high are just ahead.

At 0.3 mile the trail surface becomes smooth and even again. Taylor Creek flows over rocks on the right. Take a 5% incline, increasing to 8% for a few feet, then reducing back to 5% and continuing for 30 feet. At 0.35 mile the trail levels out and you cross two rough wooden boards over a stream, with a 6-inch gap between the boards. The trail continues on a slight incline, deeply rutted down the center with a steep cross slope on either side.

At 0.4 mile you reach the lake and several level camping spots among the trees. The camping spots are not developed in any way; there are no amenities or toilets, but it is a great place to try out wilderness camping. Just be sure to check for fire restrictions in the summer and take all of your trash and supplies with you when you leave. Continue towards the lake, passing narrowly around a fallen tree and between two standing trees. The trail continues level, narrows to 24 to 28 inches along the lakeshore and transitions to grass. You can continue on a narrow grassy path through wildflowers along the lake. There are a few places to get down to the water and beautiful views of the lake and towering mountains above you. I recommend turning around after about 0.2 mile along the lake, as the trail narrows and enters the forest and there are some blowdowns you have to step over.

MILES AND DIRECTIONS

0.0 Begin at the trailhead.

0.4 Arrive at Taylor Lake.

0.65 Turn around before the trail enters the forest.

1.3 Arrive back at the trailhead.

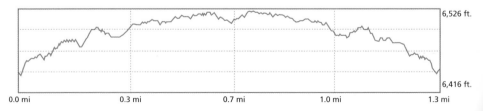

32 SISSON MEADOW

WHY GO?

Sisson Meadow is a 7.5-acre wetland meadow in downtown Mt. Shasta. Meadows once covered this area but have been lost to settlement and farming. This pocket has been restored to provide habitat for numerous wildflowers, birds, and other wildlife. There are stunning views of Mount Shasta, the Eddy Mountains, and Castle Crags. A boardwalk winds through the meadow and connects with a paved trail offering a mile of accessible strolling, with ample places to sit and enjoy the experience. I especially recommend visiting at sunrise or sunset.

THE RUNDOWN

Spoon rating: 1 spoon. Wheelchair accessible with some caution due to high thresholds and gaps in the boardwalk.
Type: Out-and-back
Distance: 1.0 mile
Elevation: 3,609 feet
Elevation gain: 45 feet
Max grade: 2%
Max cross slope: 3%
Typical width: 3 feet
Typical surface: Composite boards, pavement
Trail users: Hikers, bikers

Season/schedule: Open year-round; may be snowy in winter
Water availability: None
Sun exposure: Full sun
Amenities: Benches, picnic tables
Pet-friendly: Yes, on leash
Cell phone reception: Yes
Nearest town: Mt. Shasta
Land manager: Siskiyou Land Trust, (530) 926-2259
Pass/entry fee: None
Land acknowledgment: Winnemem Wintu

FINDING THE TRAILHEAD

Getting there: From E. Lake Street and N. Mt. Shasta Boulevard in Mt. Shasta, head 2 blocks east on Lake Street. Make a left on Alder Street, then a right on E. Castle Street. Park on the right at the corner with a small parking sign for the meadow. **GPS:** 41.315514, -122.311788

Parking: Angled parking for about 3 vehicles on E. Castle Street at the corner of Alder Street. You may be able to park on the street to deploy a ramp.

Start: The trailhead at the end of E. Castle Street.

THE HIKE

You can access the boardwalk from the end of E. Castle Street, the library on E. Alma Street, or on E. Lake Street. The only place with accessible parking is the library. I began at the E. Castle Street trailhead. The trailhead is at the end of the road—continue straight ahead past an engraved rock sign that says Welcome to Sisson Meadow. A rock in the center of the trail prevents vehicles but reduces the width to about 3 feet; the trail is 4 feet wide beyond that point. The trail starts on firm, packed dirt and you immediately have great views of Mount Shasta. After a few feet, there are two picnic tables set on dirt on the left, and you reach a trail board sign. The sign has photos and information about the

plants and animals found here and recent history about the meadow, but nothing about the Indigenous peoples.

The trail forks here. The main trail continues straight ahead for about 0.2 mile. There is a 2-inch rise onto the boardwalk, which is made of composite boards and is 40 inches wide with edge guards. It is generally level, but has slightly collapsed in a few places. You have incredible views across the meadow, which is particularly stunning in the spring and provides ample birding opportunities. Several benches and pullouts are available along the boardwalk. Mount Shasta rises ahead of you the entire way.

At 0.1 mile there is a gap on the right half of the boardwalk that is about 2 inches wide. At 0.15 mile there is another approximately 2-inch gap between the boards, and then it transitions to pavement with a 1.5-inch gap between the pavement and the boardwalk and 0.5-inch rise. The trail inclines slightly, and you get another striking view of Mount Shasta as you reach a T-intersection with a trash can and dog bag station.

The trail to the right leads out to Lake Street. The pavement has some cracks and pot-holes, but they can be navigated around. You travel between trees and flowers, then pass a school and playfield and reach the street at a crosswalk with a curb cut and tactile paver.

The trail to the left continues along the meadow with a nice view of the mountains and Castle Spire in the distance. You soon reach a circular area with flagstone and pol-ished marble boulders to sit on beneath a big pine. The trail continues paved and 6 feet wide, and you cross a 2-inch crack across the pavement. Go left at the next fork, and then the trail ends at the library. There are some picnic tables and a native plant garden. Return the way you came, enjoying a different view of the mountains on the way back.

Back at the first trail fork at the interpretive sign, go left. This path travels less than 0.1 mile on a boardwalk through the meadow, then enters a narrow section of woods—if you are using a wheelchair, you should turn around before this point. The boardwalk

View of Castle Crags

The flagstone path and sitting area at the waterfall

ends onto a flagstone path that leads to a small sitting area with flat, polished boulders next to a small waterfall. A narrow footbridge then takes you out onto Alder Street. It is a pleasant detour and a nice place to sit, especially on a warm day. Turn around and head back to the fork, going left to return to the parking area.

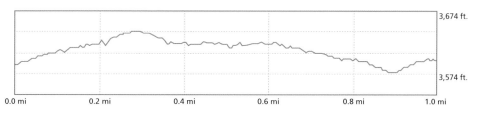

3,674 ft.

3,574 ft.

0.0 mi   0.2 mi   0.4 mi   0.6 mi   0.8 mi   1.0 mi

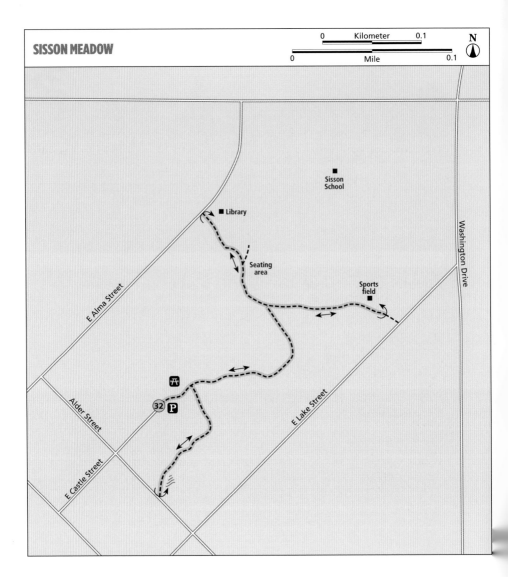

SISSON MEADOW

MILES AND DIRECTIONS

0.0 Start at the trailhead on E. Castle Street.

0.08 Reach a fork. Continue straight.

0.2 Reach a T-intersection. Go right.

0.3 Reach E. Lake Street. Turn around and continue straight at the intersection.

0.5 Reach the library. Turn around and go right at the intersection.

0.8 Go left at the fork.

0.9 Reach Alder Street. Turn around and go left at the fork.

1.0 Arrive back at the trailhead.

33 McCLOUD RIVER FALLS

WHY GO?

The McCloud River Canyon is one of the most popular destinations in the Mount Shasta area. This stunning landscape is evidence of the geological history of the area and the power of the river. This section of the canyon follows two bends in the river, with towering cliffs, basalt columns, and of course three unique waterfalls—Lower, Middle, and Upper McCloud Falls. This route takes you to all three, but you can also "choose your own adventure" on this hike.

THE RUNDOWN

Spoon rating: 2 spoons for Lower Falls to Middle Falls, 3 spoons for Middle Falls overlook to Upper Falls, 5 spoons for the entire hike. Wheelchair-accessible overlooks at each waterfall, and wheelchair accessible with caution for the first 0.7 mile.
Type: Out-and-back, scenic viewpoint
Distance: 4.4 miles (out-and-back)
Elevation: 3,240 feet
Elevation gain: 358 feet
Max grade: 20%
Max cross slope: 8%
Typical width: 3 feet
Typical surface: Firm soil, rocks
Trail users: Hikers

Season/schedule: Open year-round. Best spring through fall; snowy in winter.
Water availability: Water spigots at picnic areas
Sun exposure: Partial shade
Amenities: Accessible vault toilets, picnic tables, water spigots
Pet-friendly: Yes, on leash
Cell phone reception: None
Nearest town: McCloud
Land manager: Shasta-Trinity National Forest, McCloud Ranger District, (530) 964-2184
Pass/entry fee: None
Land acknowledgment: Winnemem Wintu (Middle Water People) have always been connected to Winnemem Waywaket (McCloud River).

FINDING THE TRAILHEAD

Getting there: From the small town of McCloud, take CA 89 south for 5.5 miles. Turn right on Fowler Public Camp Road, at a Forest Service sign for Fowlers Campground and Lower Falls. Turn right in 0.7 mile to stay on Fowlers Road, then turn left into the parking lot. **GPS:** 41.240208, -122.025038

Parking: Paved, circular parking lot with space for about 30 cars. One ADA van-accessible spot.

Start: The Lower Falls trailhead at the entrance of the parking lot.

THE HIKE

Little has been written about the accessibility of this popular trail, so I have focused on the technical details over what you may experience along the way. For ease of reading, I have separated the description by each of the three waterfalls. Every waterfall has its own day-use and parking area, so it is possible to choose a section to hike or to view the waterfalls from their individual accessible overlook. My recommendation for an easier,

Lower McCloud Falls

more accessible hike to see all three waterfalls is to start at Lower Falls and hike to Middle Falls. Turn around and then drive to Upper Falls and hike around the day-use area.

LOWER FALLS

The trail begins at a trail board next to the restroom. It is paved and passes through a picnic area with accessible tables. The trail forks as you approach the overlook—there's a slight crack and dip across the pavement if you go straight ahead, so you may want to take the right loop. Either way leads you to the overlook of Lower Falls. The waterfall drops 15 feet into a wide pool in a narrow basalt canyon. The barrier at the overlook is a fence with vertical metal poles and there is a bench, but the view from sitting height is slightly obstructed. A print interpretive sign provides information about the Winnemem Wintu, who have lived here since time immemorial. The river is sacred for the Winnemem Wintu, whose name for the lower falls is Nurunwitipom, so please be respectful during your visit. Stairs lead steeply down to the canyon edge and a trail along the river.

Continue on the paved trail to the left of the overlook. It continues about 4 feet wide, closely following the road with nice views down to the river. At 0.15 mile the trail takes a slight decline and then there is an unprotected eroded outer edge, followed by a few more cracked areas with unprotected eroded outer edges. The trail is 3 feet wide through these sections.

At 0.2 mile this trail meets the river trail at an angle. There is a slight decline as you connect with the lower trail with a 6-inch-section with a steep cross slope as you approach, so be very careful if you are using a wheelchair. The level section is about 3 feet wide. The trail continues paved and 4 feet wide on a slight incline. You're moving away from the river and traveling through low shrubs. There are some exposed rocks on the right as you approach a large pine ahead of you. The trail switchbacks gently right and inclines at 8% for about 15 feet, then continues on a 5% incline for another 20 feet. It levels out next to a rock wall on the left and you cross a 2-inch-wide, 0.5-inch-deep crack across the trail, then incline again at 8% for 15 feet. The trail switchbacks gently left, and then you are at the top of the river canyon.

At 0.35 mile the trail curves left on a slightly uneven 5–8% incline, and then curves right and levels out. The trail widens to 5 feet, but there are a couple unprotected drop-offs about 6 inches high. At 0.4 mile the trail inclines slightly, then you reach Fowlers Campground. Accessible vault toilets are on the left. The trail continues paved and generally even along the edge of the campground with the river on your right. There are a couple cracks across the width of the trail.

At 0.45 mile the trail comes to a T-intersection. Go right to a small overlook—there is an old 3/4 log bench here and an interpretive sign on the left about the campground, which was once a Winnemem Wintu village site. Continue to follow the paved trail through the campground along the river, which is generally 4 feet wide and level with a few unprotected edges. At 0.6 mile there are a couple dips and cracks from roots, but they are passable. Another toilet is located at the end of the campground. The paved trail ends at 0.7 mile. Wheelchair users may be able to continue another 0.1 mile, but I recommend turning around here.

MIDDLE FALLS

Continue straight ahead at the end of the campground, towards a sign that says Middle Falls. The trail becomes natural soil surface with some loose dirt on top and widens to 6 feet, continuing level for a few feet. It then declines slightly and there are several exposed rocks up to 4 inches in the center of the trail that can be navigated around. Continue on a generally 3% decline as you travel through the forest with the river just below you on the right. After 100 feet or so, you come to another set of exposed rocks rising 4 to 6 inches with about 2 feet of clearance on the side. At 0.75 mile there is an eroded drop-off on the right with a steep cross slope. The trail levels out briefly and then takes a rolling incline of 2–5% and continues generally 4 to 5 feet wide.

View of Middle McCloud Falls from the rocky trail

At 0.8 mile three large rocks are on the left with 3 to 4 feet of clearance on the right. The trail then narrows to 3 feet with some exposed rocks rising 4 inches above the trail. The trail may be a little brushy with encroaching vegetation and pinched to 30 inches. In another 100 feet, there are several boulders along the trail and exposed rocks. The trail continues level with several areas of exposed rocks that could catch your toes or mobility aid, so walk carefully.

At 0.9 mile you start a generally 2% incline as you continue to follow the river upstream. Level out briefly and then at 1.0 mile pass between two large boulders on either side of the trail. Continue on a long 2% incline with more exposed rocks in the surface. In a couple hundred feet, take a 5% decline for a few feet and then you have a nice view up the river to the exposed cliffs. The trail is then pinched to less than 2 feet as you pass next to a large boulder on the left and then lots of exposed roots and rocks. Pass a large fir and the trail continues on a 3% incline for a few feet, levels out, then inclines at 8% for about 15 feet. It levels out again briefly with a steep drop-off on the right, then takes an 8% incline for 50 feet.

At 1.2 miles the trail levels out. There are many more exposed rocks in the trail. At 1.25 miles you pass through an area strewn with big volcanic boulders. The trail is generally level, but uneven with exposed rocks. You may start to hear and see the waterfall up ahead as the trail inclines at 3–5%. You reach the bottom of Middle Falls at 1.4 miles. To get down to the river, you have to climb down a bunch of rocks; it is a popular swimming spot and can be very busy. There are a couple places to carefully step off the trail and watch the waterfall. Turn around here for the easiest hike.

Continuing past Middle Falls, the trail begins a difficult 0.3-mile-long section of steep, narrow switchbacks. It's often busy with hikers traveling in both directions and no wide

Middle McCloud Falls from the overlook

places to step off of the trail. Switchback sharply left; there are a lot of rocks in the trail, and it inclines at about 15% for a few feet, then continues narrow and rocky. Take a 20% incline with some exposed rocks for a few feet, then the incline reduces to 10% with some loose dirt and rocks in the surface. At 1.45 miles the trail levels out slightly but continues rocky and narrow, then continues on 5–8% grades with some level areas. Cross a very narrow, rocky area with large boulders on both sides and large exposed rocks on the surface of the trail. Switchback sharply right, stepping up, on, and around rocks.

At 1.5 miles the trail evens out a little bit and gets less rocky but continues on a 12% incline with level areas for a couple hundred feet. You then cross over a large, exposed rock in the center of the trail and pass narrowly between two more boulders. The trail continues about 30 inches wide, uneven and rocky with a sharp drop-off on the right and occasional eroded edges that narrow the trail to 2 feet or less. Take a 12% incline, increasing to 20% for a few feet, then continuing at 10%.

At 1.57 miles the trail continues on a rolling 10% incline, rocky with a sharp drop-off, then switchbacks left. There's a view above the falls here, but not a good place to pause and appreciate it. The switchback is rocky and narrow with a couple eroded drop-offs on a short 20% incline. The trail continues narrow on a slight incline. At 1.65 miles it switchbacks right and comes to a steep set of stairs with thirty-three steps with a 6-inch rise. You are now at the top of the canyon. The trail continues rocky and generally levels out.

At 1.7 miles you reach the overlook for Middle Falls. A paved trail leads from the parking area to the paved overlook—this is where you will come in if you park at the Middle Falls lot. Continue straight on the paved path. The overlook is high above the falls, with a view up- and downriver. There is a bench and a barrier with vertical metal poles. The pavement ends abruptly just after the bench.

The McCloud River at the Upper Falls

UPPER FALLS

Continuing past the Middle Falls overlook, there is a 2-inch lip from the pavement onto natural dirt surface. The trail is about 4 feet wide as it continues along the edge of the cliff above the river, with a metal fence on the edge—the edge has eroded in a few places, leaving a hole beneath the fence, so take care not to catch a pole or a cane like I did! The trail continues level but is a little rocky, with nice views of the river and the surrounding

MCCLOUD RIVER FALLS

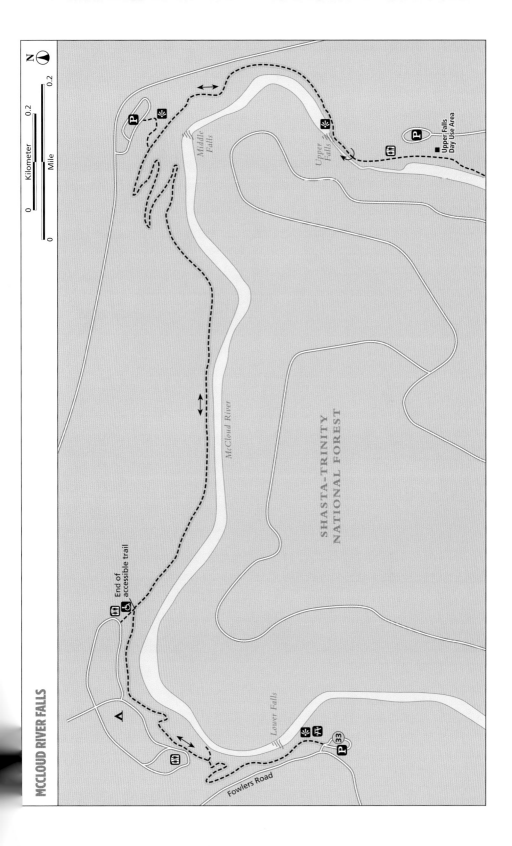

N

Kilometer
0   0.2

Mile
0   0.2

Middle Falls

McCloud River

SHASTA-TRINITY NATIONAL FOREST

Upper Falls

Upper Falls Day Use Area

End of accessible trail

Lower Falls

Fowlers Road

P 33

Upper McCloud Falls

mountains. The barrier ends at about 1.9 miles and the trail narrows to about 2 feet in some sections with a rocky, sharp drop-off above the canyon. You then start a slight decline and enter a forested area with some shade. Continue on a slight rolling decline as you pass next to a really cool exposed rock face on the left. The trail narrows to 2 to 3 feet and continues rocky with some sharp drop-offs as you follow the exposed cliff.

Narrow, rocky trail on the switchbacks above Middle Falls

At 2.0 miles the trail starts to open up again, continuing on a long 3–5% incline. Cross a section of an old slide. The trail is about 28 inches wide here with a steep cross slope and sharp drop-off for about 100 feet. At 2.1 miles you reach the Upper Falls overlook area. The trail transitions to pavement and follows the edge of the cliff with several overlooks above the river protected by the same metal barrier along the edge. The trail forks to loop around the day-use area—the left side leads directly to the parking lot, where there are toilets and picnic tables. The right side continues along the river with a few more viewpoints. The pavement ends at 2.2 miles. The trail continues for 13 miles beyond this point, but this is our turnaround spot.

MILES AND DIRECTIONS

- 0.0 Begin at the Lower Falls trailhead. Continue past the overlook.
- 0.7 Reach the end of the paved trail. Continue straight to Middle Falls.
- 1.4 Reach the base of Middle Falls. Take the switchbacks uphill.
- 1.7 Reach the overlook for Middle Falls.
- 2.1 Reach the overlook for Upper Falls.
- 2.2 The paved trail ends. Turn around.
- 4.4 Arrive back at the trailhead.

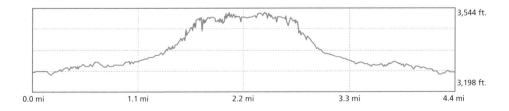

34 LASSEN VOLCANIC NATIONAL PARK SCENIC DRIVE

WHY GO?

Located within the volcanic landscape of the Southern Cascade Range, Lassen Volcanic National Park is an underappreciated wonder. It is a rugged, living landscape of hydrothermal activity, volcanoes, forests, and over 745 species of plants and animals. The park is fairly remote but a worthwhile destination on its own or while driving the Volcanic Legacy Scenic Byway. There aren't many accessible trails, but the park makes for a great scenic drive with a printed guide and audio tour of the route. There are four accessible campsites and four accessible camping cabins if you'd like to stay overnight.

THE RUNDOWN

Type: Scenic drive
Distance: 30 miles one-way, allow at least an hour for the drive.
Elevation: 6,700 feet
Typical width and surface: Two-lane paved road with no guardrails
Season/schedule: Open year-round, but CA 89 through the park closes in the winter. Only the Southwest and Manzanita Lake areas are accessible by vehicle from November to May; some facilities begin closing in October.
Water availability: Water fountains at visitor centers
Sun exposure: Full sun
Amenities: Visitor centers, audio tour

Pet-friendly: Yes, on leash where vehicles are permitted (roads, parking areas, and pullouts)
Cell phone reception: None
Nearest town: Chester
Land manager: Lassen Volcanic National Park, (530) 595-4480
Pass/entry fee: Entrance fee or federal recreation pass
Land acknowledgment: The Atsugwei, Yana, Yahi, and Maidu made summer homes and hunted on Kohm Yah-mah-nee, meaning "snow mountain" in the Maidu language, for thousands of years. The mountain (now known as Lassen Peak) remains a sacred place for Indigenous people.

FINDING THE TRAILHEAD

Getting there: From Red Bluff, travel 46 miles east on CA 36. Turn left on CA 89 / Volcanic Legacy Scenic Byway and continue 5 miles to the national park entrance station. **GPS:** 40.435662, -121.534015
Start: Kohm Yah-mah-nee Visitor Center

THE DRIVE

I highly recommend downloading the NPS App and saving the park for offline use before your visit. There is very limited cell service in the park. Downloading the park into the app will allow you to access maps, directions, trail information, and the audio tour while offline. The app is a pretty useful tool in general, so check it out! If you can't use the app, downloadable audio and text files are available on the park website at www.nps.gov/lavo/learn/photosmultimedia/audio.htm.

View of the Sulphur Works and scenic highway

You can enter the park from the southwest or northwest entrance, but the auto tour is set up to begin from the southwest entrance, which is where I suggest beginning if you can. Once you pass through the entrance kiosks, you immediately reach stop 1: Kohm Yah-mah-nee Visitor Center. The visitor center is open year-round and offers easy access to winter recreation. It is ADA accessible and includes an information desk, tactile exhibits, theater, store, and cafe with free Wi-Fi. There are gendered restrooms with accessible stalls and one accessible family restroom that is locked—ask at the information desk for

Top: View along the Lassen Volcanic National Park scenic highway
Bottom: Balsam root at an overlook

the key. A short, paved path leads to audio-described signage that interprets the geological timeline of the park.

Just past the visitor center, you arrive at the second stop: Sulphur Works. There is a paved parking area on the left with two accessible spots and accessible vault toilets. Follow the sidewalk from the parking lot to overlooks of bubbling, steaming pools of mud and sulphur on both sides of the road. The pools are protected by wooden fences, but the sidewalk is less than 6 feet wide at the viewing area, the soil is very dangerous to touch, and you are next to the road, so be very careful.

You next pass two pullouts—a viewpoint of Diamond Peak and a vista of Little Hot Springs Valley. The Diamond Peak viewpoint is a small pullout at a curve on the right, with views of Lassen Peak, East Sulphur Creek, and the steep face of Diamond Peak. Little Hot Springs is a large pullout with views of a steep valley. Wildflowers cover the scene throughout early summer. Bring binoculars and you may spot bears and hydrothermal activity along the creeks.

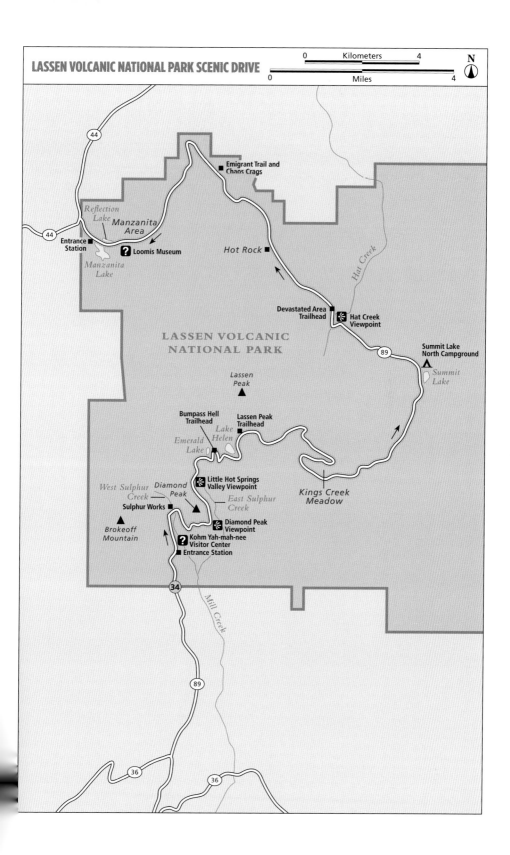

LASSEN VOLCANIC NATIONAL PARK SCENIC DRIVE

Kilometers
0   4

Miles
0   4

N

44

Emigrant Trail and
Chaos Crags

Reflection Lake
Manzanita Area

44

Entrance
Station

Manzanita Lake

Loomis Museum

Hot Rock

Hat Creek

Devastated Area
Trailhead

Hat Creek
Viewpoint

LASSEN VOLCANIC
NATIONAL PARK

89

Summit Lake
North Campground

Summit Lake

Lassen Peak

Bumpass Hell
Trailhead

Lassen Peak
Trailhead

Lake Helen

Emerald Lake

Little Hot Springs
Valley Viewpoint

West Sulphur Creek

Diamond Peak

Sulphur Works

East Sulphur Creek

Brokeoff Mountain

Diamond Peak
Viewpoint

Kohm Yah-mah-nee
Visitor Center
Entrance Station

Kings Creek
Meadow

34

Mill Creek

89

36

36

View of Brokeoff Mountain

Lassen Peak

About 5.5 miles from the visitor center, you pass glistening green Emerald Lake. Shortly after, you arrive at the trailhead for Bumpass Hell, with a small paved parking lot with accessible parking and vault toilets. The Bumpass Hell Trail gains and loses elevation on moderate grades for the first mile, and then descends very steeply to the basin that features hydrothermal activity. But there are nice views from the parking area, including an overlook of Brokeoff Volcano, Lassen Peak, and a glacial erratic boulder that seems to defy gravity. You may pick up some cell service here.

Immediately past Bumpass Hell, you reach Lake Helen. A road on the left leads to a small parking area with some picnic tables and beautiful views of the sapphire lake. At 7 miles you reach the Lassen Peak trailhead and parking area, with vault toilets and trash cans. There are beautiful views of Lassen Peak, and snow lingers around the parking area well into summer, making it a popular photo and playing spot. The peak is at 10,457 feet elevation, and the parking lot is at about 8,500 feet.

At about 15 miles from the visitor center, you pass Kings Creek meadow. There are a couple small pullouts from which to view the meadow, which is incredible at any time of year. Please stay on paved areas and do not enter the meadow for any reason—plants have a very limited period of time to grow in this environment, and damage to the soil can kill them. After Kings Creek, you come to Summit Lake and a campground. The north side has a few day-use picnic tables at the edge of the parking lot, with a view of the lake.

About 18 miles from the visitor center, you reach Hat Creek. There is a small parking lot on the right with views of the meadows and Lassen Peak towering above you. A short way past Hat Creek you arrive at the Devastated Area Trail. This is the park's only wheelchair-accessible trail, and it has a large paved parking lot with accessible parking, picnic tables, and vault toilets. The trail is firm natural surface with some small loose gravel on top. It is a 0.5-mile loop through an area that was devastated in the 1915 eruption of Lassen Peak. Interpretive signs with built-in audio description units provide information on the eruption, the rocks around you, and the landscape. There are beautiful views of the volcano through the trees.

Two miles past the Devastated Area, you pass Hot Rock on the left, a huge block of lava that erupted from the volcano and tumbled down the mountain. Evidence of past wildfires are seen on the opposite side of the highway. There are pullouts on both sides of the road. Pass two more viewpoints for the Emigrant Trail and Chaos Crags, and then at about 27 miles you reach the Manzanita area. The Loomis Museum, Discovery Center, restrooms, and campground are here. There is a large parking area on the left and a few pullouts. Reflection Lake is on the right side of the highway, and Manzanita Lake is on the left. This is a great place to stop before leaving the park. You can drive up close to Reflection Lake, which offers views of Lassen Peak and Chaos Crags. A level trail circles Manzanita Lake, but it is not fully wheelchair accessible.

At 30 miles you exit the park on the northwest side. You may pick up some cell service near the entrance station; this is your last chance to map your route out of the park if you haven't saved a map. When you get to the T-intersection, go left for the quickest way back to I-5 at Redding, or right to continue on the Volcanic Legacy Scenic Byway towards Mount Shasta.

SACRAMENTO VALLEY AND SIERRA FOOTHILLS

The Great Valley of California is truly a geological wonder. Extending over 400 miles and bordered by the Cascade Range, Sierra Nevada, Techapi Mountains, and the Coast Ranges, it is a semiarid region that has long been a haven for animals and humans. The Sacramento Valley is the northern portion of the Great Valley; it stretches from the city of Redding to Sacramento. Several rivers flow through the valley, including the Sacramento, Feather, Yuba, Bear, and American. The city of Sacramento sits to the north of a large "reverse delta"—an estuary where many rivers and creeks come together to flow out through a strait and into the bay. This natural drainage and water storage system has supported food production for thousands of years and has become the agricultural center of the West Coast in the last 200 years. Some of the ecological function of the natural drainage system has been altered to control flooding and support agriculture; much of the valley is crisscrossed by levees and the rivers have been dammed. Folsom Lake, one of the most popular recreation sites in the valley, was created by the Folsom Dam.

The Sierra Foothills are a narrow stretch of land between the Great Valley and the High Sierra. The foothills rise in elevation to a maximum of 5,000 feet. The area is semiarid with a mix of habitats including grasslands, oak woodlands, and pine at the higher elevations. The foothills play a crucial role in wildlife and human migration, serving as a buffer zone between hot summers in the valley and heavy winter snowfall in the mountains. It was also a primary site for the California Gold Rush—often referred to as Mother Lode Country, the Sierra Foothills were heavily mined during the height of the gold rush. Many of the small towns that dot the foothills began as mining camps, including Auburn, Nevada City, and Placerville.

Maidu is the name used by European settlers to describe the Indigenous people who lived in the valley and foothills and spoke a group of related languages called Maidu. Maidu means "people" in that language. The Maiduan includes distinct groups of related people: the Mountain Maidu, the Konkow Maidu, and the Nisenan. The ancestral homelands of the Nisenan encompass much of the southern Sacramento Valley and Sierra Foothills, including the present-day counties of Yuba, Nevada, Placer, Sacramento, and El Dorado. Nisenan territory includes the Consumnes River to the south, Kyburz and the Sacramento River to the east, Gold Lake to the north, and the South Fork Feather River to the west and includes Marysville Buttes, which is sacred for the Nisenan (www.nisenan.org). The Nevada City Rancheria was created as a reservation for the Nisenan but was terminated during the Termination Act era. The tribe is fighting for re-recognition. The Konkow Maidu lived along the drainage area of the North Fork of the Feather River, in present-day Butte and Yuba Counties. The Konkow Valley Band of Maidu Indians are currently an unrecognized tribe, but are engaged in revitalization efforts through the Konkow Maidu Cultural Preservation Association, which includes a language preservation project.

35 BUTTERMILK BEND TRAIL

WHY GO?

The Buttermilk Bend Trail is a very popular destination for spring wildflowers, which carpet the hillsides March through May. Wildflower identification signs help visitors learn more about the diversity of plants that grow here. The trail offers incredible year-round views of the Wild and Scenic South Yuba River, which flows through a deep granite canyon, and there are several benches to rest and appreciate the experience. It is identified as a wheelchair-accessible trail, but I recommend this hike only for experienced wheelchair hikers and people who are comfortable with heights and steep drop-offs.

THE RUNDOWN

Spoon rating: 3 spoons. The trail is wheelchair hikeable with caution. It is generally level, but narrow with unprotected drop-offs and a few areas of exposed rocks.
Type: Out-and-back
Distance: 1.9 miles
Elevation: 580 feet
Elevation gain: 194 feet
Max grade: 15%
Max cross slope: 5%
Typical width: 4 feet, minimum 3 feet
Typical surface: Firm soil, gravel
Trail users: Hikers
Season/schedule: Open year-round, sunrise to sunset. Best fall through spring.
Water availability: Water fountain, creek (always use an appropriate filter)

Sun exposure: Full sun
Amenities: Picnic tables, benches, restrooms, vault toilets, visitor center
Pet-friendly: Yes, on leash but not recommended due to narrow trail
Cell phone reception: None
Special notes: The sound of the river can be very loud in the spring when it is at peak flow, with a constant rushing sound reverberating up the canyon. This may be soothing or irritating depending on your sensory experience.
Nearest town: Grass Valley
Land manager: South Yuba River State Park, (530) 432-2546
Pass/entry fee: Day-use parking fee or California State Parks annual pass
Land acknowledgment: Nisenan

FINDING THE TRAILHEAD

Getting there: From Grass Valley, take CA 20 west for approximately 8 miles to Pleasant Valley Road and turn right. Continue another 8 miles and turn right into the north parking lot. **GPS:** 39.293564, -121.192522

Parking: Paved parking lot with space for about 30 cars. Four ADA spaces, 1 van accessible.

Start: The trailhead next to the ADA parking on the northeast side of the north parking lot.

THE HIKE

The trailhead is in front of the ADA parking spots at the northeast corner of the parking lot. There is another trailhead on the south side of the parking lot, but that trail is steep and rocky. Start at the trail access information sign, which indicates that this is an accessible trail for 0.7 mile. While it is generally level, the trail is narrow and travels along a steep cliff, so I recommend it only for experienced wheelchair hikers and those who are comfortable with heights and steep drop-offs.

The trail begins on some loose gravel and winds gently uphill on maximum 8% grades. Cross a footbridge with a 1.5-inch rise. The trail transitions to firm soil and continues on a 2–5% incline with some uneven areas. Cross another footbridge over a small stream and pass a bench at approximately 0.2 mile. You then pass a fork on the right where the not-accessible trail meets with the main trail. Continue straight on the generally level and even 4-foot-wide trail. You are traveling along the hillside with an unprotected drop-off on the right for the entire length of the trail. Cross a section that has become rutted and uneven due to use in muddy conditions.

At 0.3 mile the trail narrows to 3 feet next to a large rock. Pass a bench at a large rock outcropping. You start to get a view of the river below. After 100 feet or so, the trail widens back out to 4 feet. Cross over an armored crossing; there are some exposed rocks, but it is pretty level. The trail narrows again to 3 feet. At 0.4 mile there is another bench against the hillside and an overlook of the river. The trail is a little rough here, with some loose gravel. There are pine and manzanita, and lots of wildflowers in the spring. The trail continues generally 4 feet wide, curving along the hillside with some gentle rolling grades up to 3%, but always with an unprotected drop-off above the river and few places to step or pull off.

At 0.5 mile the trail widens at another armored crossing with smooth, exposed rocks up to 1.5 inches high. It is a challenge to cross in a wheelchair. The trail narrows to generally 3 feet wide and continues to curve left and right with some loose gravel on the surface. At 0.55 mile it generally widens to 4 feet but is pinched to less than 36 inches with a flat exposed rock on the edge of the trail—you may be able to cross it in a wheelchair with caution. The trail continues 3 feet wide, traveling high above the river with views of the surrounding mountains. You pass closely next to an exposed rocky cliff face, and then at 0.6 mile pass a bench with armrests and a nice view overlooking the river rapids.

At 0.7 mile you cross a level footbridge over a creek. The trail on the opposite side takes a 5–8% incline for about 50 feet. It is pretty uneven with a steep cross slope and may have a deep rut down the edge. You then reach the creek, with a nice flat area beside it. There is some shade and rocks to sit on. This is the end of the most accessible portion of the trail.

If you continue on, the trail curves sharply right and inclines at 10%. You then take a very eroded 15% decline with some large, exposed boulders and loose rocks that you have to step around. This section of trail is a little more shaded. It narrows to about 30 inches and continues with lots of exposed rocks and boulders above the river. There are areas where the outer edge has eroded and the trail is less than 2 feet wide.

At 0.9 mile you reach a waterfall and a very eroded crossing with an exposed metal culvert. You have to step down steeply from the top of the culvert onto an eroded, rocky trail. There are a couple rocks you can sit on at the base of the waterfall. It is a pretty spot, but definitely a challenge to navigate. Beyond this point, the trail continues rocky

Buttermilk Bend Trail

A rock along the edge of the Buttermilk Bend Trail

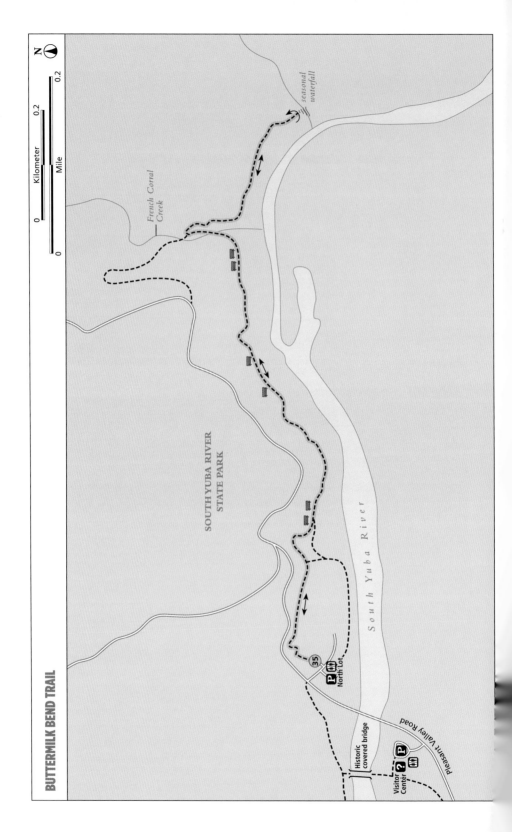

BUTTERMILK BEND TRAIL

N

Kilometer
0   0.2   0.2

Mile
0   0.2

seasonal waterfall

French Corral Creek

SOUTH YUBA RIVER STATE PARK

South Yuba River

35

North Lot

Historic covered bridge

Visitor Center

Pleasant Valley Road

View of the South Yuba River

and eroded with some steep cross slopes, then ends in less than 0.5 mile, so I recommend turning around here.

If you would like to visit the historic area and the visitor center, you can cross the road from the parking lot and take the trail to the left (it is a bit steep and may be deeply rutted with some loose gravel, so I don't recommend it for wheelchair users), or drive back across the river and turn right into the visitor center parking lot. A gravel path leads from the parking area to an electronic payment kiosk. Continue past the kiosk towards the Bridgeport Covered Bridge, the longest single-span covered bridge in the world. To the left are the visitor center, restrooms, water fountain, and historic structures. Go right and cross the covered bridge. The bridge is made of closely placed horizontal boards with two reinforced tracks of vertical boards in the center. There is a wheelchair-accessible mat on the left. It is a bit dark on the covered bridge, so bring some extra light if you need it. A couple windows provide a nice view of the South Yuba River. There is a picnic table on the right just beyond the bridge.

MILES AND DIRECTIONS

0.0 Begin at the trailhead sign on the northeast side of the parking lot.

0.7 Cross a long footbridge over the creek. This is the end of the most accessible portion.

0.9 Reach a waterfall with a rough crossing. Turn around.

1.9 Arrive back at the trailhead.

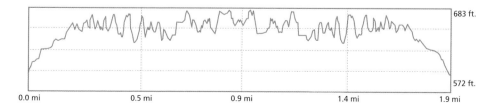

36 QUARRY TRAIL

WHY GO?

This is a great accessible hike with stunning views of the Middle Fork of the American River. The trail follows the route of a gold rush–era flume but gets its name as the site of a former limestone quarry. There are accessible toilets and picnic tables along the way, and it ends at a big picnic area with some remnants of the route's extractive history. With the exception of the first 300 feet or so, it is almost entirely flat and wide.

THE RUNDOWN

Spoon rating: 2 spoons. Wheelchair accessible with some caution due to a prolonged maximum 8% grade at the beginning.
Type: Out-and-back
Distance: 2.7 miles
Elevation: 650 feet
Elevation gain: 144 feet
Max grade: 8%
Max cross slope: 5%
Typical width: 9 feet, minimum 5 feet
Typical surface: Compacted gravel
Trail users: Hikers, bikers, equestrians

Season/schedule: Open year-round, sunrise to sunset. Best fall through spring.
Water availability: None.
Sun exposure: Full sun except for partial shade in the morning
Amenities: Accessible toilets, picnic tables, shade pavilions
Pet-friendly: Yes, on leash
Cell phone reception: Yes
Nearest town: Auburn
Land manager: California State Parks, Auburn State Recreation Area, (530) 885-4527
Pass/entry fee: Day-use parking fee or California State Parks annual pass
Land acknowledgment: Nisenan

FINDING THE TRAILHEAD

Getting there: From Auburn, take CA 49 south for 2.5 miles. It is a curvy two-lane road. CA 49 turns right and crosses the American River. In 0.4 mile, turn left at a sign for Quarry Road Trail and park in the pay parking lot (free with an annual pass). There is free parking along CA 49. **GPS:** 38.912209, -121.035212

Parking: Gravel parking lot with 1 ADA van-accessible spot.
Start: The trailhead at the end of the road.

THE HIKE

There are two places to begin this trail—at the gate below the parking lot, or the accessible route directly in front of the accessible parking spot, bypassing the gate. The trail is used as an access road, so you may encounter state vehicles. It starts about 5 feet wide on a gradual decline, increasing to 8% as it meets the main trail and widens to 8 feet. The surface is packed gravel, but there may be some loose rocks and gravel. The trail continues on a 5% decline, then you reach an accessible vault toilet at 0.1 mile and the trail curves left, crossing over a culverted stream. Continue on an 8% decline with some loose gravel.

Limestone cliffs above
the American River

The Quarry Trail along
the American River

At 0.17 mile the trail levels out and you have nice views of the river to the left. You then come to a section where the old, paved roadbed is exposed, with a few pieces rising an inch above the surface, but it can be bypassed with care. Continue on the compact gravel trail. There are some areas with morning shade and trees growing along the top of the hill, but for the most part it is fully exposed.

At 0.25 mile take a 5–8% decline for about 50 feet, then curve right. You then reach an accessible portable toilet and accessible picnic table at 0.3 mile. This is a great spot with

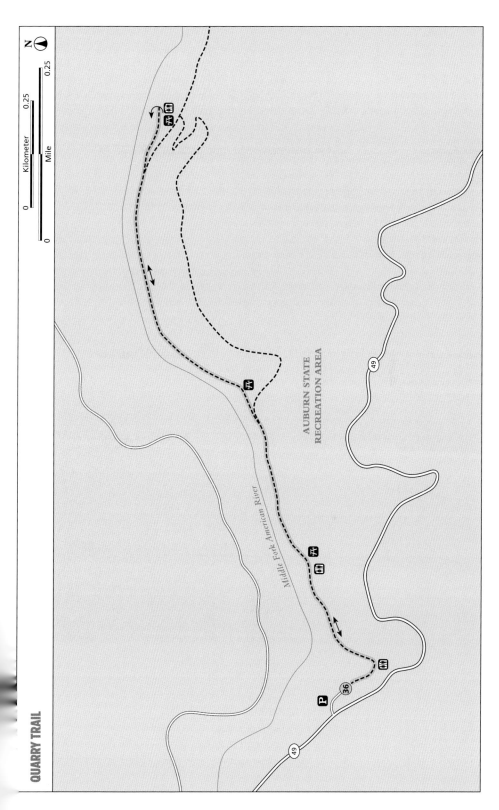

QUARRY TRAIL

Middle Fork American River

AUBURN STATE
RECREATION AREA

49

P

36

49

N

0   Kilometer   0.25

0   Mile   0.25

some partial shade to appreciate views across the canyon. At 0.4 mile there may be some large potholes in the road, but they can be navigated with at least 3 feet of clearance. The trail continues generally level, with the hill rising above you on the right and the river below you on the left.

At 0.5 mile there is a culvert that may be partially exposed on the side and a couple more potholes, but these are also easy to bypass. River rapids are below you. At 0.6 mile the trail gets a little uneven at a former washout. A trail that leads to the old quarry forks uphill on the right—just continue straight on the 8-foot-wide gravel road, then reach another accessible picnic table at 0.7 mile. It is placed on gravel in a wide grassy area on the right.

The trail then curves slightly left with a 2–5% cross slope for a few feet. There is a sharp drop-off on the river side of the trail, but it's generally protected by a raised mound, and the trail is at least 8 feet wide so you can stay close to the hillside if you prefer. The trail continues level and even on compacted gravel with great views of the river and the surrounding hills. You may notice a stream cascading down the opposite side of the canyon at around 1.0 mile, and big exposed limestone rocks above the river.

At 1.3 miles the trail forks—the right side goes steeply up the hill. Continue straight ahead. The trail widens to 9 feet and gets a little uneven with some areas of 5% cross slope. At 1.35 miles you arrive at a large staging area that has portable toilets, picnic tables, trash cans, and shade shelters. Print interpretive signs identify the plants and animals found in the foothills and provide information about the quarry and gold mining history of the area, including the concrete structure that rises above you. This is a great spot to hang out, have a picnic, listen to the river, and watch birds soaring above the canyon. Turn around and head back to the parking area when you're ready.

MILES AND DIRECTIONS

0.0   Begin at the trailhead in front of the accessible parking spot.

0.65 Continue straight at the fork.

1.3   Continue straight at the fork.

1.35 Reach the picnic area. Turn around.

2.7   Arrive back at the trailhead.

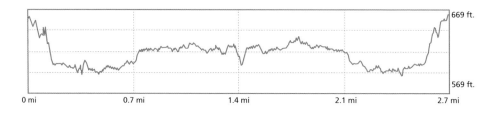

669 ft.

569 ft.

0 mi   0.7 mi   1.4 mi   2.1 mi   2.7 mi

WHY GO?

The American River Parkway (also called the Jedediah Smith Memorial Trail) is a 32-mile-long multiuse path that travels between Beal's Point at Lake Folsom and Discovery Park in Sacramento. The entire route is generally wheelchair accessible, but the first 3 miles from the lake loses about 150 feet in elevation and follows the highway for a while, so I recommend starting in Historic Folsom if you want to take the entire route. This section, from Hagan Community Park to River Bend Regional Park, is almost entirely flat and avoids major roads while offering access to amenities and beautiful views of the river and wildflowers.

THE RUNDOWN

Spoon rating: 1 spoon. Paved, level bike trail with benches.
Type: Out-and-back
Distance: 5 miles
Elevation: 70 feet
Elevation gain: 89 feet
Max grade: 5%
Max cross slope: 2%
Typical width: 8 feet
Typical surface: Pavement
Trail users: Hikers, bikers
Season/schedule: Open year-round, sunrise to sunset
Water availability: Water fountains
Sun exposure: Partial shade

Amenities: Benches, picnic tables, usable restrooms, trash cans
Pet-friendly: Yes, on leash
Cell phone reception: Yes
Special notes: Law enforcement may patrol the trail in vehicles or on bikes.
Nearest town: Rancho Cordova
Land manager: Cordova Parks and Recreation, (916) 842-3300
Pass/entry fee: Parking fee on weekends May–September. A free disabled and seniors pass is available from the parks department.
Land acknowledgment: Nisenan

FINDING THE TRAILHEAD

Getting there: From Folsom Boulevard and Coloma Road in Rancho Cordova, head 0.5 mile north on Coloma Road. Turn left on Chase Drive and continue 0.8 mile into the park. **GPS:** 38.603741, -121.309871
Parking: Paved parking lot with several ADA van-accessible spots.
Public transit: Sacramento Regional Transit route 21 stops on Coloma Road and Dolcetta Drive. Go left on Chase Drive and continue into the park.
Start: Next to the dog park.

THE HIKE

Hagan Community Park is the best place to begin this hike—there is lots of van-accessible parking and usable (but not fully accessible) restrooms, and parking fees are only charged on weekends. It is a popular place for families, with multiple sports fields, playgrounds and picnic areas, a pond, a dog park, and even a petting zoo and miniature train rides.

The most accessible route to the American River Parkway is next to the dog park—follow the sidewalk that winds between the playgrounds to the dog park. (If you go

The paved path in River Bend Park to the American River Parkway

around the pond and along the artificial stream, the pavement is rough and raised in some sections, but it is pretty.) Go left at the wide, paved bike path. People traveling on foot are supposed to stay to the left, people using wheels (including wheelchairs) are supposed to stay to the right, and pets are supposed to stay on the shoulder—this does not feel like the safest arrangement and separating groups with people walking on foot and using wheelchairs isn't an inclusive practice, but people on the trail seem to be accommodating.

The trail is 8 feet wide with a center stripe creating two lanes just under 4 feet each and a gravel shoulder, with a few pullouts. There are lots of benches and picnic tables along the way, and narrow footpaths that lead down to the river. The river is particularly beautiful in spring; the flow is high, the oaks and maples put out bright green leaves, and wildflowers grow in the grassy areas along the riverbank.

At 0.3 mile continue straight past a trail on the left (it connects to additional parking areas and Chase Drive). The trail then forks. Continue on the paved bike trail to the left, taking a 2% incline. (The trail on the right is a gravel foot and horse path that continues closer to the river for a couple hundred feet, and then reconnects to the bike path on a short but very steep incline.)

At 0.6 mile the paved trail crosses a bridge over Cordova Creek, with a wooden rail barrier protecting the edge. An interpretive sign explains the restoration work that is happening here. The creek used to be restricted to a concrete drainage system, but the concrete was removed, and the ecosystem has been restored by re-creating a natural creek corridor and replanting vegetation. You may notice some remnants of the concrete structures below the bridge.

Just beyond the creek, you reach another trail intersection. The paved trail continues straight ahead, and a gravel trail goes to the right and left. If you are comfortable walking

American River Parkway in Hagan Park

on narrow, rolling footpaths, I recommend making a detour to the right. The path is a bit sandy with some loose gravel, and typically 2 to 3 feet wide. It follows closely along the river, traveling through grassy hummocks with oak and black walnut trees arching over the trail. There are lots of places to get down to the river, but the social trails can get a little confusing so you may want to just stick to one path and then turn around to the bike trail when you are ready. This intersection is a good turnaround spot if you want to head back to Hagan Park.

Continuing on the paved trail, you take a 5% incline for about 50 feet and then it levels out. The trail skirts the border of River Bend Regional Park, continuing generally level as it moves away from the river. You pass some farmland and then open grassy areas, eventually becoming surrounded by more trees as you travel further into the park. Several trails fork off into the park, but continue on the paved bike path. At approximately 1.4 miles you pass a gravel trail that forks to the right and leads to a park service road—just continue straight. At 1.6 miles you pass Goethe Park Road and a gate—the paved trail curves right and takes a few slightly rolling grades.

At 1.9 miles you cross the main entrance road to the park. The trail inclines at 3–5% for a couple hundred feet. At 2.0 miles paved paths on the right lead to the main parking area and facilities at River Bend Park. The restrooms are not wheelchair accessible and don't have soap or towel dispensers. There are picnic tables in the shade. Some parking spots are designated as accessible but don't meet guidelines; there are no van-accessible parking spots.

Continuing past the park, the American River Parkway takes a 5% incline and curves left. You then cross the Harold Richey Memorial Bridge over the American River. The bridge curves on a 3–5% grade. There are vertical metal barriers along the edge and a

Top: Footpath along the American River
Bottom: View of the American River

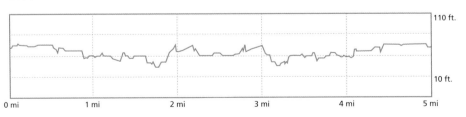

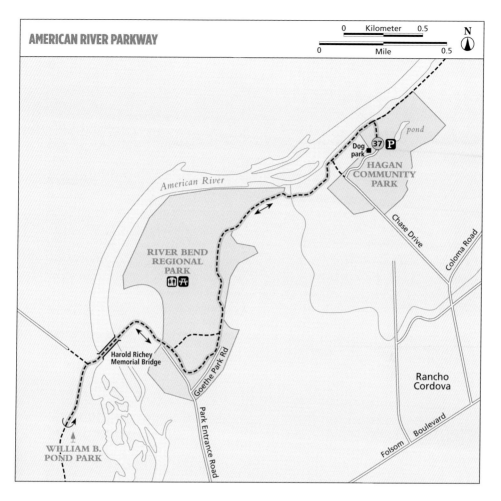

couple pullouts with beautiful views up and down the river. The trail continues into William B. Pond Park, with views of rapids and river bars. Turn around when you are ready.

MILES AND DIRECTIONS

0.0 Begin next to the dog park in Hagan Park. Go left on the American River Parkway.

0.3 Bypass two forks, continuing on the paved trail.

0.6 Cross Cordova Creek. *Option:* Take a detour on a footpath on the right or turn around.

1.9 Cross the entrance road for River Bend Regional Park.

2.0 Pass paved trails on the right that lead into the park. Cross the bridge.

2.5 Reach William B. Pond Park. Turn around.

5.0 Arrive back at Hagan Park.

SIERRA NEVADA

The Sierra Nevada is a unique landscape. While it is technically a single mountain range, its size is comparable to the largest mountain systems in the world. It is the largest mountain range in the United States and contains the highest summits in the country as well. The Sierra tower above the lowlands and can be seen from across the Great Valley and the Great Basin. A range of such size creates its own climate, and ecosystems vary widely from the west to the east and between the peaks and canyons. The Sierra Nevada is generally classified into four regions: Lake Tahoe, Western Sierra, Southern Sierra, and Eastern Sierra. Hikes in this guide are located in the Lake Tahoe and Southern Sierra regions.

This formidable and awe-inspiring landscape has been cemented into an almost poetic identity within American culture, due in large part to the writings of early conservationists such as John Muir and photographs by Ansel Adams. It is easy to understand why once you experience it. But this identity often erases the Indigenous people who lived

here for thousands of years before the arrival of settlers and the harm done to their communities in the name of conservation and public lands. John Muir was another problematic figure within the early wilderness and conservation movement; he often wrote about Native people in either disparaging or inspirational ways with little consideration for their role in shaping the landscape he so admired, or for the ongoing genocide enacted upon them. The national parks were created through the murder and forced removal of Indigenous people from their homelands, including military actions such as the Mariposa War, which led to the first non-Native people entering Yosemite Valley.

Lake Tahoe is the largest alpine lake in North America. Its crystal blue waters, pine forests, and meadows draw crowds year-round for hiking, swimming, and skiing. The basin was formed by faulting, and Ice Age glaciers further carved the landscape. The Wá·šiw (Washoe) have lived in this area since time immemorial and consider dá?aw (Lake Tahoe) as the center of their geographic and spiritual world.

The Southern Sierra is home to the largest trees in the world—giant sequoia. It is a rugged landscape defined by deep canyons and granite cliffs. The San Joaquin and Kern Rivers flow through the region, and there are mixed conifer forests, alpine lakes, and meadows. The Southern Sierra includes the ancestral homelands of the Mono (Monache), Yokuts, Tübatulabal, Paiute (Nüümü), and Western Shoshone. The Tübatulabal people have always lived in the area surrounding the North and South Forks of the Kern River. The Tübatulabal speak Pahka'anil, a Shoshonean language.

38 FRAZIER FALLS

WHY GO?

This paved, accessible trail travels through a stunning alpine landscape of glacier-carved granite cliffs. The waterfall is the most popular draw and the trail can be very busy, especially when the waterfall is flowing strong. But it is a worthwhile visit at any time to experience the wildflowers, pine-scented air, and expansive views of the northern Sierra Nevada. There are many benches along the way to rest and appreciate the landscape. Pack a picnic to enjoy at the picnic area with access to restrooms and trash cans.

THE RUNDOWN

Spoon rating: 1 spoon. Wheelchair-accessible paved trail with grades up to 8% and several benches.
Type: Out-and-back
Distance: 1 mile
Elevation: 6,190 feet
Elevation gain: 80 feet
Max grade: 8%
Max cross slope: 2%
Typical width: 5 feet with pullouts
Typical surface: Pavement
Trail users: Hikers
Season/schedule: Open spring through fall. The waterfall is best viewed in spring once the road opens, but there can be snow on the trail well into June.

Water availability: None. The creek is difficult to access and unsafe.
Sun exposure: Partial shade
Amenities: Accessible vault toilets, picnic tables, trash cans, benches (*note:* locations of benches on the map are approximate)
Pet-friendly: Yes, on leash
Cell phone reception: None
Nearest town: Graeagle
Land manager: Plumas National Forest, Beckwourth Ranger District, (530) 836-2575
Pass/entry fee: None
Land acknowledgment: Wá·šiw (Washoe)

FINDING THE TRAILHEAD

Getting there: From Graeagle, head south on CA 89 for 1.5 miles. Turn right on Gold Lake Highway, a paved two-lane road, and continue 1.5 miles. Turn left on Frazier Falls Road. This is a curvy, wide, single-lane paved road. Continue 4 miles to the trailhead on the left. **GPS:** 39.70836, -120.64629

Parking: Small paved parking area with 1 designated accessible spot. Additional parking along the road in dirt pullouts.

Start: Frazier Falls trailhead

THE HIKE

The paved trail starts on a very slight decline with a 2% cross slope for a few feet and then levels out. You pass next to a large pine and then come to four picnic tables—one is generally accessible on packed gravel, the rest are on grass or packed earth. Pass a trail sign that says the creek is 0.25 mile and the falls is 0.5 mile, then the trail inclines at 8% for a couple feet before reducing to a 5% incline. You are traveling through a forest of wildflowers, juniper, pine, and fir. The trail levels out briefly and then declines at 5–8%,

Frazier Creek

Frazier Falls

The bridge over Frazier Creek

Overlooking the granite cliff and Frazier Falls

curves sharply left, and continues on a 5% decline for about 40 feet. The trail levels out and you pass a very low bench.

There are lots of exposed granite terraces and boulders all around you. The trail inclines at 6% for a few feet, levels out briefly, and then inclines slightly again. There is another bench on the left at a reasonable sitting height. You then descend slightly, then incline at 6% for a few feet. Curve left with a 2% cross slope and then right. You are now at the creek, almost directly above the waterfall. A slight drop-off is on the left but is semi-protected by rocks as you approach the bridge. The trail declines at 5%, increasing to 8% for about 5 feet at the bridge. There is a level transition on either side; the boards are a bit rough and slightly raised, but it is accessible. Pass an interpretive sign on the left about Frazier Creek, and then the trail starts a rolling 8% incline for about 45 feet, with level areas every 15 feet or so.

Pass a bench on the left. The trail curves sharply left, then slightly right, and inclines at 8% for a few feet before curving sharply right. There are a couple places where the outer edge of the trail has eroded with unprotected drop-offs a few inches high. Another bench is on the left as you continue level through a shady area of pine and fir. The trail curves sharply left as you leave the pines and takes a long, slightly rolling 5–8% incline. It levels out briefly as you pass a high unprotected drop-off on the left, with some boulders that stick out below the trail.

Curve right and take a slight incline, and then you have views of the granite cliffs ahead of you. Another bench on the left overlooks the mountains. The trail takes a 2–5% decline, curving left and right a few times, and then there's a shaded bench and an overlook with an interpretive sign about glaciers. This is the first view of the falls. The trail then declines at 8% for a few feet to the viewpoint of the waterfall, which cascades 248 feet down the granite cliffs. The overlook is wide and paved, with a metal fence barrier with vertical poles. There are great views of the valley and across the mountains, so you have plenty to appreciate even if the falls aren't flowing strongly. A few rock steps lead steeply and unevenly down to another viewpoint. Turn around when you are ready and head back to the trailhead, appreciating a different angle on the landscape.

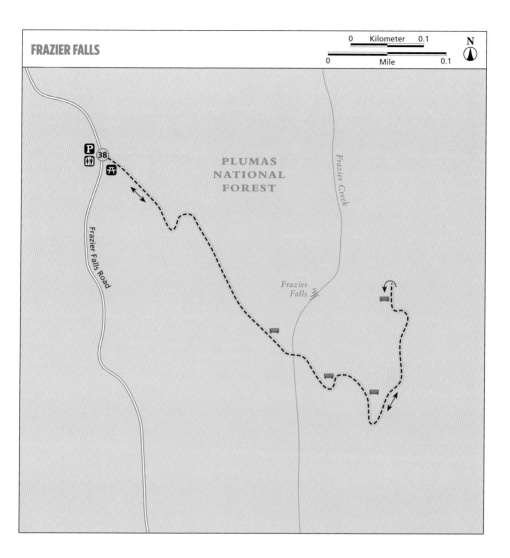

FRAZIER FALLS

PLUMAS NATIONAL FOREST

Frazier Creek

Frazier Falls Road

Frazier Falls

MILES AND DIRECTIONS

0.0 Begin at the trailhead.

0.25 Cross Frazier Creek on a sturdy bridge.

0.5 Arrive at the Frazier Falls overlook. Turn around.

1.0 Arrive back at the trailhead.

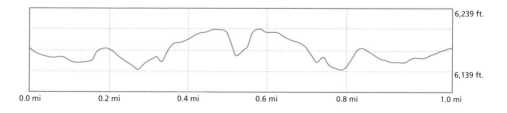

WHY GO?

This level portion of the Meeks Bay Trail travels along meadows on the north side of Meeks Creek, with hills rising up to 600 feet above you. Lots of glacial erratics are scattered along the hills, and pine and juniper trees tower above you. Efforts have begun to restore the meadow ecosystem through traditional ecological knowledge practices with the Washoe Tribe. In the meantime, there is still much to appreciate on this hike.

THE RUNDOWN

Spoon rating: 3 spoons. Generally level and firm trail with some obstacles for first 1.7 miles, then slightly steep and rocky. Partially wheelchair hikeable with all-terrain equipment.
Type: Out-and-back
Distance: 3.9 miles
Elevation: 6,243 feet
Elevation gain: 125 feet
Max grade: 10%
Max cross slope: 5%
Typical width: 6 feet, minimum 3 feet
Typical surface: Firm soil and sand
Trail users: Hikers

Season/schedule: Open year-round, best spring, after the snow melts, through fall
Water availability: Creek (use an appropriate filter)
Sun exposure: Full sun
Amenities: None
Pet-friendly: Yes, on leash
Cell phone reception: Spotty
Nearest town: South Lake Tahoe
Land manager: US Forest Service, Lake Tahoe Basin Management Unit, (530) 543-2600
Pass/entry fee: None
Land acknowledgment: Lake Tahoe is known as dáʔaw to the Wá·šiw (Washoe), and sits at the center of their geographic and spiritual world.

FINDING THE TRAILHEAD

Getting there: From South Lake Tahoe, head north on CA 89 for 16 miles. The parking lot is on the left across from Meeks Bay Resort. **GPS:** 39.03738, -120.12654

Parking: Gravel parking area with room for 6 cars. Additional parking along CA 89. No designated accessible parking.

Start: The trail information board at the end of the parking area.

THE HIKE

The Meeks Bay Trail travels several miles into Desolation Wilderness, but the first 1.5 miles follows a service road along a meadow before it climbs a hill and reaches the creek. As such, it is generally level and wide, but there are some sections of rocks, grass, and ruts. I enjoyed this trail a lot more than I thought I would and loved traveling through so many different habitats in a short distance. There are ample wildflowers in spring, some very large juniper and pine trees, and interesting views of the surrounding ridges. The most difficult part is the last 0.2 mile, when the trail ascends and descends a hill in the forest

Top: View of Rubicon Peak across the meadow
Bottom: Meeks Bay Trail along a meadow

and then crosses the rocky creek bed. But the views of the creek and cliffs at the end are worth it. There is a detour to a waterfall, but the trail is difficult to navigate. There are no benches or good places to sit, so bring a collapsible chair if you need to rest.

Start at the trail information board next to the green gate. There is a map and permit station—a free day-use permit is required for Desolation Wilderness, but this hike does not enter the wilderness. Go straight through the metal gate (it was open during my visit, but there is approximately 32 inches of clearance around the gate if it is closed). The trail starts level and 6 feet wide on compacted soil with 0.25 to 0.5 inch of loose sand on the surface. There are a couple inch-high roots and rocks in the trail, but they can be

Left: Meeks Bay Trail through the forest
Right: Meeks Creek

bypassed. It is a very pleasant hike from the beginning, with grassy meadows and pine and juniper trees growing on the hills. Rubicon Peak peeks above the hills on the left.

At 0.3 mile the trail gets a little rough, with exposed rocks up to 3 inches high and tire track ruts. It may be a challenge to navigate with a wheelchair or scooter. It evens out again after a couple hundred feet, then at 0.4 mile the trail inclines briefly at 8%. You enter a more forested area with ferns and lots of cool rocks scattered up on the hill. At 0.5 mile the trail opens up to a view of a mountain peak ahead of you. There are a few more rocks in the trail, but they're easy to get around. At 0.55 mile the trail gets a little sandy and uneven with some patchy grass, but generally continues level and 5 to 6 feet wide.

At 0.7 mile the trail gets a little rougher, with some loose sand, grass, and rocks. It then becomes more of a double track, with a raised section in the middle and two slightly rutted sections on either side. At 0.8 mile a root crosses the trail; it is 4 inches high at most and 1.5 inches at the least, but you would have to go into the grass to bypass it. At 0.9 mile the trail gets a little rocky and then curves left. At the end of the curve, it takes a 5% decline for a few feet, with some exposed rocks rising 2 to 6 inches in the center of the trail. The trail then opens up with nice views of the surrounding mountains. There is some loose sand up to 2 inches deep on the surface of the trail.

At 1.1 miles the trail takes a slight incline, gets a little uneven and rooted, and then levels out after about 50 feet. At 1.2 miles there is a large rock across the trail with about 2 feet of clearance on either side. The trail continues generally level. At 1.3 miles you have a last look at the meadow on the left. The trail then inclines at 2–5% and

gets a little rocky for about 100 feet. At 1.4 miles a fork on the right goes uphill to the Tahoe-Yosemite Trail—continue straight ahead on the 5-foot-wide Meeks Bay Trail.

The landscape starts to shift as you enter the forest. Take an 8% incline for 15 feet, and then the trail levels out. At 1.5 miles take a 2% incline for a couple hundred feet, then level out and continue passing through trees with several cut-out blowdowns. At 1.6 miles the trail narrows to 3 feet and becomes a bit uneven on firm soil with some rocks. You pass narrowly between ferns and other low plants, and the trail narrows to a minimum of 2 feet in some areas. Continue on a rolling 2–5% incline, increasing to 8% for a few feet and crossing over exposed roots. The incline continues at 8–10% for a few more feet. At 1.68 miles the trail is a bit washed out on one side with some exposed roots. It then widens back out to 6 feet and continues on an 8–10% incline with lots of exposed rocks.

Rocky section of Meeks Bay Trail

At 1.7 miles the trail generally levels out but continues rocky, with some rocks up to 6 inches high. Take a slight decline, and then the trail curves right and left. Pass a large boulder on the right, continuing on a rocky trail with some deep, loose small rocks in the surface and a slight drop-off on the left—I recommend hiking poles for this section. You are traveling along the edge of a hill above the creek. At 1.85 miles it levels and evens out a bit as you continue through a lush forest. At 1.9 miles there's a steep dip in the trail, and then you may notice the remains of an outhouse on the right—this used to be a Girl Scout camp. The trail continues level and about 3 feet wide.

At 1.95 miles you reach a creek bed—it is very rocky, with one short section that requires stepping up and across some large rocks, but it is level. The trail continues slightly rocky beyond, and you may begin to notice the sound and feel of rushing water. You then arrive at Meeks Creek. This is a beautiful spot with tall cliffs rising through the trees and lush growth along the creek. The trail is a bit steep to get down to the creek,

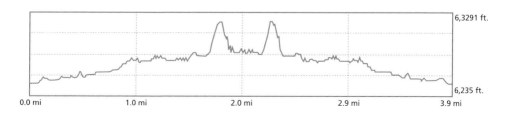

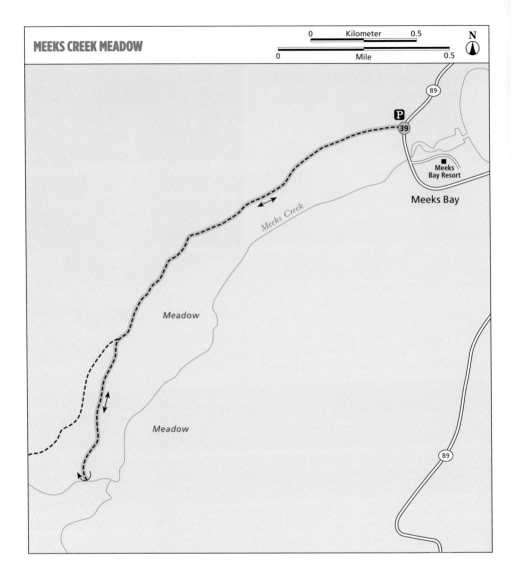

but there are a few spots to enjoy the view and get some water to filter if you need it. When you're ready, turn around and hike back the same way to the trailhead.

MILES AND DIRECTIONS

0.0   Begin at the Meeks Bay trailhead information board.

1.4   Continue straight past the fork for the Tahoe-Yosemite Trail.

1.95 Reach Meeks Creek. Turn around.

3.9   Arrive back at the trailhead.

40 SONORA PASS SCENIC DRIVE

WHY GO?

This route offers many of the same iconic Sierra Nevada views as other nearby passes, but with fewer crowds and an easier drive. You head up to the summit of Sonora Pass and then back down, traveling along the Stanislaus River with meadows, forests, and towering mountains above you. I've included several accessible stops for rest breaks and recreation, including the Columns of the Giants Trail and Donnell Vista. Be sure to fill up your gas tank and bring water and any other supplies you might need—there aren't any services along the route.

THE RUNDOWN

Type: Scenic drive
Distance: 35 miles one-way. Allow at least an hour for the drive
Elevation: 6,300 feet to 9,600 feet
Typical width and surface: Two-lane paved road
Season/schedule: Typically opens in late May or June and closes with the snowfall in November
Water availability: None
Sun exposure: Full sun
Amenities: Vault toilets, picnic areas; services in Bridgeport and Sierra Village

Pet-friendly: Yes, on leash at the recreation sites.
Cell phone reception: Spotty
Nearest town: Bridgeport and Sierra Village
Land manager: Stanislaus National Forest, Summit Mi-Wok District, (209) 965-3434
Pass/entry fee: None
Land acknowledgment: This route crosses Wá·šiw (Washoe), Nüümü (Northern Paiute), and Me-Wuk (Central Sierra Miwok) ancestral lands.

FINDING THE TRAILHEAD

Getting there: To begin this scenic drive, start in Sonora Junction at the intersection of CA 108 and US 395.
Start: Set your odometer on CA 108 at US 395 in Sonora Junction.

THE DRIVE

You can start the scenic drive from the west end of CA 108 at Sierra Village, but this guide begins at the east end at Sonora Junction. From US 395 and CA 108 in Sonora Junction, head west on CA 108. At 2 miles stop at the Sonora Bridge Meadow Picnic Area on the West Walker River. There are picnic tables in the meadow, a vault toilet with a 2-inch rise onto it, and a footpath that leads to the river, along with nice views of the mountains. Continue on CA 108, crossing a bridge over the Walker River. You then pass a Marine Corps training center on the right and start winding up the mountains on a curvy two-lane road.

At 7 miles you reach the Leavitt Meadows Trailhead on the left. The gravel parking area has gendered accessible vault toilets that you can pull up next to. There are nice

Top: Sonora Bridge Meadow Picnic Area
Bottom: Donnell Vista

views of the river. Pass the Leavitt Falls Vista on the left at 9 miles, then cross a cattle guard at 13.7 miles. The road continues curvy and climbing up the mountain.

At 15 miles you reach the summit of Sonora Pass at an elevation of 9,600 feet. In comparison to nearby passes, this drive is not too bad—it is a bit curvy, but there aren't any major drop-offs, and the views are stunning the entire way. You pass mountains and valleys, meadows, and waterfalls. Shortly after the Sonora Pass sign, you reach a paved forest road on the right. This leads to a staging area for the Pacific Crest Trail. There are vault toilets (not wheelchair accessible) and picnic tables with great views from the parking lot.

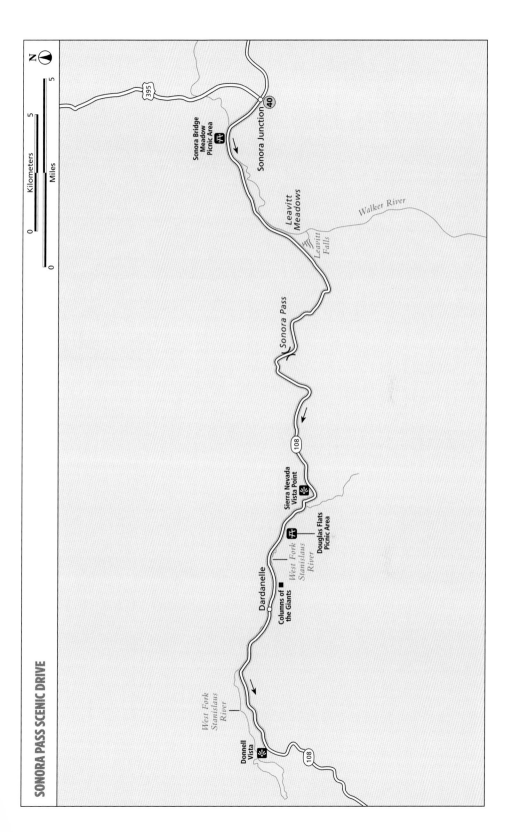

SONORA PASS SCENIC DRIVE

N

Kilometers
0   5   5

Miles
0   5

395

40

Sonora Bridge
Meadow
Picnic Area

Sonora Junction

Leavitt
Meadows

Walker River

Leavitt
Falls

Sonora Pass

108

Sierra Nevada
Vista Point

Douglas Flats
Picnic Area

Dardanelle

West Fork
Stanislaus
River

Columns of
the Giants

Donnell
Vista

West Fork
Stanislaus
River

108

View of the Sonora Pass scenic highway

The highway gets a little curvier as you start descending the pass. At 22 miles you reach the Sierra Nevada Vista Point at a large pullout on the right at a curve. This is a good spot to take a break. There are nice views, but you have to walk on the top of boulders for the best vista of the mountains and valley. An interpretive sign provides information on the emigrant settlers who used the pass. The road gets less curvy as you continue on, and you start traveling along a creek on the left. Craggy peaks tower above the road, and there are a couple more pullouts to stop and take in the views. At 24 miles you pass the Kennedy Meadows Campground.

At 26 miles you arrive at the Douglas Flats Picnic Area. I highly recommend stopping here. There is a paved parking lot with two ADA parking spots, gendered accessible vault toilets, and accessible picnic tables. The picnic tables sit along a paved path, under a few trees in a meadow—this area is recovering from a wildfire, so take care with the sensitive landscape. A short but steep paved path continues from the end of the picnic area to an overlook of the river with two benches.

At 28 miles you reach the Columns of the Giants Trail, another stop I highly recommend. It has the same incredible geological features as the Devils Postpile formation, but it is wheelchair accessible and much less busy. Turn left at the Pigeon Flat Campground sign, then immediately right and park in the paved parking lot. There is one van-accessible parallel-parking spot. Follow the trail towards the creek. It is 0.25 mile long, paved, and generally level with a couple short 5–8% grades. You cross the Stanislaus River on a wooden bridge, then travel briefly uphill with an unprotected drop-off above the river. Wind through a meadow with fire-scarred trees, being careful to stay on the trail to protect this sensitive and recovering landscape. The exposed talus slopes start to come into view, and then the columnar basalt cliff towers above you. Numerous print interpretive signs explain the volcanic and glacial forces that created this unique formation. Bring binoculars if you use them to get a good view of the rocks, and watch for hawks flying overhead.

At 30 miles you pass Dardanelle Resort on the left and several more campgrounds. You're traveling through a pretty area of pine forests and hills on a relatively straight road. At 35 miles you reach Donnell Vista, your last recommended stop. There is a large paved

Top: Columns of the Giants
Bottom: View of the Sierras from the highway

parking lot with two ADA spots and gendered accessible vault toilets. A 0.25-mile-long wheelchair-accessible paved trail winds around a bluff above the Middle Fork Stanislaus River, with sweeping views of the river canyon, Donnell Reservoir, and the mountains. While the trail is a loop, it is wheelchair accessible as an out-and-back beginning at the accessible parking spots. There are several viewpoints along the way, and it ends at a large overlook of the river. Print interpretive signs describe the history of the U-shaped canyon, the Miwok who used this route for travel and hunting, and the settlers who crossed the mountains.

CA 108 continues another 45 miles to Sonora, but this is the last of the accessible recreation sites on the route, so it makes a good turnaround spot.

41 GENERAL GRANT TREE TRAIL

WHY GO?

The General Grant Tree is one of the largest trees in the world. The giant sequoia towers 268 feet high and has a circumference of 107.5 feet at the ground. The tree is an awe-inspiring presence in the forest. Located in a large grove of giant sequoia, this is one among many striking features on this trail, which includes a fallen tree you can walk through and a historic cabin. The forest is not particularly lush—a few ferns, sorrel, and small trees grow along the trail—but this makes the giant sequoia stand out even more. The trail is very popular, and crowds tend to congregate around the General Grant Tree to take photos. Braille and tactile signage line the paved 0.5-mile loop.

THE RUNDOWN

Spoon rating: 1 spoon. Wheelchair accessible with caution due to a steep grade at the beginning and end of the loop.
Type: Loop
Distance: 0.5 mile
Elevation: 6,340 feet
Elevation gain: 30 feet
Max grade: 10%
Max cross slope: 5%
Typical width: 6 feet
Typical surface: Pavement
Trail users: Hikers
Season/schedule: Open year-round. Best spring through fall.
Water availability: Water fountain
Sun exposure: Partial shade

Amenities: Restrooms, benches, trash cans, tactile signage
Pet-friendly: No
Cell phone reception: None
Nearest town: Yokuts Valley (limited services in Grant Grove)
Land manager: Sequoia and Kings Canyon National Parks, (559) 565-3341
Pass/entry fee: Entrance fee or federal recreation pass
Land acknowledgment: Sequoia and Kings Canyon National Parks are the homelands of the Mono (Monache), Yokuts, Tübatulabal, Paiute, and Western Shoshone.

FINDING THE TRAILHEAD

Getting there: From Fresno, take CA 180 east for approximately 57 miles. The road gets increasingly curvy as you climb up the mountains into the park. Go through the Kings Canyon National Park entrance. In 1.5 miles, General's Highway goes to the right—stay left on CA 180, following signs for Grant Grove. Go past the visitor center and turn left on Grant Tree Road. Turn right into the parking lot.
GPS: 36.746635, -118.973152
Parking: Large paved parking lot with 5 ADA spots.
Start: The trailhead at the north side of the parking lot.

THE HIKE

The loop starts with a steep grade going both directions from the parking area. Go right, taking an 8% incline with a slight cross slope. The trail is bordered by a split-rail wooden fence and curves gently through the forest surrounded by giant sequoias. At 0.08 mile you pass the Fallen Monarch, a sequoia tree that you can walk through. At 0.1 mile the

General Grant Tree Trail

trail generally levels out. Tactile interpretive signs provide information about the giant sequoia and the recent history of the grove. Pass a bench set off on the right, and then there is a 5% cross slope for a few feet as you approach a fork. Stay on the paved trail as it curves left and takes a 2–5% incline. The pavement is a little rough and may have some loose soil on the surface.

You reach the General Grant Tree at 0.2 mile. A bench as you approach offers a good place to sit if you want to wait for a break in the crowd. The tree is protected by a wooden fence, and there is a large paved viewing area. A path encircles the tree, but you have to take steps to access it.

General Grant Tree Trail

The Fallen Monarch

Go left on the paved trail, continuing past the General Grant Tree. The trail levels out, but there are some cracked and uneven sections. At 0.25 mile it inclines again at 5% and is slightly uneven. Continue to the left, passing a fork on the right that leads to a burn scar. The trail takes another 8% incline for about 40 feet, and then at 0.3 mile you reach the historic Gamlin Cabin, which was built by settlers in 1872.

Follow the paved trail to the left past the cabin. Pass a bench on the left, and then take an 8% decline for about 30 feet, passing several large giant sequoias. You pass the Centennial Stump at about 0.4 mile. The stump is the remains of a tree that was cut in 1875 for display at the Philadelphia Centennial Exhibition. The trail then declines again at 8% on some sections of rough and cracked pavement. It levels out briefly, and then continues on a 5% decline as you pass the other side of the Fallen Monarch. The trail curves left, then levels out. Be careful at a pothole in the center of the trail with about 3 feet of space around it. The trail continues with some areas of cracked and uneven pavement. It curves left again and takes a 10% decline for about 40 feet as you approach the end of the trail and the parking area.

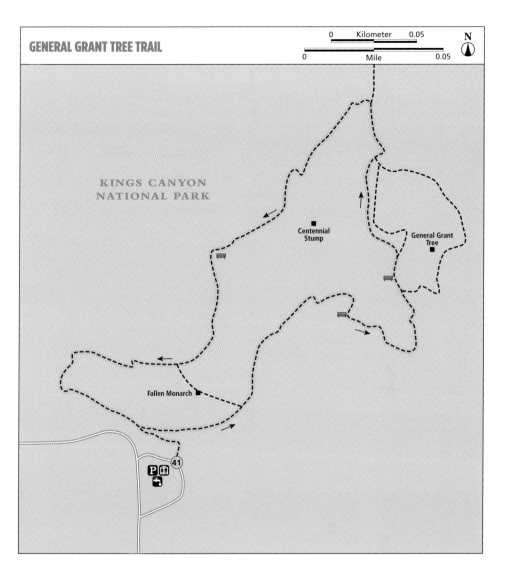

GENERAL GRANT TREE TRAIL

KINGS CANYON
NATIONAL PARK

Centennial
Stump

General Grant
Tree

Fallen Monarch

41

MILES AND DIRECTIONS

0.0 Begin at the trailhead.

0.2 Reach the General Grant Tree. Go left around the tree.

0.56 Arrive back at the trailhead.

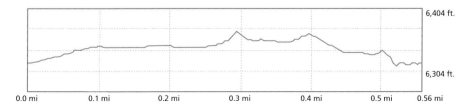

42 BIG TREES TRAIL

WHY GO?

This trail in Sequoia National Park (not to be confused with similarly named trails in nearby recreation areas) is a worthwhile destination on its own. The paved loop circles Round Meadow with ancient giant sequoias growing along the edge. Many of the trees have fluted bases to help them stay sturdy in the wet landscape. Little Deer Creek flows across the meadow, which is a sea of colorful wildflowers in spring and early summer. Numerous benches with pullouts provide resting areas to enjoy the experience. I spent well over an hour on this peaceful and awe-inspiring trail.

THE RUNDOWN

Spoon rating: 1 spoon. Wheelchair accessible, but there are some sections of rough pavement and a partially collapsed boardwalk.
Type: Lollipop loop
Distance: 0.7 mile
Elevation: 6,390 feet
Elevation gain: 43 feet
Max grade: 5%
Max cross slope: 2%
Typical width: 4 feet
Typical surface: Pavement, boardwalk
Trail users: Hikers
Season/schedule: Open year-round. Best spring through fall.
Water availability: Water fountain
Sun exposure: Partial shade
Amenities: Accessible toilets, benches

Pet-friendly: No
Cell phone reception: None
Special notes: Be careful in the accessible parking lot. People frequently walk through and stop to take photos, and drivers use it as a turnaround.
Nearest town: Three Rivers
Land manager: Sequoia and Kings Canyon National Parks, (559) 565-3341
Pass/entry fee: Entrance fee or federal recreation pass
Land acknowledgment: Sequoia and Kings Canyon National Parks are the homelands of the Mono (Monache), Yokuts, Tübatulabal, Paiute, and Western Shoshone.

FINDING THE TRAILHEAD

Getting there: From Fresno, take CA 180 east for approximately 57 miles. The road gets increasingly curvy as you climb up the mountains into the park. Go through the Kings Canyon National Park entrance, and in 1.5 miles, turn right on Generals Highway. Continue 29 miles on the curvy two-lane road through the park. If you have a disabled parking placard, you can turn right into the designated parking lot at the trailhead. If you don't have a placard, you can pick up a temporary one from any of the visitor centers in Sequoia or Kings Canyon. Otherwise, park at the Giant Forest Museum. **GPS:** 36.565338, -118.768761

Parking: Paved parking lot with 8 designated accessible parking spaces with no access aisles.

Start: The trailhead at the end of the accessible parking lot.

Left: Big Trees Trail
Right: Old-growth giant sequoia and boulders along the trail

THE HIKE

Start on the paved trail at the end of the accessible parking lot. It is blocked by plastic cones, but there is at least 3 feet of clearance around them. There are huge trees right at the parking area. You reach a trail intersection and the beginning of the loop in about 100 feet, with benches and a sign that points straight ahead to the restrooms or to the right for the Big Trees Trail. The trail on the left goes to the parking area at the museum. Go right on the Big Trees Trail.

The trail takes a 2% decline for a few feet. A giant sequoia towers directly ahead of you. You cross over a stream, and then the meadow comes into view. The first of many benches is on the right beneath the sequoia. At 0.09 mile the trail takes a 2% incline with level areas every few feet; this side of the loop generally inclines at 2–5% with level areas every few feet. There are beautiful views across the meadow, and giant sequoias rise over 200 feet high above you, with glacial erratics scattered along the hill.

At 0.2 mile you transition onto a boardwalk. The pavement has slipped on the left as you approach the boardwalk; there is about 3 feet of level space and a level transition onto the boardwalk. The boards are slightly uneven with a 0.5-inch gap in between. The boardwalk has round edge guards, but one section of barrier is broken at the end. The pavement on the other side is slightly cracked, with a narrow but deep pothole. You pass a sequoia on the right that has grown around a large boulder, giving the appearance that

View across Round Meadow

The Big Trees Trail passing next to a large boulder

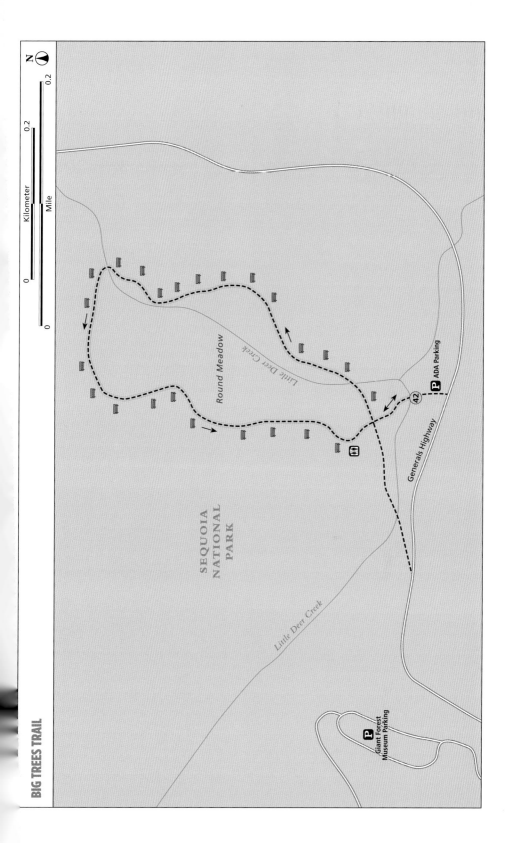

BIG TREES TRAIL

N

0   Kilometer   0.2

0   Mile   0.2

SEQUOIA
NATIONAL
PARK

Little Deer Creek

Round Meadow

Little Deer Creek

42

Generals Highway

P ADA Parking

P Giant Forest
Museum Parking

View across Round Meadow to two old-growth giant sequoias

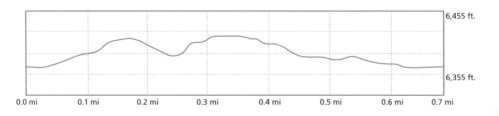

the two are merging, and then come to a longer boardwalk that is level and has pullouts next to giant boulders.

Continue traveling on a slight incline through a mix of lodgepole pine and giant sequoia with lots of wildflowers in the meadow. At 0.3 mile you reach another short boardwalk with rough pavement on the approach and a 0.5-inch lip. It has a slight cross slope with edge guards and travels across the creek as it flows into the meadow. The trail curves left and you are now at the north side of the meadow. Lodgepole pines grow close to the trail, and there are views across the meadow to the boulders.

At 0.4 mile you come to a long boardwalk. It is level onto the boardwalk, but there are some small holes in the boards. It travels across the meadow next to large sequoias, with a few pullouts and benches. There may be a 5-foot-long damaged section near the end—it is collapsed on the left side with a 0.5-inch lip, a steep cross slope, and no barrier. Shortly after, the boardwalk ends level onto pavement. Pass a bench and then a few feet beyond that there is a rough patch of pavement. The trail continues generally level with a few more areas of uneven and rough pavement. You pass many more large trees, including one that is scarred by fire with a large split in the base.

At 0.6 mile you reach the restrooms and water bottle filling station. Go left to close the loop and then continue straight to the parking area.

MILES AND DIRECTIONS

0.0 Begin at the trailhead at the accessible parking lot. Go right on the paved trail to begin the loop.

0.6 Reach the restrooms. Go left to close the loop.

0.7 Arrive back at the beginning of the loop. Go straight to the parking area.

ADDITIONAL RESOURCES

Find more trail guides, resources, and information about group hikes at www.disabled hikers.com.

Links provided in this book and trail updates can be found at www.disabledhikers.com/the-disabled-hikers-guide-to-northern-california.

National Park and Federal Recreational Lands Access Passes can be obtained at www.nps .gov/subjects/accessibility/interagency-access-pass.htm.

Information on California State Parks passes can be found at www.parks.ca .gov/?page_id=1049.

A simplified fact sheet about wheelchair and OPDMD use is provided by the Department of Justice at www.ada.gov/resources/opdmds.

National Park Service rules for wheelchairs and OPDMD can be found at www.nps .gov/subjects/accessibility/mobility-devices.htm. Similar rules apply at national forests.

HIKE INDEX

THE TEN ESSENTIALS OF HIKING

American Hiking Society

American Hiking Society recommends you pack the "Ten Essentials" every time you head out for a hike. Whether you plan to be gone for a couple of hours or several months, make sure to pack these items. Become familiar with these items and know how to use them. Learn more at **AmericanHiking.org/hiking-resources.**

1. Appropriate Footwear

6. Safety Items (light, fire, and a whistle)

2. Navigation

7. First Aid Kit

3. Water (and a way to purify it)

8. Knife or Multi-Tool

4. Food

9. Sun Protection

5. Rain Gear & Dry-Fast Layers

10. Shelter

PROTECT THE PLACES YOU LOVE TO HIKE

Become a member today and take $5 off an annual membership using the code **Falcon5**.

AmericanHiking.org/join

American Hiking Society is the only national nonprofit organization dedicated to empowering all to enjoy, share, and preserve the hiking experience.